A publication of the

AMERICAN ASSOCIATION FOR HIGHER EDUCATION
A department of the National Education Association
1201 Sixteenth Street, Northwest
Washington, D.C. 20036

G. KERRY SMITH, *Executive Secretary*

The American Association for Higher Education, AAHE,
a self-governing department of the National Education
Association, promotes higher education and provides a
national voice for individual members. AAHE, founded
in 1870, is the only national higher education
organization open to faculty members and administrators—
without regard to rank, discipline, or type or size
of institution. AAHE is dedicated to the professional
development of college and university educators, to
the achievement of their educational objectives, and
to the improvement of conditions of service.

Stress
and
Campus
Response

G. Kerry Smith, EDITOR

1968

CURRENT ISSUES IN HIGHER EDUCATION

ASSOCIATE EDITORS, *Joseph Axelrod,*
Tom Erhard, Mervin B. Freedman,
Lewis B. Mayhew

STRESS
AND
CAMPUS
RESPONSE

Jossey-Bass Inc., Publishers
615 Montgomery Street • San Francisco • 1968

STRESS AND CAMPUS RESPONSE
Current Issues in Higher Education 1968
G. Kerry Smith, Editor

Jossey-Bass, Inc., Publishers
615 Montgomery Street
San Francisco, California 94111

Library of Congress Catalog Card Number 68–57441

Printed in the United States of America
by Hamilton Printing Company
Rensselaer, New York

FIRST EDITION

681014

THE JOSSEY-BASS SERIES IN HIGHER EDUCATION

General Editors

JOSEPH AXELROD and MERVIN B. FREEDMAN
San Francisco State College

Preface

We cannot seriously believe that the explosions at Berkeley and Columbia resulted from spontaneous combustion, or that they can be attributed solely to a handful of disaffected student "leaders" and "outside agitators." We are not in the midst of a brief storm that will blow over and be forgotten; rather, we are involved, whether we like it or not, in what one of this book's contributors describes as a "profound combination of revolutions."

The national forum where earlier versions of these essays were presented did not expect agreement—only insight. One of the most troubling questions confronting that forum was stated recently by Henry David Aiken: "Why does that success which has made the university so indispensable to the technetronic society dispose so many of the university's own choicest spirits to revolt so passionately against it?"

When France tottered in crisis in the spring of 1968, we were reminded not only that disturbances happen in other countries too, but that they are particularly evident in countries that are more technologically advanced. It is not surprising, then, that the impact of technology is evident in the essays presented in *Stress and Campus Response.* Along with such modern side effects as environmental pollution, we are confronted with the ironic realization that despite our achievements in science and technology, the deep-down human problems are still around; the achievements have only made them stand out in stark relief. As another contributor puts it: "It is not dissent or disruption or law-breaking or violence *per se* that is our problem. It is moral and political and intellectual confusion within the 'adult' society, which knows in its heart that the war and racism and poverty are here, and serious, and wrong—but which cannot find ways of stemming their tide, much less eliminating them."

The troubles in Paris and at Columbia had not taken place at the time of the Twenty-third National Conference on Higher Education, from which this volume emanates. Nor had the assassinations of Martin Luther King and Robert Kennedy yet scarred the national conscience. But the mood of the conference, held in March 1968 and sponsored by the American Association for Higher Education (AAHE), was as ominous as it was accurate —a mood summed up in the following words of the president of AAHE: "When a handful of students can disrupt a major university, when frustrated people turn cities into battlefields, and when youth can reject the fundamental values of a culture, a crisis is at hand."

The essays in *Stress and Campus Response* were selected by an editorial board, set up by the AAHE Executive Committee, composed of Joseph Axelrod, Tom Erhard, Mervin B. Freedman, and Lewis B. Mayhew.

September 1968   G. KERRY SMITH
Washington, D.C.

Contents

Contributors

JOSEPH AXELROD, Project Director, Center for Research and Development in Higher Education, University of California, Berkeley (on leave, San Francisco State College)

RICHARD AXEN, Professor of Higher Education, San Francisco State College

FREDERICK DEW. BOLMAN, Associate Director, Esso Education Foundation, New York

BURTON R. CLARK, Professor of Sociology, Yale University

BARRY COMMONER, Chairman, Department of Botany and Director, Center for the Biology of Natural Systems, Washington University

WILLIAM E. ENGBRETSON, Professor of Higher Education, University of Denver

CHARLES FRANKEL, Aspen Institute of Humanistic Studies, Aspen, Colorado, formerly Assistant Secretary of State for Educational and Cultural Affairs

DONALD L. GARRITY, Vice President for Academic Affairs, San Francisco State College

ANDREW M. GREELEY, Senior Study Director, National Opinion Research Center, University of Chicago

EDITH GREEN, Representative from Oregon, United States House of Representatives

THEODORE P. GREENE, Professor of History, Amherst College

S. L. HALLECK, Director, Student Health Psychiatry and Professor of Psychology, University of Wisconsin

MICHAEL HARRINGTON, Chairman of the Board, League for Industrial Democracy, New York

ROGER W. HEYNS, Chancellor, University of California, Berkeley

WILLIAM L. KOLB, Dean of the College, Beloit College

JOHN C. LIVINGSTON, Professor of Government, Sacramento State College

TERRY F. LUNSFORD, Project Director, Center for Research and Development in Higher Education, University of California, Berkeley

LEWIS B. MAYHEW, Professor of Education, Stanford University

WILLIAM MOORE, JR., Associate Dean of Instruction, Forest Park Community College, St. Louis

GLENN A. OLDS, University Dean for International Studies and World Affairs, State University of New York, Oyster Bay

EDWARD JOSEPH SHOBEN, JR., Head, Center for Higher Education, State University of New York, Buffalo

ROBERT VAN WAES, Associate Secretary, American Association of University Professors

ALVIN M. WEINBERG, Director, Oak Ridge National Laboratory

ROBERT B. YEGGE, Dean, College of Law, University of Denver

Stress
and
Campus
Response

Prologue

THE LIGHT AT THE END OF THE TUNNEL

Joseph Axelrod

The essays in *Stress and Campus Response* describe the many kinds of stress to which, in recent years, the American college/ university has been subjected. Most of the essays refer, of course, to the social conditions of our time, and most of the authors agree that these conditions are very bad and are likely to become worse. Barry Commoner's essay, which opens Part One of the volume, begins with this sentence: "There is ample, tragic evidence of a deep crisis in the human condition." And Congresswoman Edith Green's essay, which closes the volume, enumerates a number of unacceptable situations in which millions of Americans are caught but for which solutions are not even in sight.

On the campuses themselves, the response to these conditions of stress is, in Roger Heyns' phrase, "a mindless and inefficient stumbling from crisis to crisis." Most of the authors agree. Charles Frankel, for example, declares that "no thinking man could pronounce anything but a severe judgment on the present

1

condition of higher education" in the United States. And Lewis B. Mayhew begins the first of his two essays in this collection by stating that the American college/university stands on the verge of "imminent impotency."

The severe social dislocation described in the essays of the first part of the volume leaves no facet of higher education untouched. Student unrest is analyzed in the second part. The third part describes the dysfunction in institutional organization and governance and suggests remedies. And the fourth part gives examples of curricular changes that reflect the breaking down of the wall that had earlier separated the campus from the world outside. Finally, the fifth part recombines all of these strands into a new whole and, analyzing the present in terms of the future, establishes a new order of priorities for the years ahead.

The four essays of Part One are jointly titled "A Society in Crisis." The first two essays are by noted scientists, Barry Commoner and Alvin M. Weinberg. Weinberg believes that the American college/university cannot, and should not, take upon itself a job society desperately needs done—namely, working toward rational solution of our difficult social problems. The sociotechnological institute—the "think tank"—he says, is far better equipped to do this job. Commoner's essay takes the opposing view; he lays emphasis on the enormous social responsibility that the American college/university cannot avoid accepting. But he believes a solution cannot be determined until the deep connections between the technological and the human sides of what he calls the "dual crisis" have been explored.

If one takes Commoner's argument as the frame of reference, the third essay of Part One, by Michael Harrington, can be regarded as a specific case study. Harrington concentrates on a single problem, poverty, and shows what the college/university must do if it is to help society—and what risks it runs if it does. Charles Frankel, in the essay that closes the first part of the book, takes on perhaps the most difficult task of all: to explore some crucial but not very obvious facets of the relationship between the American college/university and what government officials and newspaper people call the national interest. One of the tests by which our country's foreign policy can be judged, Frankel asserts, is its impact on higher education. And when we apply this test, we find our country has failed badly.

Part One thus succeeds in delineating some of the crises of our society. The sensitive reader will find the picture it paints grim. But beyond that picture, he will perceive something else as well: the incredible inadequacy of the American college/university for providing meaningful leadership in a society that desperately needs guidance from those most capable of giving it. The reader must wonder whether, since the college/university has not been able to supply leadership for American society at large, it has at least offered the leadership higher education itself needs. And that is the large question of the second, third, and fourth parts of the book.

Part Two is devoted to students, and it concentrates on the specific topics which at this moment have crowded the others out: student rights, dissent, defiance, violence. Robert Van Waes and Robert B. Yegge open the section with two essays on student rights and freedoms. Both Van Waes and Yegge discuss the *Joint Statement on Rights and Freedoms of Students* endorsed by major associations and councils in higher education, including the American Association for Higher Education. Van Waes' essay provides a nice bridge between Part One and Part Two, for he sees close relationships tying student freedoms to the college/university as an instrument of social reform. Yegge's hypothetical case study (a student is arrested by the morals squad of the local police in an off-campus apartment, and the verdict of a campus review committee is suspension) points up countless legal intricacies that will be of interest to readers who do not sit on disciplinary committees as well as to those who do.

Part Two continues with six essays analyzing student unrest. Taken together, these essays constitute a powerful statement about student activism.[1] Terry F. Lunsford's essay, which opens this group, defines and condemns privatism. (The word *privatism* may be new to some readers. It describes the response of otherwise responsible adults who leave the political field entirely in the pos-

---

[1] Another is the collection of papers that appeared in the July, 1967, issue of *The Journal of Social Issues.* Those papers, and several others added to them, will appear in book form in 1969, edited by Edward E. Sampson and Harold A. Korn (Jossey-Bass Series in Higher Education). Joseph Katz' New Dimensions in Higher Education monograph (No. 30) titled *The Student Activists,* which appeared in a preliminary edition in 1967, is presently under revision.

session of angry student activists and their repressers, after which they sit comfortably and watch television news programs and shake their heads and deplore the increasing polarization in America.) Theodore P. Greene, in the second essay of this group, recounts a fascinating historical parallel: the dilemma John Cotton faced in Massachusetts more than three hundred years ago. Richard Axen, in his essay, shows the surprisingly close relationship between peaceful dissent and powerless dissent, and he suggests a radical solution.

Continuing the discussion of student activism and alienation, S. L. Halleck presents a series of hypotheses explaining student unrest. Each hypothesis is attractive and true, in one way or another. But the most powerful explanations—the ones Halleck finds most valid—are the ones that are, he says, "most difficult to live with optimistically." Edward Joseph Shoben, Jr., explains why he believes the new student morality is now decaying at its center. His presentation includes a brief but profound discussion of civil disobedience and the conditions under which it is justifiable and even beneficial. Lewis B. Mayhew, closing Part Two, suggests that the solution lies in a tight constructionist interpretation, under which college officials would limit their concerns to educational matters only.

Meanwhile, as the authors of Part Two point out, the situation has become increasingly more tense in the struggle between the college/university Establishment and the New Left in the years between nonviolent Berkeley (1964) and violent Columbia (1968). More severe student unrest on more campuses has elicited an increasingly punitive reaction on the part of college/university officials. The only solution is to find a way to put this tremendous energy and motivation and power of students to constructive uses, through some form of "participatory democracy." But the realization of such a solution is not yet in sight.

One would suppose that in moving from student unrest to problems of institutional organization—the subject of Part Three —the reader might be able to breathe more easily. He does for a moment, but he soon discovers that calm exists only in the physicians' waiting room, that inside the offices all is in turmoil, and the physicians appear unable to heal themselves. Or, to state the matter bluntly: Everywhere on our college/university campuses there is what the experts diagnose as severe dysfunction. There is no cure for it, they tell us, but the replacement of the old organizational structures with new ones that will allow—no, necessitate—more efficient modes of functioning.

But we are kept where we are, the essays of Part Three show us, by a vast irony. Like a healthy heart rejected by a body whose own heart can no longer serve it adequately, new structures, if they come ready-made, are rejected by the standard system. And if an attempt is made to build up new structures from within the system, a different obstacle obtrudes: The present structures refuse to accommodate the very processes by which the new structures might be developed. In short, we are caught in a system designed for another world and for another century. It stubbornly refuses our efforts to change it. And the only movements we can make with comfort are short-run adjustments to problems as they arise.

Roger Heyns opens with a startling assertion: give administrators more power, not less. If administrators are to become real leaders, instead of consensus seekers and mediators, the academic community must give them more power, and must do so voluntarily. William L. Kolb's essay goes on to define the kind of leader the undergraduate teacher must be, and Frederick deW. Bolman's essay analyzes the various dimensions of administrative leadership.

As Part Three moves to a discussion of the faculty's role in governance, John C. Livingston suggests that the very language in which we now conceive of the problem reflects an outmoded way of looking at the world. And Burton R. Clark argues that faculty governance will flourish only within an organizational structure that promotes collegial authority. But the present structures, he says, are perfect for promoting paranoia.

The severe organizational dysfunction on the American campus appears to be of no interest whatsoever to the news commentator on television—unless, of course, he can catch a politician openly dictating to a college president which faculty he may hire. Even that situation, however, is far less newsworthy than the subject of dissident students who break down a door or go limp and allow themselves to be carried to the paddy wagon. But of these two kinds of problems, those relating to institutional organizations are, in certain ways, the more basic. And for many readers, therefore, the essays of Part Three will be of paramount interest.

In Part Four we turn from problems of organization and governance to curriculum. Curricula are the unique possession of educational institutions. No other organization has them. Many social institutions share common features with schools—organizational tables and flow charts; computerized record keeping and centralized purchasing; budgets that are either too fat or too lean; staff members who are overambitious or totally unmotivated; a clientele that is resigned, tranquilized, restless, or occasionally satisfied; a general public that is distrusting, respectful but remote, totally apathetic, or occasionally appreciative and supportive —but only schools have curricula.

It is no wonder, then, that we guard this possession closely. If it loses its identity, we may lose ours. If it loses its power (it is the curriculum, after all, that determines the path to the degree), we lose ours as well. So we guard it closely—so closely as to keep it unchanged in any basic way. But curricula are highly changeable (although the ritual is complex), in small, innocuous ways. Curriculum committees spend hundreds of man-hours weekly approving new courses and revising old programs or substituting one form of bookkeeping for another. The curriculum committee may even introduce a new academic calendar. And sometimes it initiates (or merely approves—but its approval is a great event on campus) whole new concepts: showing course lectures on television; or holding course lectures in the buildings where students live; or presenting course lectures informally to small-class audiences rather than to large-auditorium audiences. Occasionally, however, a revolutionary concept actually is initiated (or approved) by a curriculum committee—for example, allowing a student to earn course credit not by listening to lectures but by studying "independently" a set of printed materials.

The pressures from students and from some faculty have been mounting, and on many campuses basic curricular changes· —usually initiated from quarters other than faculty senates or administrative offices—are in the making. Part Four reports how some of these changes have taken place in response to concerns with large moral issues of the day, with community problems in urban areas, and with intercultural and international understandings. These concerns represent three areas in which curricula have moved toward greater "relevance."

The Reverend Andrew M. Greeley sets the stage for Part Four. He presents, in the essay that opens the section, a provocative argument: Young people are "too moral" for the ready-made ethical systems the adult world now makes available to them, but they do not have the wisdom to invent adequate systems for themselves. Hence, educators—and particularly those of us in higher education—must undertake the responsibility of teaching moral wisdom. But unfortunately, we are unwilling or unable, Greeley states at the end of his essay, to carry out this responsibility.

The essays that follow Greeley's tell of experiences on a number of campuses where the concerns expressed by Greeley are taken seriously. Donald L. Garrity describes program innovations at San Francisco State College; Willam E. Engbretson traces new trends in teacher education; William Moore, Jr., tells of a new program for academically disadvantaged students at Forest Park Community College in St. Louis.

Part Four ends with two essays touching on the international dimension. Joseph Axelrod recommends a general requirement in intercultural studies to replace the current standard requirement in foreign languages. Glenn A. Olds shows why American programs abroad often fail, and he outlines a way by which the overseas undergraduate program can become a truly crosscultural experience. But neither of these authors is entirely optimistic. Part of the fault appears to lie with undergraduate faculty, who are not well-enough educated and who suffer as much from the myopia of ethnocentrism as the students whose perspectives they are supposed to broaden.

The twenty-three essays of the first four parts of the book leave the reader with the most serious question that college/university faculty and administrators have ever faced: Is planned change possible? Is college/university reform *really* possible?

The two essays of Part Five supply part of the answer. Lewis Mayhew, the author of the first essay in the section, hovers between faith and despair—faith in the ability of the leaders of American higher education judged by past successes in meeting difficult problems, and despair over the enormous discrepancy between our current activity and the ideals we proclaim. Mayhew, however, lays out a program for the immediate future. And Edith Green's essay, which closes the volume, while also not very optimistic, is similarly positive in its approach. National priorities are totally "inverted," Congresswoman Green declares, and they need to be reversed. She hopes that this reversal will come about by 1980, that we will by then "find the solution in Vietnam and get the priorities of this nation back in order again." If we do, then we can direct our energies toward a 1980 that we will control. If we do not, says Congresswoman Green, then we must be overwhelmed by an Orwellian 1984 that will control us.

PART ONE

A Society in Crisis

The four authors of Part One represent the four major disciplines: life sciences, physical sciences, social sciences, and the humanities. The two natural scientists are Barry Commoner, a center director at Washington University and chairman of the American Association for the Advancement of Science (AAAS) Committee on Science in Promotion of Human Welfare; and Alvin M. Weinberg, the Oak Ridge National Laboratory director and a recipient of the E. O. Lawrence Memorial Award for his contributions to nuclear reactor theory. The two authors who represent the social sciences and the humanities are Michael Harrington, chairman of the board of the League for Industrial Democracy and author of *The Other America;* and Charles Frankel, philosopher and former Assistant Secretary of State.

Section One contains essays by the two scientists, presenting sharply divergent points of view about the role of the university in a society in crisis. Commoner and Weinberg agree on

9

only one major point—that the American university is now largely inadequate for meaningful leadership in the solution of this country's social problems. On all other major points covered in the essays, the two authors stand at opposite poles.

Barry Commoner begins his essay, "The Dual Crisis in Science and Society," with the startling declaration that our civilization is incompetent not only in meeting social problems but also—and dangerously so—in the sphere of technology. Hence the dual crisis of his title. The essay, at its most profound level, is an attempt to explore what the author calls "the deep connections" between the two sides of the crisis. Only by understanding these connections, Commoner believes, can we move toward solution— on either the technological or the human side—of problems such as (in his own phrase) the terrifying deterioration of our cities.

Commoner's central point deals with the social responsibility of American colleges and universities. Although he respects the concept of faculty intellectual independence, he deplores the easy path to "a mandatory disinterest" that most professors choose to travel. This disinterest, he feels, has a twofold bad effect. It cuts the faculty off from the urgent needs of society as well as from their students.

In the daring final paragraphs of his essay, Commoner condemns his own generation for its insensitivity and inhumanity, while characterizing the new generation as both more sensitive and more humane. Students, he says, are far more able than their professors to define "what it is that we must try to escape." Professors need to learn from students "the sharpness of their definition of the issues," while students need from their professors "the competence and steady purpose that is the gift of experience." Working together, Commoner concludes, the two generations can secure what is so gravely threatened by the dual crisis in science and society.

In "The Think Tank and the University," Alvin M. Weinberg presents an opposite view: the university, at present, stands remote from the problems of our society, and it ought to stay that way. Weinberg believes the sociotechnological institute—what is popularly called the "think tank"—is far better equipped than the university for the job that society needs done, namely, the rational handling of difficult social problems. American higher education, he says, would do violence to the university tradition if it involved itself in social problems. It has, in any case, an important enough role to play without involving itself, that role being the preparation of the specialists who are needed to staff the think tanks.

Weinberg paints a picture, for the future, of an entire national network of these institutes, whose effectiveness, he asserts, will become even greater as they make closer contact with "hardware organizations." The author presents so convincing a picture as to raise a question, which the reader will undoubtedly find on his mind even before Weinberg expresses it: Is it possible that a society whose fundamental doctrines are formulated in a network of national sociotechnological institutes can remain a democracy? Weinberg raises this question and does not treat it lightly. But, quite predictably, he moves toward an affirmative answer.

Michael Harrington begins his essay, "The University and the Problem of Poverty," with a reference to Commoner's theme —the social responsibility of colleges and universities. The reference is appropriate; within the broad structure of Commoner's argument, Harrington's essay is, in one sense, simply a case in point. Concentrating on a single serious domestic problem— poverty—Harrington attempts to demonstrate why it is the university's responsibility to join forces with those elements in the community that are combatting the problem. Indeed, Harrington recommends that the university must enter into what he calls "a radically new relationship" with those elements. But there is a price, Harrington points out. In accepting this challenge, the university will necessarily involve itself in disturbing political conflict.

Charles Frankel's essay, "The Educational Impact of American Foreign Policy," appears at first glance to play a counterpoint to Harrington's; the one deals with a domestic theme while the other deals with American foreign policy. On one level, the two essays do enter into this kind of relationship, but Frankel's essay goes far beyond the limitations of such a parallel. He begins quietly, even humorously. But the reader is soon aware that behind his easy rhythms there beats a profound pessimism, and fairly soon the center of his concern becomes apparent: the relationship between the American college/university and "the national interest."

This relationship, which is relatively simple and clear when regents and presidents discuss it, takes on, in Frankel's essay, the most profound implications and the most complex textures. We are all, of course, aware that short-term policies in Washington necessitate the setting of short-term purposes for hundreds of the nation's campuses; and Frankel does not linger long over that point. He moves quickly on to ask why things are *so* wrong in the relationship between the federal government and higher education. And he answers his question by saying that the major cause is our nation's foreign policy.

Through a dazzling progression of ideas that cannot be adequately summarized, Frankel proceeds to the assertion that one of the tests by which American foreign policy is to be judged is its impact on higher education. What is good for higher education is good for the country's foreign policy, Frankel declares. And by such a test, our country fails badly.

The four essays of Part One, taken together, constitute a powerful dose. They succeed in delineating some of the crises of our society. But their major function in this volume is to give some stunning insights into the inadequacy of American colleges and universities in providing meaningful leadership for our society.

Joseph Axelrod

Section I

Technology and Survival

~1~

THE DUAL CRISIS IN SCIENCE AND SOCIETY

Barry Commoner

There is ample, tragic evidence of a deep crisis in the human condition. We struggle to live and to create in the shadow of death and destruction. More than two-thirds of the world population is either undernourished or on the verge of starvation. Even in the wealthiest nation in human history—the United States of 1968— many citizens are still struggling to emerge from poverty and win a just share of the nation's wealth. Spurred by such want, in the last fifty years the world has been shaken by a series of revolutions that have drastically changed the economic, social, and political structure of most of its nations—the USSR, China, India, nearly all of Africa and the Middle East, and most of Latin America. In that period of time the world has endured two great wars; in the last decade this nation has undertaken two major wars in the Far East, and one of them, in Vietnam, continues its desperate course. In the last half century the world has been in constant turmoil, which year by year has spread, become more complex, and vastly more dangerous.

The achievements of science and technology contrast vividly with the quality of life: we can nourish a man in the supreme isolation of outer space, but we cannot adequately feed the children of Calcutta or of Harlem. We hope to analyze life on other planets, but we have not yet learned to understand our own neighbors. We are attempting to live on the moon, but cannot yet live peacefully on the earth.

This is a terrible and frightening paradox: in the world of nature man exhibits—apparently—a magnificent competence; but in his own world, in human society, man appears to be a gross incompetent. The usual explanation of this paradox is that we are competent in the realm of science because no value judgments are demanded, and that we are tragically incompetent in dealing with each other because this does require adjustment between personal values and the social good—an adjustment of which we are frequently incapable.

I should like to propose another explanation: that the contrast between our technological competence and our ethical ineptitude is only apparent. We are tragically blind, I believe, not only about our fellow men, but also about important aspects of nature; we are dangerously incompetent not only in our relations with each other, but also in our relations to the natural world; our survival is threatened not only by a growing social crisis, but also by a technological crisis. And I believe that we must understand the deep connections between these crises if we are to learn how human values can guide the power of science and technology toward the improvement of the human condition and, indeed, if we are to survive these recent acquisitions of power.

One of the striking features of modern life is a deep and widespread faith in the efficacy of science and in the usefulness of technological progress. But there is now at least one good reason to question this faith: the phenomenon that has just begun to capture the public attention that it merits—environmental pollution. The rapid deterioration of the environment in which we live has become a chief determinant of the quality of our lives. We all know the dismal list: air pollution; pollution of water by urban and industrial wastes and by runoff of farmland fertilizer; multiple hazards of widespread dissemination of insecticides, herbicides, and fungicides; radiation hazards from fallout due to nuclear testing; and—for the future, if we make the catastrophic blunder—the consequences for the biology of man, beast, and plant of the massive nuclear, chemical, and biological weapons of modern war. These issues exemplify a general fault in the large-scale application of modern science to technology. We used to be told that nuclear testing was perfectly harmless. Only now, long after the damage has been done, we know differently. In October 1956, President Eisenhower had this to say about nuclear testing: "The continuance of the present rate of H-bomb testing, by the most sober and responsible scientific judgment, does not imperil the health of man." In October 1964, eight years later, President Johnson, in connection with the nuclear test-ban treaty, said:

> This treaty has halted the steady, menacing increase of radioactive fallout. The deadly products of atomic explosions were poisoning our soil and our food and the milk our children drank and the air we all breathe. Radioactive deposits were being formed in increasing quantity in the teeth and bones of young Americans. Radioactive poisons were beginning to threaten the safety of people throughout the world. They were a growing menace to the health of every unborn child.

Clearly, in 1956 the government thought that there was no harm associated with nuclear tests; but we exploded the bombs *before* we knew the biological and medical consequences.

This pattern is characteristic of many other accomplishments of modern science and technology. We produced power plants and automobiles, which envelop our cities in smog—before anyone understood its harmful effects on health. We synthesized and disseminated new insecticides—before anyone learned that they also kill birds and might be harmful to people. We produced synthetic detergents and put billions of pounds into our surface waters—before we realized that they would not be degraded in disposal systems and would pollute our water supplies. We are now, in Vietnam, spraying herbicides on an unprecedented scale —with no knowledge of their long-term effects on the life of that unhappy land. We are fully prepared to conduct a nuclear war— even though its effects on life, soil, and the weather may destroy our civilization.

Clearly we have compiled a record of serious failures in recent encounters with the environment. This record shows that we do not yet understand the environment well enough to make new large-scale intrusions on it with a reasonable expectation of accurately predicting the consequences.

This failure raises two important questions about the relations between science and technology and human values. First, what are the relative roles of science and human desires in the resolution of the important issues generated by our failures in the environment? Next, what are the causes of these failures, and how do they illuminate the dual crisis in technology and human affairs?

How can we resolve the grave public issues generated by our assaults on the environment? Sometimes it is suggested that since scientists and engineers have made the bombs, insecticides, and autos, they ought to be responsible for deciding how to deal with the resultant hazards. More cogently, it is argued that scientists and technologists are the only people who can resolve these issues. Here is the rationale of this position: scientists have the relevant technical facts essential to understanding the major public issues generated by new technology. Since scientists are trained to analyze the complex forces at work in such issues, they have an ability for rational thought that frees them, to some degree, of the emotions that encumber the ordinary citizen's views of these calamitous issues. And because the scientist is now in a particularly favorable position to be heard when he speaks—by government executives, congressional committees, the press, and the people at large—he has important opportunities to influence these social decisions.

There is a basic flaw in this position. Resolving the social issues imposed on us by modern scientific progress requires a decision based not on scientific laws, but on value judgments. What scientific procedure can determine, for example, whether the benefits of nuclear testing to the national interest outweigh the hazards of fallout? How can scientific method determine who is right—the proponents of urban superhighways or those who complain about the resultant smog? What scientific principle can tell us how to make the choice—which may be forced upon us by the insecticide problem—between the shade of the elm tree and the song of the robin? Certainly, science can validly describe the information to be gained from a nuclear experiment, the economic value of a highway, the medical hazard of radioactive contamination or of smog. However, the choice of the balance point between benefit and hazard is a value judgment; it is based on ideals of social good, or morality, or religion—but not on science. And if this balance is a social and moral judgment, it ought to be decided, not by scientists and technologists alone, but by *all* citizens.

How can a citizen make such judgments? These issues require a confrontation between human values and rather complex scientific data: the ecology of strontium-90 and herbicides, the chemistry of smog, the interactions between urban waste and runoff of farmland fertilizer. But most citizens are poorly prepared to understand such scientific matters. The solution demands of the scientist a new duty. I believe that scientists, as the custodians of the technical knowledge relevant to these public issues, have an obligation to bring this information before their fellow citizens in understandable terms. By this means scientists can place the decisions for the grave issues they have helped to create in the proper hands—an informed citizenry.

This duty is now recognized by many scientists in the United States. There is a growing movement among them to inform the public about the scientific basis of major social issues such as military and domestic aspects of nuclear power and environmental contamination. To the academic community in St. Louis, it is a source of pride that scientists and citizens in our own city have pioneered in this important work. And, at my own university, we have begun in some courses to teach science not simply as a discipline sufficient unto itself, but as the substance of the new political, social, and moral issues that trouble the modern world.

Nowhere is the urgency of this new task more clearly seen than in the matter of nuclear war. The scientific facts now available tell us that the entire system of nuclear war is incapable of fulfilling the prime purpose of national defense—preservation of our society. Our present military system's reliance on nuclear power is therefore futile. But the horrible face of nuclear war can be described only in scientific terms; it can be pictured only in the language of megatonnage and roentgens. The scientist has an obligation to help his fellow citizens penetrate the technological mask that hides the self-destructiveness of nuclear war. If he fails in his duty, the scientist will have deprived humanity of the right to sit in judgment on its own fate.

For these reasons I believe that the new duty of the scientist to inform his fellow men is the key to the humane use of the new powers of science. By this act the scientist can open the momentous issues of the modern world to the judgment of humanity. And it is only this judgment that has the strength to direct the enormous power of science toward the welfare of man.

How can we account for our recent failures in the environment, and what can we learn from such an inquiry about the relationship between science and technology and human values? These failures reveal a fundamental difficulty in the area of basic research on which we must rely for knowledge about the biological systems that are at risk in the environment. Biology has become a flourishing and well-supported science in the United States; it is producing a wealth of new knowledge, and is training many scientists skilled in its new methodology. But modern biological research is now dominated by the conviction that the most fruitful way to understand life is to discover a specific molecular event that can be identified as "the mechanism" of a particular biological process. The complexities of soil biology or the delicate balance of the nitrogen cycle in a river, which are not reducible to simple molecular mechanisms, are now often regarded as uninteresting relics of some ancient craft. In the pure glow of molecular biology, the biology of sewage is a dull and distasteful study hardly worth the attention of a "modern" biologist.

It is not surprising, then, that in contrast to the rapid increase in our knowledge of the molecular features of life, research on environmental biology has been slow. For example, the fundamental biology of soil nitrogen is still so poorly understood that we cannot, even today, draw up a reliable balance sheet to describe the fate of the huge tonnage of nitrogen fertilizer added yearly to the soil—much of which runs off the soil and contaminates the water.

For these reasons I believe that if we are to succeed as inhabitants of a world increasingly transformed by technology, we must reassess our attitudes toward the natural world on which our technology intrudes. Primitive people always see man as a dependent part of nature, a frail reed in a harsh world, governed by immutable processes that must be obeyed if he is to survive. The knowledge of nature primitive peoples achieve is remarkable. The African bushman survives in one of the most stringent habitats on earth; food is scarce, water even more so, and extremes of weather come rapidly. In this environment the bushman survives because he has an incredibly intimate understanding of the environment in which he lives. A bushman can, for example, return after many months and miles of travel to find a single underground tuber, noted in his previous wanderings, when he needs it for his water supply.

We claim to have escaped from such dependence on the environment. Where the bushman must squeeze water from a searched-out tuber, we get ours by the turn of a tap. Instead of trackless wastes, we have the grid of city streets; instead of seeking the sun's heat when we need it, or shunning it when it is too strong, we warm ourselves and cool ourselves with man-made machines. All this tends to foster the idea that we have made our own environment and no longer depend on the one provided by nature. In the eager search for the benefits of modern science and technology we have become enticed into a nearly fatal illusion: that we have at last escaped from the dependence of man on the balance of nature.

The truth is tragically different. We have become not less dependent on the balance of nature but more dependent on it. Modern technology has so stressed the web of processes in the living environment at its most vulnerable points that there is little leeway left in the system. Unless we begin to match our technological power with a deeper understanding of the balance of nature, we run the risk of destroying this planet as a place suitable for human habitation. Despite our vaunted mastery of nature, we in the "advanced" countries are far less competent inhabitants of our environment than the bushmen are of theirs. We are brilliantly successful at managing those processes that can be confined to a laboratory or a factory, but this success dwindles at the doorstep.

Perhaps *the* basic inadequacy of modern science is its neglect of systems and processes that are intrinsically complex. Certainly this failing is evident in our environmental problems. The systems at risk in environmental pollution are natural and, because they are natural, complex. For this reason they are not readily approached by the atomistic methodology characteristic of modern biological research. Water pollutants stress the total ecological web that ties together the numerous organisms that inhabit lakes and rivers; their effects on the whole natural system are not adequately described by laboratory studies of pure cultures of separate organisms. Smog attacks the self-protective mechanism of the human lung; its noxious effects on man are not accountable by an influence on a single enzyme or even a single tissue. If, for the sake of analytical detail, molecular constituents are isolated from the smashed remains of a cell, or single organisms are separated from their natural neighbors, what is lost is the network of interrelationships that crucially determines the properties of the natural whole. Therefore any new basic knowledge that is expected to elucidate environmental biology, and guide our efforts to understand and control pollution, must be relevant to the entire natural biological systems in which these problems exist.

Nor is our neglect of complex systems limited to environmental biology. A further neglect is quickly revealed, for example, by a brief inquiry into the state of modern computer science. Shortly before he died, Norbert Wiener, the mathematician who did so much to develop cybernetics, the science of designing computers, warned us about the problem. He cited, as a parable, experience with computers that had been programmed to play checkers. Engineers built into the electronic circuits a correct understanding of the rules of checkers, and also a way of judging (from a stored record of its opponents' moves) what moves were most likely to beat the human opponents. The first results of the checker tournaments between the computer and its human programmers were that the machine started out playing an accurate but uninspired game that was easy to beat. But after about ten or twenty hours of practice, the machine got the hang of it, and from then on the machine always won. Wiener concluded that it had become technically possible to build automatic machines to carry out very complex activities that elude the comprehension of their operators and that "most definitely escape from the complete effective control of the man who has made them."

Recently this difficulty has become painfully evident to the specialists who are attempting to manage the operation of the current generation of electronic computers. They are extraordinarily frustrated men. They have at their disposal beautifully designed machines, capable, in theory, of complex interdigitation of numerous mathematical operations. However, the operators have not yet learned how to operate these machines at their full capacity for complex computations without encountering inexplicable errors. A spectacular example of a similar difficulty is the New England power blackout of November 1965, in which a complex powerline network, designed to effect an even distribution of generating capacity over an 80,000 square mile area, failed. Instead of providing outside power to a local Canadian power system that had suffered a relay failure, the network acted in reverse and caused every connected power system to shut down. And a frightening potential catastrophe is the possibility that the complex, computer-guided missile systems—which can in minutes thrust us into the last World War—are equally susceptible to such failures.

There is, I believe, a common cause for our failures in situations as diverse as a power network and fallout. A power network or a computer is a machine of enormous internal complexity. What the failures tell us is that it has now become possible to construct machines that are so internally complicated as to overreach our present capability to understand complex systems. Our inability to understand the fallout problem or environmental pollution has a similar source, except that here the complex system involved is not made by man, but by nature.

It is not a coincidence, I believe, that the scientific and technological problems that affect the human condition involve inherently complex systems. Life, as we live it, is rarely encompassed by a single academic discipline. Real problems that affect our lives and impinge on what we value rarely fit into the neat categories that appear in the college catalogue: medieval history, nuclear physics, or molecular biology. For example, to encompass in our minds the terrifying deterioration of our cities we need to know not only the principles of economics, architecture, and social planning, but also the chemistry of airsheds, the biology of water systems, and the ecology of the domestic rat and the cockroach. In a word, we need to understand science and technology that is *relevant* to the human condition.

However, we in the university community have been brought up in a different tradition. We have a justified pride in our intellectual independence, and know—for we often have to battle to maintain it—how essential this independence is to the search for truth. But academic people may sometimes tend to translate intellectual independence into a kind of mandatory disinterest in all problems that do not arise in their own minds— an approach that may in some cases cut them off from their students and from the real and urgent needs of society—such as a habitable environment.

We university scientists have a clear obligation to the society that supports us. Supported by that society, we have gained a deep knowledge of nature; our universities are the custodians of this knowledge. And as the custodians of knowledge won at social expense, we have the solemn duty to make that knowledge useful to society. We have no right, I believe, to retreat behind the walls of our laboratories, if—as it must—our knowledge of the world can help improve that world as a place for human habitation.

If we accept this duty, how can we make it jibe with the principle of academic freedom, so firmly associated with the life of learning, which holds that every scholar should be free to pursue the studies that interest him and free to express whatever conclusions the evidence and the powers of his mind may generate? Does not such protection give him immunity from the students' appeal for relevance and from the demands of society for service to its needs? Is not this protection essential to the intellectual independence of the university and the justification for its freedom from political restraints?

There are no simple answers to these questions, but a useful guide has been given by a man who has contributed much to the making of the modern American university—Alexander Meiklejohn. According to Meiklejohn, academic freedom is not a special immunity from social responsibility, but, on the contrary, a basic part of the duty the university and the scholar owe to society. The university, he believes, is an institution established by society to fill its own need for knowledge about the nature of the world and man. For no society can long endure unless it takes into account the laws of nature and the aspirations of man. The scholar's search for the truth is thus not merely an obligation to himself, to his profession, or to the university, but a duty to society. And in this search open discourse is essential, for no scholar's work is complete or faultless; and the truth—whether it relates to the mechanism of biological inheritance, to the medical effects of fallout, or to the political origins of the war in Vietnam —can emerge only from the interaction, open and unconstrained, among the views of the separate scholars that make up the academic community. The scholar's duty is not to truth for its own sake, but to truth for society's sake. As Meiklejohn says, our final responsibility as scholars and teachers is not to the truth, but to the people who need the truth.

The scholar's work, therefore, must be devoted not only to the truth, but to human needs; the scholar's duty becomes, thereby, inevitably coupled to social issues. But if we accept relevance to social need as an important criterion for the choice of a field of inquiry, we, and the society that supports us, must recognize, as a necessary consequence, that scholars will become concerned not only with social needs, but with social goals. We cannot ask a physician, a biochemist, or a historian to dedicate his inquiring mind to society's needs without at the same time expecting him to be equally inquisitive about what those needs are, and what he thinks they ought to be. He will be motivated in his work not only by a concern for the truth about nature and man, but by an equally strong sense of engagement in the problems of society. And if society expects the scholar to honor a duty toward the development of socially significant knowledge, society must equally honor his freedom openly to express a concern with social goals. Those whom we serve should see in our zeal for this freedom not the selfish exercise of privilege, but a response to these solemn obligations.

The academic world is now emerging from a long period of silence, a silence that has obscured the true purpose of the university, and has weakened its service to society. We now hear many new voices in the universities. Some speak in the traditional well-modulated language of the scholar, some in the sharper tones of dissent, and some in a new language that is concerned less with transmitting ideas than feelings. But behind nearly all the voices is a mutual concern with the quality of life. Among our students this concern is often reduced to its most elementary level—a demand for the right to life itself. And this is natural, for our students represent the first generation of human beings who have grown to adulthood under the constant threat of instant annihilation. Our own generation—yours and mine—is often criticized because we have, with our own minds and hands, created the weapon of total human destruction; we invented the first nuclear bomb, and worse, we have built and deployed for instant release enough of them to ensure the destruction of humanity. But an even greater sin is that our generation has become numb to the frightful meaning of what we have done. We can speak, with relative calm, of the choice between a war that kills fifty million people or one that kills a hundred million; the very effort to apply logic to a situation that is in its entirety totally inhumane, is, in effect, a confession of our own inhumanity.

The newer generation, our students, have a different way of sensing these things. If nuclear death threatens our generation with an earlier end to an already in part fulfilled life, it threatens theirs with the total loss of a life yet to be fulfilled. They, far better than we, can sense the total inhumanity of the civilization that we share. If they fail to suggest a reasonable way out they have at least defined what it is that we must try to escape. We need the sharpness of their definition of the issues; they need from us the competence and steady purpose that is the gift of experience. Together we can, I believe, secure for all of us what is so gravely threatened by the dual crisis in science and in society—a technology that serves the life of man and a society that cherishes the right to life.

2

THE THINK TANK
AND THE
UNIVERSITY

Alvin M. Weinberg

These are tough times. Our country is wracked by racial unrest and by Vietnam, by decaying cities and by unabated pollution, by crime and by hippyism. Even these social stresses are small when measured against the twin catastrophes that are now so commonly predicted: widespread and permanent famine caused by the uncontrolled growth of population, and a polarization of the world into antagonistic races. One need not invoke the ultimate catastrophe—thermonuclear war—to conclude that times are indeed tough.

I shall not suggest solutions to these complex social problems; rather, I shall suggest a certain kind of new institution that

27

might help deal with these questions: this is the modern "think tank."

Think tanks, ordinarily regarded as inventions of the nuclear age, are really very old. Francis Bacon in the *New Atlantis* described what we would now call a think tank. He called it Solomon's House, an institute that sent several representatives abroad every twelve years to obtain knowledge "especially of the sciences, arts, manufactures, and inventions of all the world . . . thus you see we remain a trade not for gold, silver or jewels, but only for God's first creature which was light. . . ."

Perhaps the most influential of the modern think tanks, and the best known, is RAND, located in Santa Monica. RAND was organized in 1947 by the Air Force to examine "intercontinental warfare, other than surface." Over the years it has gradually broadened its terms of reference, and it now concerns itself with many matters that are not directly connected with the national defense. In the most telling sense, RAND has over the years developed coherent doctrine with respect to our entire defense posture. Perhaps most important, it has provided a language in which much of the debate over arms limitation and strategic defense is conducted. The current techniques of programming, planning, and budgeting that are used governmentwide originated in some of the cost-benefit analysis carried on by RAND.

RAND has been so successful in part because it sits outside government and is removed from the hurly-burly of putting out fires yet is considered part of the Air Force family; and in part because it has been able to examine problems coherently and in their entirety rather than in fragmented pieces.

RAND's success has stimulated many other think tanks to hang out their shingles. The Army's Research Analysis Corporation (RAC), the Navy's Center for Naval Analysis (CNA), the Defense Department's Institute for Defense Analysis (IDA), Mitre, the Systems Development Corporation (SDC), the Hudson Institute, TEMPO—all of these institutes have been predominantly, but not exclusively, agents of the military concerned with military planning of the broadest sort. In recent years some of the civilian agencies have been considering setting up their own think tanks. The Department of Housing and Urban Development is in the process of setting up an Institute of Urban Development to help formulate policy, and the recently established Medical Advisory Board of the National Academy of Sciences may be the forerunner of a think tank for the Public Health Service.

The state of California has already used systems engineering organizations to analyze important public questions. Early last year, four aerospace companies completed reports on crime, mental health care, state information systems, and disposal of wastes. These experimental studies were then assessed by SDC. It will be interesting to see what effect the studies will finally have on California's legislation in these important social areas.

The think tank, insofar as it can provide underlying coherent doctrine, represents an important step in the direction of rational handling of difficult social problems. But think tanks are not all-knowing. As a *New Yorker* cartoonist (January 13, 1968) had a government official say, "Best think tank in the country, and their conclusion after two years, thousands of dollars, and millions of words is 'God only knows!' "

And, in fact, think tanks may be a little too remote from actual hardware technological development to enable them to contribute fully to the formulation of viable doctrine. For modern social problems have both social and technological components. Their most effective resolution will often require a judicious melding of the knowledge of social scientist and engineer, of economist and physicist, of sociologist and biologist.

For example, crime is largely a social problem, but would any coherent and modern approach to the control of crime neglect the new technological possibilities for quick communication and nonlethal incapacitating agents now available? Our cities could be saved if people's prejudices were softened, but in the meantime better technological approaches to building houses and to controlling the physical environment of the city surely would be included in a rational approach to urban problems. The whole strategy for staving off thermonuclear war clearly involves developments in nuclear weapons and rocketry as well as in negotiations, not to mention the Washington-Moscow hot line, an imaginative application of communications technology.

Think tanks as presently organized, though they have many able engineers and physical scientists on their staffs, suffer because their contacts with technologies tend to be derived contacts. An economist is not qualified to judge how feasible a new reactor is going to be; he must make his judgment on the basis of either his own imperfect technical knowledge or on the advice of a reactor expert he trusts. If the economist studying nuclear power operates in an environment where there are no actively working reactor experts, his estimates of the future of nuclear power are likely to be in error. The literature of nuclear power economics in the 1950's was sprinkled with predictions that nuclear power would cost about twice what we now believe it will cost.

There is another reason why the think tanks of the future might be improved by closer contact with hardware organizations. The coherent doctrines of the future will often require entirely new technological inventions designed for a specific social purpose. For example, a strategy for rebuilding the ghettos cries for a simple way to rehabilitate old houses. Communication by underground tunnel would require new ways of digging tunnels. Thus a truly imaginative coherent doctrine will often require a specific kind of technology, and such a technology can come only in an institution organized for technological innovation.

It is on this account that I have urged the creation of national sociotechnological institutions or laboratories to help develop the coherent doctrines we shall need to cope intelligently with today's desperate sociotechnological problems. Each institution would be both a think tank and a national laboratory—a combination of RAND and ORNL (Oak Ridge National Laboratory), or TEMPO and Argonne, or IDA and NBS. It would have both software and hardware types; it would have computers for the social scientists and electron microscopes for the hard scientists. Its coherent doctrines would not only apply existing technologies, and make projections on the basis of the expected innovations of technology by outsiders; it would also be based often on its own technological projections and innovations.

Perhaps a couple of examples from our experience at ORNL may help clarify the sort of thing I have in mind. At ORNL we have been examining the problem of civil defense. This is an unpopular, even repellent subject since, as Herman Kahn has stressed, we hate to think about the unthinkable. Yet thermonuclear weapons exist, and they will not go away. We really have no choice but to examine civil defense—soberly, dispassionately, scientifically.

Our small group of social scientists, natural scientists, and engineers has been subjecting civil defense to integrated, broad analysis. In what sense is civil defense feasible? Would a credible civil defense make thermonuclear war more or less likely? Could civil defense shelters, which we visualize as interconnected underground tunnels, serve also as utility tunnels?

These are difficult, sticky questions. In trying to answer them one is constantly confronted with the intimate interaction between technology and social questions. The feasibility of civil defense depends not only on the existence of adequate shelters but also on the attitudes of people who are to inhabit the shelters; conversely, the attitudes of people toward shelters is influenced by the adequacy of the shelters. Or the whole national position toward civil defense—whether it is to be taken seriously or to be rejected as it largely has been—depends first of all on whether civil defense can be made to work.

In our studies we have found that a key element is a technological invention—the interconnected tunnel grid system. The details of such an interconnected tunnel system require knowledge of civil engineering, municipal design, thermonuclear weapons effects, and other diverse specialties. The options available to the social scientists in looking at social aspects of civil defense were enlarged by this invention.

A second example of how a coherent doctrine might be developed in a sociotechnological institute is afforded by a recent study of the application of nuclear power to the production of food in India. William and Paul Paddock, in their terrifying book, *Famine 1975!*, predict that widespread famine is inevitable in India by the middle of the coming decade, and that nothing can be done to avert a staggering calamity.

Yet the situation may not be really as hopeless as the Paddocks have predicted, thanks to a brilliant sociotechnological invention made by Professor Perry R. Stout of the University of California at Davis, with some help from the Oak Ridge National Laboratory. Stout points out that the entire Gangetic plain is underlaid with ground water not more than thirty feet below the surface. If this water could be used for irrigation during the eight dry months of the year, not one but two and possibly three crops could be grown annually. Moreover, if the new high-yielding wheats developed by the Rockefeller Foundation in collaboration with the Mexican government were used, the yield per crop would be tripled: the overall wheat crop might be quadrupled or even sextupled—enough to convert India from a net importer of wheat to an exporter within a decade or so. That such possibilities are not pipe dreams is suggested by experience in Pakistan during the past couple of years. About 50,000 irrigation wells have been dug in the Indus Basin of West Pakistan, and the wheat crop there has increased to the point where West Pakistan is soon expected to grow all the food it needs for its people.

The key to the scheme is power: to energize the pumps on the hundreds of thousands of shallow wells that would be needed to get at the ground water, and to manufacture the huge amounts of ammonia fertilizer that these new varieties of wheat require. What would be needed eventually are about ten huge nuclear power stations, each providing about one million kilowatts. The entire plan, as formulated by Professor Stout in collaboration with nuclear power experts at Oak Ridge, would cost around ten billion dollars. This is lots of money, but it is no more than India is expected to spend in foreign exchange for imported wheat during the next decade. Last November a team of a half dozen experts from Oak Ridge went to India to confer with representatives of the Indian AEC about the Stout plan, and other schemes involving nuclear power for producing fertilizer. The response of the Indians has been enthusiastic, and I would anticipate positive action aimed at implementing Professor Stout's plan.

I have given these two examples to show what a coherent doctrine combining both technical and social elements amounts to, and to show how people with widely different expertise are needed to formulate it. Both in the matter of civil defense and in the matter of hunger in India, the social scientist by himself would have been thwarted because his technological horizon was too limited: he could not have been expected to come up with blast-proof tunnels nor with huge nuclear reactors to provide power for pumping water and for processing fertilizer. Similarly, the engineer would have been thwarted had he tried to put his schemes into effect, because so much must depend upon proper cooperation from the people who would use either the shelters or the tube wells. Both engineers and social scientists are needed, and both I believe are strengthened by working side by side.

A national sociotechnological institute such as I have described is perhaps analogous to an engineering laboratory, where typically many different disciplines are combined to develop and build a single engineering device, such as a Saturn rocket or a big nuclear reactor. But since the matters we are dealing with have such strong social components, these institutes might best be called "social engineering laboratories." For indeed, the coherent doctrines that we envisage as the outputs of these institutes are examples of social engineering in its most modern sense: schemes for improving man's lot that embody all the expertise in all relevant fields of hard and soft science.

What role can the university play in the formulation of these coherent doctrines? Can the university itself become a national sociotechnological institute? The university obviously already possesses some of the requirements for such an institute; it is perhaps the only institution in our society that has under one roof sociologists and physicists, economists and chemical engineers, political scientists and medical researchers—in short, the people needed to devise coherent doctrines with respect to our pressing problems. But I doubt that the university can or should become a national sociotechnological institute. What might happen when the university tries to be a think tank is caricatured by Voltaire in *Candide*. "After the earthquake which destroyed three-quarters of Lisbon, the wise men of that country could discover no more efficacious way of preventing a total ruin than by giving people a splendid auto-da-fé. It was decided by the University at Coimbra that the sight of several people being burned in great ceremony is an infallible secret for preventing earthquakes." For the weakness of the university as a coherent think tank is also the essence of its strength and uniqueness: its discipline orientation and the intellectual autonomy of the professor. In the university, the intellectual inclination of the professor determines the direction in which he goes. The university is purposely cloistered and somewhat remote so that the professor can probe from an appropriately distant standpoint. Moreover the university is primarily a collection of independent scholars. Though much is said nowadays about interdisciplinary approaches, and we see institutes spring up around universities, my impression is that these do violence to the university tradition and therefore generally have tough going. An engineering laboratory, even a social engineering laboratory, requires a hierarchical organization with an organization chart; a boss who tells those under him what must be done, and employees who are prepared to do what is expected of them. But this sort of organization is anathema to the university; a professor of analytical chemistry is under no compulsion to drop what interests him in order to analyze a piece of zirconium that a colleague in the department of metallurgy is studying. Thus, although the university possesses the disciplines that go into coherent doctrines, it lacks the coherence and the interdisciplinary viewpoint that make it an appropriate seat for the development of such doctrine.

This is not to say that the university, even in its present configuration, will not contribute importantly to developing coherent doctrines. Often the most original spark, like Professor Stout's brilliant idea, originates in the mind of an isolated professor. It is the working out of the subsequent details, both technical and nontechnical, that demands a big problem-oriented institution, a social engineering laboratory. And such original thinking, such brilliant flashes will probably come more often from the unfettered university than from the hierarchical social engineering laboratories. So one surely will see an exchange of ideas and a flow of professors between universities and national sociotechnological institutes, much as we now have a continuing flow of natural scientists between the university and the present national laboratories.

But the strongest interaction between the universities and the national sociotechnological institutes will be through the university graduates who will staff the institutes. And here I believe the universities will face a challenge to their current mode and bias. For the essence of the national institutes must be their mission-orientation and search for solutions to social problems. Their approach is predominantly engineering rather than scientific; it is interdisciplinary. Its staff, to be successful, will therefore have a deep commitment to the problem at hand rather than to the profession in which they were originally trained. I speak no un-revealed truth to university administrators when I point out that this wholeness of approach, this commitment to the problem rather than to the discipline, is foreign to the university and, un-fortunately, to the modern graduates of the university.

How can the university modify itself to create in those graduates who will man the national sociotechnological institutes the required commitment and taste for solving problems through social engineering? Is it too wild to suggest that, just as the uni-versities have established schools of engineering whose graduates typically have performed the conventional engineering tasks of the day, perhaps in this new day of severe social stress we shall need schools of social engineering whose graduates will perform the social engineering of the day? Institutes that approximate such schools already exist—for example, the Center for Urban Studies at the University of Chicago. I wonder if they would not be im-proved for having more hard technology and hard science in-cluded in their curricula. Since the social problems of today require both soft and hard scientists working together, the train-ing of the young social engineer must include a fair exposure to the relevant hard science of the time, and the training of the hard-ware engineer exposure to the social sciences.

Nowadays there is growing concern about the lack of in-terest in the application of knowledge as opposed to knowledge itself on the part of the graduates of our universities. This was a recurrent theme in the report *Applied Science and Technologi-cal Progress* (June 1967) prepared by a National Academy of Sciences panel for the Daddario Subcommittee of the House Committee on Science and Astronautics. The remoteness of the basic outlook taught at the university ill fits the student for the solution of real problems. Though most of the report's concern on this point was directed at the separateness between the pure and applied natural sciences, there was a fair concern also with an equivalent remoteness in the social sciences; such concern has been voiced particularly by the demographer Kingsley Davis, who goes so far as to deny the validity of "applied" social science.

How to overcome this remoteness—how to balance the discipline-orientation of the university with the problem-orienta-tion of the institute is a recurrent, almost insoluble problem. One suggestion that may have merit comes from Arthur Kantrowitz and Edward Teller in *Basic Research and National Goals* (NAS, March 1965). These applied physical scientists urge that the industrial laboratories of applied science be made available to university students who might serve internships there, or even do their Ph.D. theses in the problem-oriented atmosphere of the applied laboratory.

A variant that appeals to me is suggested by our experience at ORNL with the MIT Practice School of Engineering. Each year we accommodate some thirty or so engineering students from MIT who spend time at our laboratory performing a succession of engineering tasks. The students spend three months at ORNL and receive credit toward their master's degree for this work. So one wonders whether, as part of the newly visualized schools of Social Engineering, one might not plan practice schools in conjunction with national sociotechnological institutes. The students would work for a time at an institute as part of their regular program.

The relation between the university and the think tank, or the sociotechnological institute, has become somewhat equivocal in the past year or so. On the one hand we see the university setting up its own institutes, such as the Center for Population Studies at Harvard, or the Center for Urban Studies at Chicago, or a host of Institutes of Science and Public Policy. These university-based think tanks are generally not hardware-oriented, so they would fall short of the institutes I have proposed. On the other hand, we see a tendency toward withdrawal of the university from connection with such institutes as the Institute of Defense Analysis, largely on the grounds that the university is out of sympathy with the aims of IDA.

Yet the university cannot have it both ways. If it wishes to participate in the formulation of coherent doctrine, it must be willing to address itself to doctrines that the society or, more accurately, the government needs to formulate. If the universities withdraw from connection with IDA on the grounds that formulation of coherent military doctrine is tainted, why should the university expect to be called upon to formulate doctrine about the city? The government cannot be so choosy about what it does and what it does not do: the university of course can, but in so doing it inevitably reduces its interaction with, and ultimately its influence upon, government.

In spite of my doubts about the university being a proper instrument for formulation of coherent doctrine, I can see an essential role that it must play in addition to training the young people who will formulate these doctrines. I refer to the university as social critic. The doctrines that are formulated, even by the cleverest and most knowledgeable think tanks and sociotechnological institutes will, after all, be fallible. There is always the severest danger that doctrines, simply because they are the only ones that have been formulated coherently, will acquire a status and acceptance that goes beyond their fundamental wisdom and sense. It will always be important for such doctrines, even coherent ones, to be criticized by those who are outside the bureaucracy, and outside the institutions that have formulated the doctrines. The individual professor must say his piece if he believes the newly fashioned coherent doctrines are wrong or dangerous or both. This certainly has happened during our present crises; and despite the discomfort the university teach-ins engender among us members of the establishment, this kind of social criticism will continue to be a necessary element of our social edifice. For just as the doctrines themselves acquire more and more technical and expert elements, so the critiques of these doctrines if they are to be responsible will require corresponding sophistication. In part, the traditional role of the press as the means of keeping the politicians honest may have to be exercised more strongly by the university, simply because it takes a university professor to understand the technical intricacies of the new modes of resolution of social problems.

I have two other points. First I ask whether a society whose fundamental doctrines are formulated in a network of national sociotechnological institutes, supported by the universities, can remain a democratic society? Will we not slide into a kind of scientific technocracy in which the will of the common man is thwarted simply because he cannot understand the details of what is going on? As Bertrand de Jouvenel has said, can democracy survive technology? This is certainly a danger; but I think it is not necessarily a fatal one. In the first place, we already operate in a technocratic environment where the details of economic policy are to most people just about as mysterious as are the details of the Apollo project; yet what we have now is still democratic government. The extent to which the technocrats preempt power from the masses will depend in good measure upon the education of the masses. With almost half of our high school graduates entering college now, I see at least some reason to be hopeful about our future masses staying well enough abreast of our technological doctrines to prevent the takeover de Jouvenel envisages. (I am told that Paul Samuelson's book, *Foundations of Economic Analysis,* has been read by several million Americans.) And secondly, we must never underestimate the inertia of politics. It is well and good for a technologist to visualize a society in which the heavy thinking is done by a network of think tanks, but it is quite something else for the coherent doctrines to survive the political process. In 1966, every professional economist I knew assured me that a tax increase was necessary; yet the realities of politics transcended and superseded the imperative of economic reason. To the formulator of neatly coherent doctrine this is patently silly and untenable bullheadedness; to the political and social philosopher this may be ultimately the only way for democracy and scientism to coexist—neither fully effective, neither fully prevailing, yet one hopes each keeping the other honest and thus preserving the political structure.

I close with an even more fundamental concern. In arguing for the formulation of coherent doctrines by think tanks and other institutions as a necessary step in resolving our profound social stresses, I make a vast and unprovable assumption: that the methods of science, of exact observation and careful generalization, of controlled experiment and quantitative analysis are relevant to the resolution of social problems. As a technologist I of course live by this faith: that rational analysis, in the spirit of modern science, must be equal to every task, even the tasks that confront us during these tough times. But I confess to a tiny doubt that we scientists may be wrong: that in dealing with very complicated social systems, and particularly with individual humans, we may have to invent new modes of attack that are not at all subsumed in our modern scientific approach. Several scientists, notably the psychologist Abraham Maslow and physicist Walter Elsasser, have begun to voice such doubts. As Elsasser puts it, modern physical science is based on the overwhelming assumption that all electrons are identical. By contrast, *no* two living cells are identical, nor are two human beings, nor are two social systems. We can predict the behavior of electrons because they are identical: though we may be able to predict the behavior of large ensembles of cells or people on the average, this may not be good enough to solve specific social problems. A remedy for rioting in Detroit may or may not work in Los Angeles; a means for resolving the fighting in Vietnam may not help at all in the Middle East. What is at issue is nothing less than the relevance or usefulness of academic social science to the solution of social problems. Certainly academic sociology is not as relevant to the problem of the ghetto as is thermodynamics to the design of a desalting plant. This is not to say that social scientists are not very useful; but perhaps what they should supply to the formulation of coherent doctrine is perspective rather than methodology, knowledge rather than analysis.

But having voiced these doubts and, by implication, having invited the universities to examine their validity, I see no choice but to proceed with the knowledge we possess. Our neat scientism with its interacting think tanks and universities and social engineering laboratories is to my mind a hopeful kind of approach. Man is imperfect and his knowledge is incomplete. If for this age of the H-bomb and rampant overpopulation and violent social stress the intellectual edifices we have erected are inadequate, so be it and we shall not survive. But we would not be human if we did not erect such edifices and thus apply human reason to the resolution of human problems.

Section II

Human and Social Ecology

3

THE UNIVERSITY AND THE PROBLEM OF POVERTY

Michael Harrington

Barry Commoner writes in this volume of the unwitting hazards of scientific technology. I want to write about the unwitting hazards of social and economic policy. Commoner writes of the necessity for value judgments relating the natural sciences to society. I would like to focus on the need for social science itself to be more conscious of its needs for value judgments and for relating to the society. And I would do so by focusing and concentrating on what is to me a terrible paradox: with the best intention in the world, desiring to abolish poverty (as I think we honestly do) and without any malevolence whatsoever, we are currently spending more money to promote poverty than to abolish it.

I would like to suggest the arguments that demonstrate my

assertion. First, I will document it; second, I will treat this incredible paradox as a problem for policy makers, particularly in colleges and universities; and finally, I will narrow the challenge even more specifically into a challenge to higher education in the United States.

So, first of all, the evidence: the federal agricultural programs were begun in the 1930's with a good social purpose, the best in the world; but one of the consequences of the way in which we spent literally tens of billions of dollars for agricultural subsidies since the 1930's was to drive millions of uneducated, illiterate, black and white poor people off the farms of the South and into the ghettos and slums of the cities of the South, North, East, and West.

As a matter of fact, recently the *Wall Street Journal* noted that in the last two years the subsidies to cotton alone have been 1.8 billion dollars. The basically rich cotton farmers (the corporate farmers, because that is who gets the agricultural subsidies) got in two years a subsidy equal to one year of the Poverty Program. And the *Wall Street Journal* is hardly a radical, revolutionary source. As the *Wall Street Journal* said, everyone in Washington knows that one of the uses to which that 1.8 billion dollars is put—and perhaps the most important social use—is to finance mechanization, to withdraw land from production, and to force people off of the land and into the cities.

Think for a moment what this means: that 50 per cent of the people in Harlem were not born there. Think what this means when you consider the problems of civil disorder. The Kerner Commission on Civil Disorders told us in its summary the rather shocking fact that in thirty-one years, this society has built eight hundred thousand units of housing for the poor, and in thirty-four years it has financed over ten million units of housing for the middle class and the rich.

Indeed, I submit that throughout America's housing programs—ever since the first one in the 1930's under the New Deal, and certainly since the one in 1949—we have given much more lavish subsidies to the middle class and the rich than to the poor, and the effect of the housing program has unintentionally, because we didn't see the consequences, been to widen the gap between the two and to increase the agony of poverty in the United States.

This was certainly true of urban renewal, particularly under President Eisenhower. Urban renewal in the 1950's was used to aid downtown businessmen, downtown office buildings, downtown department stores, and civic projects; and to remove Negroes and poor people from the sight of those institutions. It had an antisocial and counterproductive effect. Consider the paradox that at the same time the government was bankrolling the building of suburbia and thus facilitating the flight of the middle class out of the city under urban renewal, it simultaneously had a program to persuade the middle class to come back into the city. In either case, if you were middle class, you could not lose; and in either case, if you were poor, you had to lose.

And here is a problem of visibility and invisibility in a social sense: the subsidy in housing to the poor is visible. It is a big high-rise segregated barracks. Chicago has the worst one in the United States of America down on the South Side—just a big jail for poor people, where poor people can see only poor people. That is visible. We all know about that. Now, on the other hand, consider the pride of all good middle-class people, who can feel that they are virtuous and Emersonian because they are not on the dole; and yet, leaving aside the fact that suburbia was built with federal credit, as the Kerner Commission [1] tells us, consider that in 1962 the value of the tax write-off to the middle-class and upper-class homebuilder for the interest on his mortgage payment was in dollar terms equal to twice what we spent on public housing. So, not simply agricultural expenditure, but housing expenditure has actually made the access to getting out of poverty more difficult.

Next, I come to that expenditure that is the one truly socialist program that every citizen in the United States wants to support: highways. Highways are something we can always sell. Once, as a matter of fact, I suggested that we could get a radical program through the Congress of the United States if we called poor people *cars*.

We currently have a fifty-billion-dollar federal highway

---

[1] *Report of the National Advisory Commission on Civil Disorders* (New York: Dutton, 1968), Otto Kerner, Governor of Illinois, Chairman.

program. It was initiated under Eisenhower by the Republican Administration in the 1950's; and yet, as the *Manpower Report of 1967* of the United States Department of Labor and the *Report* of the Council of Economic Advisers in January 1968 told us, one of the main consequences of that highway expenditure has been to move businesses and middle-class people out of the city, to make jobs much more distant from the central city, and to isolate the black and white poor in the central city. Further, if you want to read the report of the McComb Commission in California, one of the consequences of this expenditure of federal highway funds was to incite the riots in Watts—because the transportation system in Los Angeles was built with taxpayers' money for the convenience of those who were not poor. Those who were poor had to rot in their ghettos with the jobs miles away; they didn't have cars, and there was no decent public transportation.

As an example of the governmental socialization of crisis, the National Commission on Inter-Group Relations told us in January 1968 that we as a society currently spend more money on the education of wealthy children than on the education of poor children. The lowest expenditures are in the rural backwoods of the South, where our federal agricultural program—with its displaced-persons approach—is sending these children North. The next lowest expenditure is in the slums of the cities. The suburbs get the highest expenditure. This method of spending tax money is upside down—isn't it crystal clear that governmental funds should be used for those in greatest need and not for those with greatest opportunity?

Finally, with regard to federal support to poverty, let me present a most ironic case. I am speaking of the largest single antipoverty program we have. When the Administration currently tells us how much we are spending on poverty, it uses a statistical trick. It gives a figure of about twenty-six billion dollars. The trick is that the majority of that money is money contributed by the people themselves. That money comes from Social Security and other programs of an insurance character, not from governmental grants. More than that, the irony is that Social Security, our largest single program, in terms of dollars, for giving money to the poor, is based on a regressive tax system that maldistributes the wealth in the United States. Social Security is cheap insurance for the rich and expensive insurance for the poor; and so here again we have this paradox in our society: that because we did not think of the consequences of the way in which we designed programs, these programs actually make life more difficult for the poor.

I would suggest in a very brief, sketchy theory that this is not an isolated thing, and it is not something that happens because of the ill will of some people in government who are against the poor. Of course that is not the case. What happens, I believe, is that government, in the absence of strong, conscious, and politically powerful countermeasures, intervenes according to the logic of power and commerce priorities. For this reason, government intervention will take on the character of the society; and rather than change the society, the intervention will shore it up—even when such intervention is proclaimed in the name of changing society.

For example, let me name for you the chairman and ranking members of the Senate Agricultural Committee, which presides over the subsidies I mentioned at the beginning of this paper. The chairman is Senator Allen Ellender; the ranking members are Senators Holland, Eastland, and Talmadge; and if you want to know why the agricultural programs tend to favor the rich farmer rather than the poor farmer, that is at least part of the answer. The realities of the political power of the rich farmers in the United States of America are centered in the Senate Agricultural Committee. Or if you want to know why we make some of these incredibly unthought-out investments in superhighways without considering alternative uses of funds that might also help the poor, it is of some relevance that four of the ten largest corporations in America sell either cars or gas. As a matter of fact, the most amusing case in point, to me, is now taking place in San Diego. San Diego was worried about the problem of transportation. Being a sophisticated city, it wants a systems analysis of the problems of transportation; and it has hired a private company to give it a systems analysis of its transportation problem. That company is a subsidiary of the Ford Motor Company.

Although the above instance is almost humorous, similar things happen, in the absence of strong countermeasures, throughout our society. This leads to the second point I want to make: we must have these countermeasures, and the university has a role to play as one of the forces for those countermeasures.

I think the Administration itself is obviously coming to understand the need for some kind of planning, for some kind of systems analysis. John Gardner, before he left—we had a review for McNamara when he left but apparently not even a handshake for Gardner—was proposing some kind of social cost accounting in the society. But I think even these tentative understandings on the part of the government that we have to see things systematically and in terms of social consequences are much too tame, too cautious, too timid. They rely on the assumption that the job can always be done on a basis of consensus, that there need be no conflict involved, that you can hire the Ford Motor Company to give you an objective analysis of what you need in the way of a transportation system. This strikes me as an act of faith.

I suggest that if we take the idea of social cost accounting, of understanding the social consequences of agricultural programs, or highway programs, or housing programs, before we invest the billions of dollars, then we are going to have to make some fairly radical and conflict-laden departures. For example, to change our agricultural program will require challenging certain vested agricultural interests. To change transportation policy might cause some conflict with the Ford Motor Company. And in the area of education, if we are going to have true community-of-scholars participation at all of these levels, we might challenge some of the companies now coming into the knowledge industry who want to corporatize and systematize and profitize systems analysis.

If the colleges and universities begin to make these judgments, begin to develop measures and criteria of social consequence, we will involve the administrations of the universities and colleges in conflict, perhaps even with some of their donors. I think such involvement is a dangerous business, but it has to be done if we are to escape from this truly obscene situation of spending more money to promote poverty than to abolish it.

So, I would suggest that one of the basic challenges to the university in the coming period is for it to become a center where definitions of social costs and accountability are made. It must become a center to expose these problems, to define these problems, and to suggest alternative ways of dealing with them.

We know, for example, that right now there is a struggle going on in Washington, D.C., over where a road is going to be placed; and perhaps for the first time in human history we actually might build a road and not remove Negroes in a city, because there are people who are aroused and fighting, and some of them are part of the Department of Transportation. We know, for example, that in Baltimore there is an experiment funded by the government called the "Baltimore Concept Team," where the design of a road is being considered not simply by engineers and politicians, but by a task force that will include social scientists and psychologists. I think that in this area the university can make a profound contribution to our society.

We have in America—and I think they have been extraordinarily useful—the National Institutes of Health. It seems to me that we could well endow with generous federal funds National Institutes of Social Health, in which there would be socially provided funding for the college and the university to take on this kind of pioneering research.

It might get the institution into trouble with some of its present sources of funding, but I am not suggesting that campus scholars with their Olympian knowledge should look down upon the society and the poor people in it and devise socially good programs for them. I think there is, indeed, a real danger that systems analysis in a bureaucratic and élitist sense could outrage the poor and could outrage the people generally by turning them into ciphers, by making them into IBM cards.

I think, therefore, that if the university is not to become a source of elite definitions and elite decision making and elite concepts, it must, as Barry Commoner suggested, enter into a relationship with the actual organizations of the people. It must break down the walls that so often separate higher education from the masses of people in the society. The university has to be in a relationship, it seems to me, with civil rights organizations and community action organizations and neighborhood organizations that don't want to be bulldozed. One thing is true about this society: you can no longer do anything unless you have access to expert knowledge. Everybody needs it. The corporations already have their expert knowledge; city hall has its expert knowledge; the poor do not. It seems to me that here is another part of the challenge: the university has to bring its knowledge down into these communities and not simply make up definitions of social consequence and social good from on high, but make these definitions in the course of a dialogue with the people who are down there.

For example, there are many colleges and universities that have been think-tanking it for some years for the Army, Navy, Marines, CIA, and many other institutions. How about every college in the United States having in a sense a think tank, a bank of data, and scholars and expert knowledge available to the people in the community who are engaged in struggle? Instead of simply telling the Air Force what a maximum-rocket policy is, a university could actually enter into a relationship with a group of people who are a community school board and who want to challenge the Board of Education with their sets of figures and want to challenge what the Board of Education says about the reading level of children in that school. Doesn't the university have a relationship to those people?

So, in summary: We know that not simply in the area of biological and life sciences, but in social and economic policy, the most sophisticated techniques employed by sincere and honest men with good purpose can have disastrous consequences. We have to understand that this society for some years has been—and at this moment still is—providing tax money to subsidize the very crisis that it deplores; that one of the main agencies of the crisis of the cities has been the federal government. That government, when it invested tens of billions and even hundreds of billions of dollars in roads and housing and education, did so without thought of the social consequences to those less able to defend themselves. It did so according to the priorities of established power in the society, and therefore it did so by making the life of those at the bottom of the society worse.

Defining that reality and seeking ways out seem to be one of the basic challenges that higher education in America today faces. I candidly say that if higher education accepts the challenge, it will necessarily involve itself in disturbing political conflict; but I see no other way out for our society and the crisis it faces. I do not believe that in accepting this challenge—and in even being radical and accepting the idea of conflict that it involves—

the university can look down on the poor and hand down the
solutions from on high. This challenge requires the university to
enter into a radically new relationship with groups in the community throughout the United States—not just to meet an ethical
obligation, but to develop new knowledge and to bring it to the
people.

4

THE EDUCATIONAL IMPACT OF AMERICAN FOREIGN POLICY

Charles Frankel

A number of years ago I addressed the American Association for Higher Education on the subject, "The Happy Crisis in Higher Education." The theme of my remarks was that higher education was full of problems. But I expressed the view that these problems might have a good side to them. They might wake us up. They might give us the provocation to examine the premises of our activities and to do some intellectual housecleaning that was long overdue.

There is still a crisis in higher education. Added to the old one, in fact, there is a new one. Since I am somewhat older, perhaps it is simply the changes in my metabolism that lead me to take a less cheerful view of our current situation than I did of the situation we faced some years back. But I don't really think that the grim picture I see before me is merely the reflection of my advancing years. It would be odd if any thinking man were to pronounce anything but a severe judgment on the present condition of higher education in our country.

Let us get the qualifications out of the way first. Almost a hundred and fifty years ago, a Mrs. Trollope, a British visitor to these shores, remarked: "In conversing with Americans I have constantly found that if I alluded to anything which they thought I considered as uncouth, they would assure me it was local, and not national; the accidental peculiarity of a very small part, and by no means a specimen of the whole. 'That is because you know so little of America,' is a phrase I have listened to a thousand times, and in nearly as many different places." Well, the lady was right, and so were her critics. Even before leveling my criticisms I could hear the defensive words in people's throats. I confess I could hear them in my own. Obviously, no generalization that says disagreeable things about our country could possibly apply to it without qualifications.

It is true that no nation has ever before undertaken to educate so large a proportion of its people between the ages of seventeen and twenty-two. It is true that our nation, along with others like the Soviet Union and Japan, has turned higher education into a powerful instrument for reducing class barriers. It is true that during the last ten years, and particularly during the life of the present national Administration, the public funds spent on higher education represent a new and ambitious national commitment. And it is true that American scholarship has added immensely to its luster during the last generation. In its methods, in the talent available to it, in its achievements, it is a major resource for the entire international community.

But it is precisely these truths that compel one to take a jaundiced view of American higher education's present performance. The capacities of American higher education are considerable. It is in those terms that it is not doing well. In terms of what we have in this country, in terms of what, at the beginning

of the sixties, we knew that we would have to do, we are performing badly.

The problems that existed at the beginning of the sixties
are worse now than they were then. We knew then that, in too
many places, undergraduate education had become unacceptably
impersonal. That situation makes more trouble, not less, today.
We knew at the beginning of the sixties that, for all our achievements in scholarship, something was missing. What was it? A
quality of skepticism that turns back on the conventions of each
discipline and questions them? A quality of commitment that
would make the practitioners of each discipline eager to teach it
to the young, because they would regard it as an instrument for
civilizing the mind? No matter. People who find such questions
not truly scholarly are still in command of most of our fields of
learning. And we knew at the beginning of the sixties that something systematic would have to be done to guard the university's
sovereignty. Yet the universities today are engaged more extensively than before in research and teaching that represent concessions to the highest bidder, and not expressions of any considered
decision about what is intrinsically best for the progress of education and learning.

I hope I shall not be misunderstood. I don't think that
people in colleges and universities are so preternaturally wise
that they can make the right decisions without ever being presented with alternative ideas from the outside. And I think it is
a caricature of the truth to say, as some do, that the colleges and
universities of this country have been turned into servile instruments of something known as "the military-industrial complex."
Nothing more is needed to refute that proposition than the fact
that most of those who say it are inhabitants of college and university campuses.

Equally, it is fatuous to speak as though every dollar received from a federal source had something tainted and threatening about it, something inherently corrupting of honesty and
courage. Undeniably, there are congressmen who haven't read the
Constitution of the United States with full attention, and who
therefore become confused when professors who receive federal
funds go right on acting as though they enjoyed full freedom of
expression. And undoubtedly, there are bureaucrats who tremble

when these solons squeak. But the fact remains that the federal government's support of higher educational enterprises has almost invariably been accompanied by an understanding of the conditions of academic work and by respect for the rights of the educational community. Its record, surely, is at least as good as that of most state legislatures or alumni organizations.

The erosion of educational sovereignty of which I speak has not come from censorship. It has come from the pattern of ad hoc research contracts and short-term commitments for support that reduce colleges and universities to the status of intellectual handymen selling their services from door to door. It has come from the diversification of energies, the buying up of talent, the loss of a consistent sense of priorities. And in this process the federal government has played a considerable role, though, of course, not the only role.

It is at this point that I come to the central subject of my paper: the educational impact of foreign policy, the consequences for education of the foreign policies that we follow. If the policies are short term, then educational resources will be devoted to short-term purposes. If these policies are subject to uncertainties, then an element of uncertainty is introduced into the educational community. And that has happened. It is the first and simplest effect of our foreign policies on our educational affairs.

Undoubtedly, the short-term, contractual relationships between the federal government and higher educational institutions have also had a good effect. They have permitted much good research and interesting teaching to take place that might not otherwise have occurred. But these arrangements have also meant the depletion of the educational community's limited resources. Very often, too, they have meant that the university must undertake long-range commitments even though the federal government itself offers no assurance of continued federal support.

The situation is not a good one. Efforts have been made to repair it, through changes in AID (Agency for International Development) legislation, through proposals that Senator George McGovern has put before his colleagues, and through the International Education Act, which was passed in 1966. But all these efforts have been abortive. Although some changes have taken place, we are substantially where we were five or six years ago.

In fact, in certain respects we have slipped backward. Allow me a brief discussion of principles to make plain what I mean.

The colleges and universities still preserve the major portion of their sovereignty, despite the problems that I have just mentioned. They do so because most of them have firm sources of support apart from short-term contracts. But if these institutions are to realize their full potentialities as independent centers for research, criticism, and social leadership, the federal government is going to have to play a large role in keeping them properly financed.

The support that the federal government gives should be support that is cut loose from short-term requirements or emergencies. It should have the characteristics of regularity and predictability. It should permit institutions of learning considerable discretion with regard to the use of the funds they receive. And it should be support aimed not at this or that quick result, but at the strengthening of education in its long-range purposes. Such federal support, needless to say, should not be the only kind of support available to higher educational institutions. Other sources of support are also indispensable. In unity there may be strength, but, as far as educational financing goes, in plurality there is freedom.

It is in these terms, I think, that we are now worse off than we were. A few years ago the federal government seemed to be moving with confidence and imagination toward putting the principles I have just described into practice. Now, although these principles still receive official declarations of loyalty, the government has turned back on itself, and is moving in the opposite direction. There have been substantial cutbacks in support to education, scientific research, and international exchange. Even more tragic have been the cutbacks in the hopes the American people were permitted and encouraged to entertain even as recently as thirty months ago.

Federal support to the arts and the humanities remains scandalously low, and is in peril of extinction. The International Education Act has received not a dollar with which to be implemented. The statements of intention of this Administration with regard to the initiation of a worldwide program of educational advancement are still merely statements of intention.

To be sure, you may think that it was wrong for the federal government ever to get into the business of supporting higher education; but whatever you think on that subject, you cannot think that it is good for the federal government to follow a policy of now-you-see-it-now-you-don't. It is possible to show that some things have been done; it is possible to play with figures. But it is not possible to play with people's expectations and to imagine that there will be no consequences. It is not possible to stir their expectations one year and to leave them in the lurch the next without doing damage. Much is said these days about the importance of keeping our commitments. I think that is a commendable idea. It is a principle of sound government at home as well as abroad.

I do not want to ask who is responsible for what has happened—the President, or the Congress, or perhaps Ho Chi· Minh. I think, however, that there can be no argument about *what* is responsible. The major cause of these events is our foreign policy, and, most immediately, our policy in Vietnam. This does not in itself prove, needless to say, that this policy is wrong. But it does indicate part of the price we pay for it.

Yet so far I have mentioned only the less important consequences of foreign policy. Our foreign policy is also the reason for our selective service system. That system has changed the relation of students to their teachers, to grades, to their educational experience in general. It affects the outlook, the choices, the frame of mind, probably of every student in the country, women as well as men. It subjects many of the most sensitive of them to cruel dilemmas and choices. It has contributed, as we all know, to fractiousness, indiscipline, and suspicion on a very large number of the campuses in this country. That does not prove, I would admit again, that either the selective service system or the foreign policy that requires it are wrong. It is merely another price that we are willing to pay.

But as we add up these prices, it would be natural to ask at some point, I presume, what the worth of a foreign policy is. We live in a period of cost-benefit analysis. Have we applied this method of analysis to our foreign policy? Even to ask the question is a kind of oddity. The normal approach to these matters is to determine foreign policy goals and then to ask whether we have the wherewithal to reach them. It is not often asked, if ever, what these goals are worth, or what other goals will be sacrificed. And the reason it is not often asked, of course, is that one does not ask such questions where something called "the national interest" is at stake.

And so I come to my ultimate question. What is the relation of education to "the national interest"? What do we mean by that solemn phrase anyway, which need only be introduced into a discussion to silence everyone but the man who has spoken it?

I would like you to think about a fact that is perfectly obvious when you stop to think about it: The largest single external influence on the shape and focus, the atmosphere and health, of American higher education is exerted by American foreign policy. The major decisions made in government affecting higher education are made by people who usually aren't thinking about higher education at all.

This raises a question that is the reverse of the one usually asked, but still I think it is reasonable to ask it. The fact that it is unusual to ask this question indicates how oddly we view foreign policy, how much we insulate it as an artificial thing, how much we set it aside and apply assumptions and value judgments to it that are separated from the normal business of our lives.

The question that is raised, it seems to me, is a straight-forward one. What is the impact of our foreign policy on the education of the American people? It is common to ask what contributions higher education can make to the fulfillment of this country's purposes in the international arena. And it is, of course, perfectly proper to ask such a question. But the reverse question is at least as urgent. It is astonishing, indeed, that it is not commonly asked. Indeed, this in itself is a symptom of the power of foreign policy to mesmerize us and at times to turn normal modes of thought upside down.

Am I suggesting, then, that a test of American foreign policy should be its impact on education? Yes. Not the only test, but a test. Am I saying that what is good for education, and particularly higher education, is good for the foreign policy of the country? I believe I am. And that what is bad for higher education is bad for the foreign policy of the country? Not invariably, but generally, yes. Well, then, am I not guilty of the same sort of confusion about means and ends that gained a one-time president of General Motors undying fame? No. With all respect for automobiles, there is a difference between the functions of General Motors and the functions of a college or university. There is a difference between things and people.

The essence of the conviction that separated the Greeks from those they called the barbarians was that a society is, as we now say without thinking about what the word means, a *culture*: it is a soil, a setting, in which people grow, in which the character of the individual is formed. Everything about it, therefore, has an educational meaning. Everything about it can be judged by the kind of educational impact that is exerted. The heart of liberal civilization lies in the idea that you measure the worth of a society by the quality of the human beings it produces. And crucial to a society's achievement, therefore, are its formal institutions of education.

This is the background of the Greek view that their freedom, by which they meant participation in the affairs of the commonwealth, was the first and greatest of their possessions. They liked democracy (when they did) because they thought it educational. They liked it, among other reasons, because they thought it offered the right setting and orientation for formal institutions of education. And when the Athenians looked down on the Spartans it was because the Spartans, as the Athenians thought, had reversed the proper order of things. They educated men to be warriors. They did not realize that the function of education was to make good men, and that good men would be good warriors when they had to be.

All this indicates, I think, that it is not insane to ask about a foreign policy: what is its educational impact? And I suspect that if we asked this question more insistently, we might come to assess our foreign policies with clearer eyes and a sterner intelligence.

Consider, for example, our arguments about foreign assistance. What is the case for foreign assistance in Africa or in India? Is it really because we fear the power of the people of these areas if they turn against us? Is it because they have material resources we absolutely need? Are our economic or strategic interests seriously involved? It seems to me that a hard and honest look at the facts would yield a negative answer to all these questions. We give ourselves practical reasons not because these are reasons that stand up but because they are the only sorts of reasons we are supposed to admit publicly. We give ourselves these reasons, if I may suggest it, because they are the kinds of reasons which convention tells us are practical.

But being practical, after all, merely consists, as I understand it, in doing something for a good and urgent reason rather than for a frivolous one; it consists, beyond that, in choosing one's ends so that they fit one's means and capacities. So there does seem to me to be an entirely practical reason for foreign assistance. It is a far better reason, I think, than those that are usually given.

It is simply that we do not want our children to grow up in a world in which, on one side, we Americans sit back in indifference, while on the other side, large portions of mankind will be prey to famine, epidemic, and despair. We do not want such a world because it would be possible to live in it only on one of two conditions. Either we would be ashamed, but would do nothing about it; or we would have lost our sense of shame. In neither case would we have a good environment in this country in which to bring up children. In such a world there would be a quality of retreat and indifference in higher education, a separation of conscience from learning, that would make a college or university campus an unhealthy and grossly disagreeable place to be.

I know of no better argument against isolationism. I know of no other argument that we need. It is not, I confess, a very difficult argument to follow. It doesn't measure up at all to the subtle and intricate arguments, ranging from the domino theory to the theory of games, on which our foreign policy is so often alleged to be based. Still, it does not seem to me to be beneath consideration for this reason. Indeed, it is an argument that helps me to know what I am talking about when I use the phrase "the national interest." And that is a reassuring feeling.

The educational test for foreign policy has even more utility, I think, when we ask about the impact of foreign policy not only on education in the United States, but on education elsewhere. There are some purposes which, as educators know (and, I suspect, as a great many ordinary men know), simply cannot be achieved by force. There are some purposes which are destroyed when force is used. The most important and long-distance purposes of the United States in the international arena are of this sort. Education has a chance to achieve them. And a foreign policy that makes it difficult to turn to education is a mistaken foreign policy.

Moreover, a foreign policy that is based on the presumption that it is we who shall educate others is also, on these tests, a grievously mistaken policy. It is a disturbingly innocent policy. There are some things that people cannot learn unless they learn them for themselves. There are many things they simply will not learn if others are trying to teach them. And there are also a good many things that we Americans do not know. We don't know the answers in our own country, much less the answers for others. It is the recognition of this, I suspect, that explains much of the restiveness and cynicism now on our campuses.

I do not mean to say that our present foreign policies rest entirely on these innocent presumptions. There are more sensible impulses in them as well. But these simple-minded and self-congratulatory impulses are there too, and they are the ones that get us into trouble. We are not invariably harmful, we are not even invariably useless when we go overseas. On the contrary. But our usefulness to others is proportionate, I suspect, to our recognition that there is a need to educate ourselves. The important consequence to us of a foreign policy that made education a major concern is that our own intellectual and emotional resources would be greater. Our colleges and universities would be better. They would be more cosmopolitan; more aware of alternatives; more sober; more sensitive to the sound that the American voice makes in other people's ears.

This is not the moment to spell out the ways in which the colleges and universities of this country might play their part in an educationally oriented foreign policy. That is something for the future—I hope for the not too distant future. The present moment is one in which we must ask ourselves, more simply, to contemplate two large tendencies in foreign policy. For two general possibilities have long been present on the American scene, and are before us now. They ought to be compared from the point of view of their educational significance.

On one side, we have the tendency to make foreign policy decisions in isolation from their educational impact at home or abroad. This, it is commonly thought, is realism in foreign policy. Foreign policy, according to these conventions, is not philanthropy; it cannot go in for frills. And because this presumably realistic approach takes a narrow approach to the business of foreign policy, it deprives itself of a variety of instruments that might be available. The natural consequence is that it drifts increasingly into reliance on force. It finds itself seeking to accomplish purposes through the employment of means that are not designed to achieve such purposes and that are disproportionate to the value of any of the ends that are sought.

Most immediately relevant to our present discussion, such a policy is educationally disruptive. Is it surprising that there is stress on the American campus when the increasingly dominant tendency in American foreign policy is to employ instrumentalities which Americans have been taught all their lives to condemn and abhor? Is it surprising that there is stress on the university campus when our foreign policy, if we wish to support it, requires us every day to go in for extensive rationalization and excuse giving?

I do not want to oversimplify the issue. It is a complex one. I do not think that any government can live by the standards of morality that are appropriate to the behavior of individuals. I do not mean to say that we must expect governments to be immoral. I mean to say only that the standards of morality and responsible behavior that apply to individuals are different from the standards applicable to governments—not better or worse, but different. No less a philosopher and moralist than Spinoza held this view, so I do not think that I am entirely a cynic in adhering to it.

There is, however, an important qualification that has to be added. It is a qualification that applies particularly to governments that derive their legitimacy from the consent of the governed, and to a country that took its conception in the phrase "a decent respect to the opinions of mankind." The government of such a country does not have to abide by standards that are absolutely identical with those appropriate to the individual and his private life. But these standards cannot be so different that the country's most sensitive citizens, and particularly its young people, are left stunned or bewildered. This difference in standards does immeasurable social damage. It erodes the basis of authority on which a government of this sort depends. And it produces a foreign policy too grossly out of character to be successful.

There is an alternative. There has always been one. It is to have a foreign policy that conceives the important purposes of foreign policy in educational terms. I do not assume that, overnight, we can dispense with armies or with disagreements that verge on violence. I do not suppose that that will be possible in any reasonably foreseeable future. I assume only that we cannot use violence intelligently without measuring its educational impact and asking the price.

But one can speak in more positive terms. Looking at Vietnam, looking beyond Vietnam, what are our sensible purposes in foreign policy? It is a purpose of American foreign policy, I think, to reduce the tensions between the poor and the rich countries; this requires, above all, the better distribution of information and ideas, the better distribution of educational opportunity, and, underlying all the rest, the better education of Americans in the facts of international life. A crucial instrument for such a purpose is the American college and university.

And it is a purpose of American foreign policy, I think, to move toward a system of habitual negotiation and accommodation between nations and between different social systems; in this respect again, the problem we confront is essentially educational. To deal with it requires the development of partnerships that cross the borders, the building of practical interests that hold people together and give them an interest in resisting together the divisive tendencies of political rivalries and ideological superstitions. No institutions offer more promise with respect to the building of such partnerships and interests than American colleges and universities.

I cannot help but think that there is more realism in this path than in the paths that are conventionally called realistic. Such a conception of the function of American colleges and universities would enable them to do their jobs better. It would ennoble them, and it would move to the center of this nation's relations with other nations those aspects of our national life that carry the most hope for us and for the rest of mankind.

PART TWO

Students

It should not surprise the reader to find that the eight essays of Part Two focus entirely on student rights and student activism. The opening section, which deals with student rights and freedoms, consists of two essays—by Robert Van Waes, associate secretary of the American Association of University Professors, and by Robert B. Yegge, dean of the College of Law at the University of Denver.

Robert Van Waes' essay, "Student Freedoms and Educational Reform," provides a bridge between Part One and Part Two, for Van Waes sees close relationships tying student freedoms to the university as an instrumentality of social reform. These relationships are subtle but strong, he points out, and they account for the fact that many students, as well as some faculty and administrative officers, "have become persuaded that one way to reform American society is to reform the university."

Van Waes finds it entirely reasonable that students measure colleges and universities by the criteria that the colleges and universities themselves have taught are appropriate for judging social institutions. And by these very yardsticks, he contends, students have found our institutions wanting. The essay ends with a listing of the six areas in which students believe college/university reform is vital.

Robert B. Yegge opens his essay, "Emerging Legal Rights for Students," with two preliminary points. The first point is that, for more than a decade, the courts have systematically expanded civil rights protection. The second is that students *qua* individuals are not excluded from the opinions of the United States Supreme Court. He then launches into important contemporary legal issues in student-college relationships. The author invites the reader to "shepardize" (this term will be new to most academicians), and he cites a number of court rulings while, at the same time, expounding a hypothetical situation involving the morals arrest of a student named Carleta. Carleta is a twenty-year-old Mexican-American who has been arrested by the local police in an off-campus apartment.

The Conduct Review Committee at the university becomes aware of Carleta's arrest through a newspaper story. The girl refuses to "explain" her conduct, as reported in the newspaper, to the committee, and she is suspended. The legal complexities of the case are clearly beyond the simple minds of the faculty members sitting on the committee, but Yegge patiently leads his reader through them. Although the essay is somewhat technical, it will prove interesting even to readers who are not legal-minded.

The remaining two Sections of Part Two focus on student protest and activism. The second section, entitled "Dissent and Defiance," contains three essays: the first is by Terry F. Lunsford, project director at the Center for Research and Development in Higher Education at the University of California in Berkeley; the second is by Theodore P. Greene, professor of history at Amherst College; and the third is by Richard Axen, professor of higher education and former academic senate president at San Francisco State College.

Terry F. Lunsford's essay, "Activism, Privatism, and the Moral Advantage," begins by characterizing the changes that have taken place in student protest between Berkeley in 1964 and

Columbia in 1968. The protest is now far more militant, there is far greater property damage, there is violence (the Free Speech Movement in Berkeley was essentially non-violent), and there is far greater punitive use of force. In brief, escalation and sophistication of tactics (to use Lunsford's phrases) have taken place—on *both* sides.

It is natural to ask why the protests have increased and continue to increase. But it might be more revealing, Lunsford asserts, to ask why student protest should *not* increase. As he seeks to answer this question, Lunsford presents an analysis that is both subtle and disturbing. This analysis leads the reader to one underlying cause of the basic paralysis in America today: the moral and political and intellectual confusion within the adult society.

What must we do? The responsible adult, Lunsford declares, cannot leave the political contest to angry student activists and to the backlash from the right. The responsible adult cannot afford to engage in "privatism." Lunsford's discussion of privatism—and the message that lies therein for the adult liberal—should prove memorable for readers of this volume.

Theodore P. Greene presents, in his essay, "John Cotton, Anne Hutchinson, and the Student Power Movement," a fascinating recountal of the dilemma Reverend John Cotton faced in Massachusetts more than three hundred years ago. The similarity between this situation and the problem with which college administrators of today must cope—paralysis in the face of ambiguity—is startling. Greene's suggestion for resolving the ambiguity is "not to haul students into court . . . but to influence their own style, their own approach, by the nature of our response." He illustrates this principle by describing the College Council at Amherst, on which students occupy half the seats.

Richard Axen agrees with Greene about the importance of faculty and administration response to student protests and how this response may be used to *educate*. A major theme in Axen's essay, "Faculty Response to Student Dissent," is the harm—educational and political—that comes from our hysteria in the face of a demonstration of student power. We will permit, we cry, as much dissent as students wish to voice, so long as it is peaceful dissent. But in Axen's analysis, there is a close relationship between peaceful dissent and powerless dissent. And he wonders, therefore, about the purity of our reverence for peaceful protest. A sensible way to stop a revolution is to correct some of the obvious conditions that breed converts to the cause, Axen maintains, and in the final portion of his essay he offers concrete examples of long-overdue campus reforms. Some readers will undoubtedly disagree with Axen's position, but all readers will find the essay bright, direct, and provocative.

The final Section of Part Two, entitled "Explanation and Judgment," consists of three essays which do exactly that. The first essay, devoted to explanation, is by S. L. Halleck, director of student health psychiatry and professor of psychology at the University of Wisconsin. The second and third essays, devoted to both explanation and judgment, are by Edward Joseph Shoben, Jr., head of the Center for Higher Education at State University of New York at Buffalo, and by Lewis B. Mayhew, professor of education at Stanford University.

As the title of Halleck's essay, "Twelve Hypotheses of Student Unrest," shows, a variety of hypotheses are presented—or rather, as Halleck says, groups of hypotheses—that seek to explain student unrest. Some of them are sympathetic to students, others are critical of students, and three are "neutral." But none of the twelve hypotheses, Halleck believes, is to be rejected. "There is some truth," he says, "to the most critical as well as the most sympathetic." Indeed, one of his purposes in the essay is to demonstrate the "futility of searching for simple explanations of highly complex phenomena." Still, the three neutral hypotheses are the ones that will strike the reader as the most inclusive, the most profound, and the most satisfying.

One would do an injustice to these hypotheses to attempt a summary of them. This is especially true of the three neutral hypotheses. Suffice it to say that in the first of these explanations, student unrest is related to modern technology; in the second, it is related to the new media; and in the third, it is related to faith in scientific rationality. Halleck himself favors the neutral hypotheses (rather than the ones favorable to students or critical of them) as "the most intriguing and the most powerful valid explanations of student unrest." But he offers a disconcerting comment about them: "At the same time, they are the most difficult to live with optimistically."

That comment must give us pause. It becomes especially significant in the context of Section Five, with the essays of Shoben and Mayhew immediately following Halleck's.

"Thoughts on the Decay of Morals," the essay by Shoben, renders an unfavorable judgment on the new student morality. Shoben explains that his judgment of student activism has taken this turn only fairly recently. Until recently, he says, a healthy re-thinking of ethical ideas has been generated by the confrontation between the student sector and traditional society. This confronta-tion in the past has been, he believes, an authentically *moral* one, but something has now gone wrong and—in Shoben's thesis—the new morality is decaying at its center.

The demonstration of this thesis leads Shoben to a thor-ough examination of the concept of civil disobedience. This por-tion of the essay ought to be required reading for student-faculty seminars. Shoben lists the circumstances under which a planned violation of law may be acceptable, justified, or even beneficial (there are seven sets of such circumstances), but he argues that these conditions are not being met by the student activist move-ment today.

Mayhew's essay, "A Rendering of Accounts," suggests a resolution to the dilemma expounded in the essays of Sections Four and Five. Mayhew begins his essay by saying that "American higher education stands on the verge of imminent impotency unless new ways of dealing with restless students are discovered," and he then reviews what he calls "the litany from 1964 to 1968." He analyzes the causes of student unrest and arrives, finally, at a recommendation for solution of the problem.

Mayhew suggests, for all college officials, "a tight construc-tionist interpretation," under which they would limit their con-cerns to "defensible educational matters through use of clearly defined powers and recognized procedures, leaving all other mat-ters to individuals." As is characteristic of his writing about higher education, Mayhew takes pains to show how his ideas can be translated into action. He presents a whole stream of concrete examples that would make possible the application of his princi-ples—even in a crisis—without panic or paralysis, without hysteria, and without the necessity of converting colleges into churches, clinics, or family meeting rooms. If the policy he recommends is followed, Mayhew contends, order may yet be restored and accounts finally settled.

Joseph Axelrod

Section III

Rights and Freedom

⚔ **5** ⚔

STUDENT FREEDOMS AND EDUCATIONAL REFORM

Robert Van Waes

Students have always been somewhat more interested in reforming academic life than their professors or college administrators. The U. S. National Student Association, for example, discovered the need for academic freedom for students shortly after it was founded two decades ago. The American Association of University Professors began to get interested in 1960 and by 1965 had produced a statement of its own. In retrospect, it seems unpardonable that the AAUP should have waited forty-five years to turn the coin of academic freedom to its other face.

In November, 1966, thirty-three representatives from ten national organizations met in Washington, D.C., under the auspices of the AAUP to explore the feasibility of creating some kind of consensus in this long neglected area. Since that time that consensus has been promoted with great diligence and unusual success. In July, a committee representing several national organizations of higher education produced a *Joint Statement of Rights and Freedoms of Students* which was endorsed by USNSA in August, received the approval of the Council of the AAUP in October, and was recently endorsed by the Association of American Colleges and the American Association for Higher Education. Other organizations are expected to lend their approval.

Thus, within less than a year, one of the most significant documents in the history of higher education will have been framed and approved. To the extent that the *Joint Statement* recognizes new student rights in the classroom, in extracurricular activities, in the students' status as citizens, and in the area of academic due process, it is a harbinger of that revolution in institutional relationships without which our colleges and universities are not likely to reform the world that lies beyond the campus gate.

But this is only the beginning. It is one thing to praise the new freedoms outlined in the *Joint Statement,* but quite another to bury *in loco parentis* by speedily and effectively implementing the new standards on particular campuses. The five sponsoring organizations will promote that effort in their several constituencies but, in the last analysis, the new relationships of the student to the campus and to other components will rest on local implementation. The first of new demands in the area of student academic freedom is that professors and administrators, as well as students, take these proposed standards seriously and act, in good faith, to implement them on local campuses.

A second consideration is implicit in the *Joint Statement.* A section on "Student Participation in Institutional Government" states: "As constituents of the academic community, students should be free, individually and collectively, to express their views on issues of institutional policy and on matters of general interest to the student body. The student body should have clearly defined means to participate in the formulation and application of institutional policy affecting academic and student affairs. . . ."

Three comments might be offered about those two sentences, both of which are considered of paramount importance by students and by myself. First, the concept is not new. The *Tripartite Statement of Government of Colleges and Universities* issued in December 1966, by the AAUP, the American Council on Education, and the Association of Governing Boards contained a specific recognition of students "as an institutional component coordinate in importance with trustees, administrators, and faculty and pledged to assist in defining the student role in institutional governance at an early date. Second, it seems only reasonable to recognize that students who have been taught the worth of democratic principles, the importance of developing a critical intelligence, and the merit of traditional humanistic values would insist on measuring colleges and universities, as well as other social institutions, by these yardsticks. That they have found our educational institutions wanting is clear; to them colleges and universities appear as inadequate as the other social and political mechanisms of our time. Indeed, they believe that all of these institutions have directly contributed to our current social crisis. It is possible that they are quite correct. Finally, it seems clear that many students—and some professors and some administrators—have become persuaded that one way to reform American society is to reform the university.

What can we learn from student criticisms of institutional life? What could we accomplish by providing a permanent role for students in the governance of our institutions? How can they help us achieve the reform necessary to combat the social ills of modern America?

We need to listen to student complaints to determine the sources of their frustration and dissatisfaction. Students begin with a general criticism of several aspects of contemporary life: They are baffled and frustrated over the war in Vietnam, the sag in the civil rights movement, the existence of poverty in the midst of plenty, and they are baffled and frustrated about their educational experience.

So far as Vietnam, civil rights, and poverty are concerned, they probably feel little differently from most members of the educational community. But on the educational issue, they have been lonely and unwelcomed. We have seldom gone behind their rage and rhetoric to unmask the truth of their claims.

They object to size and impersonality. They seek identity, moral affiliation, and a genuine sense of community. *They object to curriculum.* They regard much of it as irrelevant to the solution of the anguished problems of the real world, and they wish relevance, commitment, and leverage. *They object to teaching methods.* They reject canned knowledge, packaged formulae, learning by fiat, and the lack of genuine dialogue. *They object to outdated social rules.* They seek escape, rather than continuation, of adolescence, and wish to be independent, developing adults, with full responsibility for their acts. If they can save themselves, then they may be equipped to save the world. *They object to neglect of rights and freedoms:* in classroom, student government, student publications, student organizations, as citizens, and in disciplinary areas. They strive for dignity, privacy, respect, and justice. *They object to lack of a significant role in institutional government.* They believe in student power, which they define as their right to contribute according to their interest, their stake, and their competence in institutional matters that affect their lives.

This last point is a crucial one. If students can criticize and actually share in the governance of our colleges and universities, then they—and we—will have an opportunity to confront institutional problems in a context that will be both less dramatic and less explosive but probably more fruitful. Indeed, the traditional strength, freshness of view, and idealism of youth can thus provide the high octane that fuels a long overdue reform of our colleges and universities.

6

EMERGING LEGAL RIGHTS FOR STUDENTS

Robert B. Yegge

Since the end of World War II, institutions of higher learning in the United States have undergone a series of dramatic changes in size, characteristics of student body, curriculum, research activities, role in the community, and so on. In this process of change, trustees, faculty, administration, and students have been searching for a definition of their appropriate role, their responsibilities, and their rights. Students have argued for a far more influential part in the education process, as well as for greater freedom in their personal lives. Faculty members have attempted to build new concepts of the scholar and of their place in the administration of the educational institution. Trustees have found it imperative to clarify their ideas about control of the university and the protection of academic freedom. And administrators have found the balancing of competing objectives ever more complex as they attempt to manage what are essentially new types of organizations. The matter of maintaining order, and at the same time freedom, on the American college and university campus is the challenge.

There has been much valuable discussion concerning these changing relationships, but one element of the problem has been frequently ignored. The law governing the education enterprise has received very little attention, although it is apparent that many of the most fundamental issues involve questions of legal rights and duties.

One excuse for ignorance of the law is frequently offered: inapplicability in the academic setting. Not everyone agrees with this principle, however. There seems to be a difference of opinion over whether the law should be involved in the educational system. On the one hand, some argue that law courts are a last resort, to be used only when human relations fail, thus insisting that law should have virtually no standing in the academic setting. On the other hand, others (notably the ACLU) argue that the legal process is fully applicable to the actions of universities and colleges, thus insisting that law and legal process should be allowed to check power exercised by universities and colleges.

Whichever position one takes, the fact of ultimate legal redress exists. And there are some ideas emerging, inchoate, in the legal arena to which the academy must pay more than passive obedience. Accordingly, at least two matters must be considered: the present state of law in the process of higher education, and the future nature and content of law applicable to the academic institution.

As for the present status of law and the appropriate legal remedies applicable, it is important to note, first, that the courts have systematically expanded civil rights protection for more than a decade. And students *qua* individuals are not excluded from the opinions of the United States Supreme Court. Today, students seem to present priority claims for attention. Consideration of the legal issues in the student-institutional relationship should raise some other questions. Then, let us "shepardize," [1] as the lawyers

---

[1] "Shepardize" is a legal research technique for finding recent cases that cite prior court rulings.

say, the student-institutional question in a legal framework.

Status quo may be Latin for "the mess we're in." We must begin to examine the academic institution's rules with respect to students in light of law. We should consider, at least, what the law says about fiduciary relations *(in loco parentis)*, privacy questions, conduct and disciplinary questions (for example, equal protection), fair rules and fair procedure (for example, due process) with respect to a whole host of matters, including admission, grading, and discipline. Should the academy not at least consider these matters, it may be that the courts will assert their powers to protect fundamental constitutional rights of members of the academic community, even if an earlier assumption will be discarded that regards the academic community as something special to which the law could not be intensively applied.

Consider this hypothetical situation. Carleta, a twenty-year-old junior of Mexican-American stock, was arrested in a raid by the morals bureau of the local police department in an off-campus apartment. Although Carleta did not reveal the charge, college officials assumed that the raid was for questioning in connection with a narcotics violation. Based on a newspaper report of the raid, the Conduct Review Committee of the university was convened to consider whether Carleta should be suspended from the university as a result of her arrest. Carleta was summoned to the office of the dean of students and told about the purpose of the meeting. At the beginning of the "hearing," Carleta was advised that the hearing was to give her an opportunity to explain the total situation and alleviate concerns which the Committee had as a result of the arrest. She was told further that unless explanations could be offered, the Committee would have no choice but to assume that she was involved in behavior reflecting unfavorably on her and the university.

The hearing was held. Carleta offered no information regarding knowledge of use of drugs or narcotics. The hearing dealt solely with her relationship to an alleged misfit male friend and with the newspaper report on the raid. The student was charged with the requirement of explaining her conduct as reported in the newspaper.

The Conduct Review Committee decided to suspend Carleta. Their grounds were these: (1) Something sufficiently serious must have been going on or the police would not have obtained a warrant. (2) Carleta did not or could not provide the Committee with any information that would alleviate its assumptions. But the record of the Committee hearing showed no evidence that Carleta was ever charged by the local authorities, that Carleta was ever notified of the university rule allegedly violated, or the potential penalty for violation, and what evidence might be presented against her, if any.

One need not be an expert in legal matters to surmise that some important questions regarding fiduciary relationships between Carleta and the university *(in loco parentis),* and fair play and procedure (due process) are raised by this hypothetic problem.

In 1934 the United States Supreme Court unanimously upheld the university's form of self-government.[2] Indeed, the university possesses special regulatory interests of a sort, which require protection only in the academic setting.[3] Early in our legal history, the courts recognized the need for certain autonomy by the university. *In loco parentis* is a fiction that the courts developed in order to find authority for institutions of higher learning to make certain rules governing student conduct. The authority authorizes rules of two types: First, there are the rules designed to protect the order and intellectual atmosphere of the university (for example, scholastic achievement, driving on campus, cheating on exams). The courts have always found, and appear determined to continue to find, sufficient governing power to uphold these regulations within certain limits.[4] Second, there are rules regulating the conduct of the student in activities not directly related to the university (for example, smoking, drinking, criminal activity). In 1924, the Florida court announced: "As to mental train-

---

[2] *Hamilton v. Regents of University of California,* 293 U.S. 245 (1934).

[3] See: R. H. Cole, H. A. Linde, and R. M. O'Neil, "Statement to the Committee on Academic Freedom of the Berkeley Division, December 15, 1964," in Seymour Lipset and Sheldon Wolin (Eds.), *The Berkeley Student Revolt,* Garden City, N.Y.: Doubleday, 1965, pp. 273–280.

[4] *Gleason v. University of Minnesota,* 104 Minn. 359, 116 N.W. 650 (1908); *Goldberg v. Regents of University of California,* 57 Cal. Rptr. 463 (Ct. App. 1967).

ing, moral and physical discipline, and welfare of the pupils, college authorities stand *in loco parentis.* . . ." [5] Today, however, in this second type of rule, the doctrine is seldom relied upon. The California Court of Appeals has indicated that the fiction is inapplicable.[6] One devastating criticism of the principle is that it allows the university power to do something which parents themselves cannot do: sever all relationship.[7]

In the case of Carleta, the university would be on thin legal ice to base its action on the second sense of the *in loco parentis* relationship. Moreover, Carleta might challenge the powers of the university to legislate concerning her off-campus behavior, with some support in the developing jurisprudence.

The university should ponder seriously whether it really desires for its students to stand *in loco parentis.* The announcement of a university that it will assume the duties and responsibilities of overseeing the conduct and morals, on and off campus, of its students may give the university power to legislate concerning student behavior and adjudicate violations of those rules adopted. At the same time, however, this posture may impose the affirmative requirement on the university that it act to prevent the undesired behavior. Default in performance of this duty may render the university liable for misfeasance or malfeasance. *Ergo:* when you want the cake, you have to eat it too.

When resolving disputes between colleges and their students, the courts have considered two matters: the contractual relationship between student and institution,[8] and constitutional due process. The contract is considered to be embodied in college bulletins, materials signed during the registration process, and so on.[9] In consideration of student acceptance of obligations, the university agrees to confer the appropriate degree after the stu-

---

[5] *John B. Stetson University v. Hunt,* 88 Fla. 510, 102 So. 637 (1924) at p. 640.

[6] *Goldberg v. Regents,* supra.

[7] See Goldman, "The University and the Liberty of Its Student," 54 K.L. Rev. 643 (1965).

[8] *Booker v. Grand Rapids Medical College,* 156 Mich. 95, 120 N.W. 589 (1909).

[9] *Anthony v. Syracuse University,* 244 App. Div. 487, 231 N.Y.S. 435 (1928).

dent successfully completes the required course of studies.[10] In the case of Carleta, the university might have relied on a specific obligation and imposed condition, contained in the university catalogue, pre-empting arrest while a student and approving summary exculpatory "hearing," if indeed such obligation and condition existed.

If we assume that the university rule allegedly violated is the general conduct rule, there is another problem. A typical general conduct rule, contained in most college and university catalogues, reads: "A student is expected to conduct himself, both within and outside the university, in a way that will reflect favorably on himself and on the university." At best, the rule is overly general. It is likely that such a rule could be viewed by a court as too vague to be enforceable—a fate that legislatively established rules have met with increasing frequency in recent years.[11]

The applicability of constitutional due process in the university setting was slow in developing: there was early failure of the courts to recognize the right to receive an education as a constitutional right protected by the Fourteenth Amendment.[12] It was not until 1961 that the right to receive an education was determined to be a constitutional right protected by the Fourteenth Amendment.[13]

The due process clause has been held to apply only to state action. Accordingly, public universities and colleges have been required to apply a rational relationship test between the act attempted to be controlled and the rule prescribing the control most commonly associated with the due process clause.[14] The

---

[10] *Gleason v. University of Minnesota,* 104 Minn. 359, 116 N.W. 560 (1908).

[11] For a discussion of judicial construction of a vague statute in a civil case, see *Lone Star Gas Co. v. Kelly,* 165 S.W. 2d 446 (Tex. Comm. App. 1942).

[12] *Board of Trustees of University of Mississippi v. Waugh,* 105 Miss. 623, 62 So. 827 (1913).

[13] *Dixon v. Alabama State Board of Education,* 294 F. 2d 150 (5th Cir., 1961).

[14] *Goldberg v. Regents of University of California,* 57 Cal. Rptr. 463 (Ct. App., 1967).

criterion that courts have considered when passing on the validity of regulations or actions of private colleges has been whether or not the regulation or action constituted a breach of contract by the college.[15] Consequently, the courts have looked to see whether the private college officials had the power to make the rule or take the action [16] and whether or not such power was exercised in an arbitrary or unreasonable manner.[17] For Carleta, under either test, one must strain either to find that due process has been met or to find rule and reasonability.

Over the years, the idea has developed that some form of notice and hearing is required in a student disciplinary matter. In the public institution, it has been decided that notice of charges and grounds must be given and the rudiments of an adversary proceeding must be preserved.[18] For Carleta—assuming for the moment she was going to a public institution—the court mandate was not observed.

---

[15] *Carr v. St. Johns University,* 17 App. Div. 2d 632, 231 NYS 2d 410 (1962).

[16] *John Stetson University v. Hunt,* 88 Fla. 510, 102 So. 637 (1924).

[17] *Robinson v. University of Miami,* 100 So. 2d 442 (Fla. Ct. App. 1958).

[18] *Dixon v. Alabama State Board of Education,* 294 F. 2d 150 (1961).

In *dicta,* the following safeguards were suggested:

1. Notice, containing a statement of the specific charges and grounds which, if proven, would justify expulsion under the college's regulations;
2. A hearing that must amount to more than an informal interview with an administrative authority, and which must preserve at least the "rudiments of an adversary proceeding": (a) an opportunity for the student to present his own defense against the charges and to produce either oral testimony or written affidavits of witnesses in his behalf; and (b) if cross-examination of witnesses is not allowed, the student "should be given the names of the witnesses against him and an oral or written report on the facts to which each witness testified."

See William W. Van Alstyne, "Student Rights and University Authority," *The College Counsel,* Vol. II, No. 1 (1967) p. 58.

There is growing dissatisfaction with the doctrine that perpetuates a distinction between public and private institutions in disciplinary matters. The courts are inquiring whether the "private" institution is actually private.[19] Moreover, private universities are not all the same. There are church-related, church-affiliated, church-established, church-dominated, and a host of independently established private institutions of higher learning. One cannot assume that all private institutions will be treated alike by the courts. For example, questions of state interference in religious activity, among other questions, can be raised in the legal setting.

Even if one assumes that private universities *are* all the same, at least the ones not connected with a church can still be regarded as quasi-public, responsible to the community and not to private interests. In accordance with that view, they should be held to the same degree of public responsibility, if not to a higher degree. Whatever the type of private university, I would predict— and within the present decade—judicial abolition of certain fictional distinctions in disciplinary matters.[20]

One thing seems clear. The legal changes in differential or similar treatment of institutions, as well as legal changes in many of the areas of lego-institutional mandates, if left solely in the courts, might emerge not on the basis of overall planning but on a piecemeal basis, mostly as a result of the strengths and weaknesses of individual cases (and their advocates) that are presented to the courts.

The action of the Conduct Review Committee was to suspend Carleta. It will be recalled that Carleta was not advised

---

[19] See *Carr v. St. John's University,* 34 Misc. 2d 319, 231 N.Y.S. 2d (1962). *Guillory v. Administrators of Tulane University,* 212 F. Supp. 674 (E.D. La. 1962).

[20] In efforts to bring actions of private institutions within the operation of the Fourteenth Amendment, it is argued—in some cases successfully—that the private institution is either engaged in an operation of such public nature or that there is sufficient involvement to find the actions of the institution to be state actions. See *Guillory v. Administrators of Tulane University,* 212 F. Supp. 674 (E.D. La. 1962). Cf. *Pennsylvania v. Board of Trusts,* 353 U.S. 230 (1957).

before the hearing that this ultimate sanction might be applied. Furthermore, there seemed to be a lack of concern by the committee for the potential disposition of the alleged arrest by the local authorities. In fact, the record is silent on whether she was ever charged following the arrest. We could therefore, speculate on some aspects of fairness.

Our traditional notions of freedom from double jeopardy might be applicable in connection with the situation.[21] Might Carleta argue, before a court (if she were subsequently charged and tried) that the university had imposed the stiff penalty of suspension, and therefore the civil authorities could not put her in jeopardy of penalty again by trial?

The university has traditionally relied on academic sanctions for all university-established rules. Are these sanctions appropriate, necessarily, for adjudicated violations of all rules including conduct destructive to order and intellectual atmosphere as well as conduct allegedly offensive, yet not directly related to the university?

Carleta was of Mexican-American heritage. It might be interesting to know whether other students suffering the same civil plight as Carleta have been dealt a similar punishment.[22] Such analysis might raise questions about equal protection—a constitutional doctrine emerging in the educational setting.

The problem of preserving individual rights has been emphasized in a series of recent United States Supreme Court decisions bearing popular names such as Gideon,[23] Miranda,[24] Escobedo,[25] and most lately, Application of Paul L. Gault.[26] It is this latest case, Gault, that I think is most significant for universities

---

[21] For example, see *State v. DiGiosia,* 3 N.J. 413, 70 A. 2d 756 (1950).

[22] In *Frank v. Marquette University,* 209 Wisc. 372, 245 N.W. 125 (1932) the court faced this problem; the court refused to order production of records of other student disciplinary cases, thus impliedly permitting possible differential treatment.

[23] 372 U.S. 335 (1963).

[24] 384 U.S. 436 (1966).

[25] 378 U.S. 478 (1964).

[26] 87 Sup. Ct. 1428 (1967).

to recognize. Gault emphasizes some of the important protections that the United States Supreme Court will recognize—possibly in a proper university test case.

Paul L. Gault was a fifteen-year-old minor charged with juvenile delinquency in the state of Arizona. (Most of the disciplinary cases in which we are involved in the university deal with minors.) The authorities took Paul into custody on a hearsay report that he had used profane language on the telephone. The boy had been before the juvenile court at an earlier time. A summary hearing was held for Gault without giving him or his parents any opportunity to know the charges. The complaining witness was not summoned and indeed was not required to attend by the specific direction of the juvenile judge.

The United States Supreme Court, through Mr. Justice Abe Fortas, struck down the conviction of Paul Gault, affirmed by the Arizona Supreme Court, expressing shock in the proceeding. The court reiterated its view expressed in *Kent v. United States*,[27] that the Juvenile Court Judge's exercise of the power of the state as *parens patriae* was not unlimited:[28] ". . . the admonition to function in a 'parental' relationship is not an invitation to procedural arbitrariness."[29]

Mr. Justice Harlan concurred in the result reached in Gault, yet dissented to a strict standard in dealing with juveniles under the so-called "protective custody" of the Juvenile Court. He announced less strict standards, which he found in Gault were violated, as follows: ". . . first, timely notice must be provided to parents and children of the nature and terms of any juvenile court proceeding in which a determination affecting their rights or interests may be made. . . ."[30] Thereafter Harlan recited a right to counsel and to a written record of the proceedings.

The failure of the Committee to give Carleta notice of the issues to be considered by the Committee prior to the hearing violates basic constitutional and humane notions of fairness. And the assumption by the Committee that Carleta was guilty until she

---

[27] 383 U.S. 541 (1966).
[28] 87 Sup. Ct. 1428 at 1445 (1967).
[29] 383 U.S. at 555.
[30] 87 St. Ct. at 1467.

proved herself innocent reminds us of the Star Chamber proceeding of English history, the result of which, in part, precipitated the American revolution. The use of a newspaper account of an event as evidence is the classic example of legally inadmissable hearsay. The notion that the press versions of an event represents a fair hearing is dangerous and potentially unfair.

I would suggest that the Conduct Review Committee reached its decision about Carleta in violation of basic fairness. If Carleta had employed counsel at any point in the proceedings, the entire matter would have been made a test case in which the university would have been made to look, at best, undemocratic.

I have, through the hypothetical case of Carleta, tried to illustrate by thesis: With increasing justification, the law is becoming involved in the educational process. First, the law is being thrust upon the university or college by persons employing the legal process to secure rights alleged to be accorded them. For example, organized students are urging their legal rights. The National Student Association Congress in September 1967 resolved:

> The system of higher educational institutions restricts the student's rights to democratic self-government. The student's control in determining those policies which affect his curricular and extracurricular activities is either weak or nonexistent. Furthermore, students are not afforded their rights as citizens in the college and university community. Students have been subject to search without warrant, arbitrary social regulations by administrations, double jeopardy by administration and civil courts. In addition, a United States Supreme Court decision of June 1967 has granted to all minors those rights which have heretofore been granted to United States citizens in legal proceedings.[31]

The Student Association is implementing a "student power desk," a part of which will be a "legal area" which will engage in research relating to the legal status of students in the context of the power movement.[32]

---

[31] See "Higher Education and National Affairs," American Council on Education, Vol. XVI, Number 31, September 15, 1967, pp. 6–7. Gault is the case to which reference is made in the passage cited.

[32] *Ibid.*

Second, the courts are beginning to insist that bodies exercising heretofore unrestricted power uphold principles of fairness as embodied in our constitutional restraints on government. As Louisell has observed, ". . . if the university's end result is fundamentally unfair and therefore illegal, . . . courts . . . are . . . open . . . to redress grievances should university remedies be found wanting." [33] In summary, ". . . the other basic constitutional guarantees of individual liberty—including provision of both state and federal constitutions that guarantee freedoms of expression (speech, press, assembly, and petition)—apply to actions of the state [I add: private] universities just as they do to actions of any other branch of the state government." [34]

Third, organized efforts are abundant in the area of embodying procedures, at least partially borrowed from the legal system, in statements of rights and freedoms of students. A summary review of the *Joint Statement of Rights* by five student, faculty, and institutional associations [35] reveals the solid legal foundation of that statement. Therein are found directives that due process, equal protection, privacy, freedom of expression be observed, and *in loco parentis* be modified, if not abolished.

Fourth, the law is beginning to recognize contemporary reality. While this development is significant, it should not lure the academic enterprise into a sense of false security. If there was ever a time in legal history for wise and active innovation in lego-educational legislation and case law, it is now. Universities, aided by the developing (yet altogether too few) forward-looking law faculties, must assume an active role in legal reform in this area.

---

[33] David W. Louisell, "A Statement of the Legal Issues, Jan. 12, 1965," in Lipset and Wolin, *op. cit.,* pp. 280–283.

[34] Cole *et al.,* in Lipset and Wolin, *op. cit.*

[35] *Joint Statement on Rights and Freedoms of Students,* drafted by a committee representing American Association of University Professors, Association of American Colleges, U.S. National Student Association, National Association of Student Personnel Administrators, and National Association of Women Deans and Counselors (1967).

Section IV

Dissent and Defiance

7

ACTIVISM, PRIVATISM, AND THE MORAL ADVANTAGE

Terry F. Lunsford

The tone and character of student protest has changed, subtly but dramatically, in the past several years and months. Student protests are more militant, more frequent, occur on more campuses, cover more issues, and involve more students directly than they did several years ago. There is more threatened or actual disruption of classes and administration. More incidents of property damage occur in the course of protests. More officials of colleges, of the Dow Chemical Company, and of the armed forces have been detained by crowds, and for longer periods. More public invective has been hurled. More conviction is expressed that the students' causes are just; more moral statements of draft refusal and of complicity with civil disobedients have been registered. More violence has occurred, started by student protestors, by antiprotestors, or by the police. Outside police have more frequently and more quickly been called into campuses. Arrests and indictments have increased. And the punitive use of force by police to disperse crowds and "teach lessons" to protestors has risen sharply.

In short, there has been escalation and sophistication of tactics by both protestors and official authorities in the student-protest scene. That scene presents a far graver tableau today than it did a few years ago, when the so-called Berkeley riots of the almost entirely nonviolent Free Speech Movement captured national attention.

It is clear that student protest is intimately related to issues that go far beyond the college or university campus: the war, racial inequalities, poverty, a bureaucratized society. Of these, the major issue, of course, is the war. The large majority of the recent campus protests have been directed at the makers of napalm, at the armed forces' recruiters, and at Selective Service induction stations. As rising military manpower demands bring the draft closer to college campuses, and hundreds of young men come face to face with the prospect of fighting and dying in a war they believe to be both useless and immoral, this issue may yet become even more explosive.

The other issues, however, must not be overlooked. Fast increasing in militancy and bitterness are black students' determined attempts to force upon the white society's attention the countless inequities to which blacks are still subject in this country. And there have also, of course, been recent student demonstrations—though these have not been numerous—turning on rules of campus conduct, housing regulations, and other local issues.

It is natural to wonder why: why are protests increasing? I should like to suggest that it may be more revealing to ask the obverse question: why should the student protests *not* increase, *not* toughen their resistance? If they should not, it is not for a number of reasons that *might* be given:

1. It is not because their causes are unjust, or trivial, or are problems that are rapidly being solved. Instead, I suggest that student activists in this country have the clear moral advantage in their opposition to the established society—and that the society

is forced generally to admit it. The major targets of student attack —war, racism, poverty, bureaucracy—all are acknowledged by the most influential opinion makers and by broad segments of the society to be serious problems that require major correctives. But few such correctives are in sight, and that also is widely admitted.

2. It is not because the students are personally unaffected, and so should leave these matters to others concerned. Blacks, draft-age students, relatives and friends of ghetto dwellers, human units in bureaucratic processing—all are plentifully represented among student protestors. Indeed, if World War III results from our present foreign policy, all of us will be affected.

3. It is not because lawbreaking is contrary to American traditions, or unobservable in "respectable" adult society. From the flagrant illegalities of Southern race relations and the scandal of General Electric's executive price-fixing to the legend of Prohibition and the current fraud of narcotics law enforcement, U.S. students have many reasons for seeing the law not as a final good or a blind goddess, but as a variable and manipulable instrument of group purposes. In the tradition of Henry David Thoreau and the worldwide legend of Gandhi, these same students find powerful precedents for placing moral law higher than the law of the state, when personal conviction demands it.

4. It is not because the United States is a nonviolent culture. The unparalleled violence of Hiroshima and Nagasaki, the bombings and napalm outrages of our Vietnam effort, the daily diet of television brutalities, the obsession with a six-gun version of our frontier heritage, the murders of nonviolent civil rights workers in the South, the venom of Northern urban residents and police against peaceful demonstration marches—these and many more provide an ample American tradition of violent "settlement" for disputes. Indeed, one wonders how so much passionate student energy has avoided a *more* destructive expression in the present crisis.

5. It is not because the leaders of nation and campus have been truthful and worthy of the trust for which they long. News manipulation, the credibility gap, the exposure of secret spying in the U-2, the Bay of Pigs and numerous other CIA affairs have all been well publicized on the national and international scene. On the .campus, official doubletalk, outright public untruths, and

transparent fictions of impartial benevolence have marked many a student-administration conflict.

6. Finally, it is not because student protests have been ineffective in bringing response from campus officials. Indeed, it is the clear lesson from most of the student-protest incidents on American campuses that only when student activists have pushed hard and insistently have significant gains been won—for campus political expression, for security of student records from government investigators, for student participation in campus governance, for re-examination of racially discriminatory practices, for procedural regularity in student discipline, and for a host of other student goals.

In other words, there are few or no *positive* reasons why students should relax their activism, as an unnecessary or futile effort. Instead, a number of *negative* reasons are usually given to advise more student quietism on political fronts. Students are told that they will encourage anarchy by their civil disobedience, or social chaos by moving from disagreement to dissent. They are warned to be more moderate lest they invite a backlash from the political right, and a new area of political witch-hunting in American life. They are told that they violate all canons of polite discussion, ignore good manners, and disrupt others' rights to go their own ways, to drive freely through the streets, to attend their classes undisturbed, or to discuss employment with whatever companies they wish.

Each of these negative responses represents a reasonable, legitimate viewpoint, and suspects a danger in the present climate of confrontation and hostility. Whether some of these objections are overdrawn (such as the image of impending anarchy) or trivial (such as the inconvenience to a motorist when a street is blocked by protestors) is part of an argument in which reasonable men can engage. At the level of the principles involved, I believe that subordinating freedom of expression to higher values, as some student activists are ready to do today, poses one of the most difficult problems for our political and educational future. But that is not because expression in this country is unqualifiedly free, or because this abstract right is not greatly sullied by the realities of a social process that forbids dissenters access to many avenues of expression unless they create sensational news events by disruption, nudity, or exaggerated threats. The danger is, rather, that the dissenters' own subordination of free expression will give moral credence to a further round of restrictions on freedom of expression by those who give highest priority to "law and order" at whatever price.

Short of such a punitive backlash supported by large segments of society, such negative responses as I have described are understandable when forceful protest threatens much of the established order. But there is an overriding problem in relying exclusively on negative responses to principled civil protest: it leaves the protestor in command of the moral heights, and provides him with intellectual and emotional ammunition to continue his assault. This, I suggest, is the basic paralysis of America today: it is not dissent or disruption or law breaking or violence *per se* that is our problem. It is moral and political and intellectual confusion within the adult society, which knows in its own heart that the war and racism and poverty are here, and serious, and wrong—but which cannot find ways even of stemming their tide, much less eliminating them.

In precisely such a situation of moral uncertainty and frustration, I believe, those who have power and responsibility are strongly tempted to cover their uncertainty by a strong and authoritative response to those who intensify the frustration. Thus we are in grave danger that much of adult society, precisely because of its own doubts and frustrations, will use the few incidents of student violence, property damage, or personal inconvenience as a moral basis for severe repressive measures against unpopular youthful dissent generally. There is evidence that this is happening already, in the police sweeps of the San Francisco Haight-Ashbury district, in the use of punitive force by police (now being investigated on several campuses), in the anticipation by police of riots where others see only peaceful protest, and in more sophisticated measures—such as the selective expulsion and imprisonment of political leaders among students and other dissenting groups.

Some ask, but what has this to do with the campus? The academic world is this country's stronghold of liberal and humanitarian values, of concern with ideas and ideals. We are suffering punishment from student protestors not for our own sins but for those of the larger society, in which we actually are the young idealists' greatest allies. This is perhaps the dominant response that I hear from academic people with whom I have talked recently about the major issues of protest—this, and a pervasive wish that the protests will soon stop, go away, and leave us all in peace.

Unfortunately, few careful observers of the student scene believe that the protests are likely to go away soon. Certainly they will not, unless severe repressions occur, or until the protestors are better understood and some of the issues they address have been faced.

Such an understanding, I believe, must give greater attention to what some student activists call American "privatism." This word refers to an overwhelming emphasis on private, individual concerns such as career advancement, specialized expertise, and freedom from messy and ambiguous political and moral issues. When such an orientation becomes widespread, it is argued, then it becomes impossible to deal with issues in a public, political context—where untidy compromises, the awareness of power, and uncertain outcome are heavily involved. Thus, the argument continues, comparatively small proportions of eligible American voters even bother to go to the ballot box, except in major national elections. "Politician" is almost a swear word to many citizens. In polite society, religion and politics were for many years routinely avoided as subjects of conversation, lest they bring passion and disagreement into the social gathering. And political scientists have for many years debated the unreality of the political bases for this country's two great political parties, which overlap each other dramatically on many basic and divisive issues.

These tendencies may be seen, of course, as the obverse side of some very positive attributes of Americans, such as individualism, self-reliance, concern for personal privacy, and a mistrust of demagoguery. The point of argument is that problems arise which cannot be solved without surmounting private concerns and making personal sacrifices in light of the shared interests of the political community. There is no guarantee in such a model of public participation that conflict will be avoided or injustice to the weaker avoided. But there is hope in such a model for the revival of a meaningful public dialogue about the purposes and ideals of our nation, its communities and institutions, and the world. The alternative to be feared is a passive, privatist acceptance of what government officials tell us is "necessary"—which means also accepting government by the relatively uninformed, mass public opinion through which those officials are elected. For many student activists, the specialized academic researcher and the narrowly loyal institutional bureaucrat are outstanding examples of the trained incapacity for meaningful political participation that privatism represents.

A basic message of the student activists, then, is that we cannot escape politics, messy and troublesome as it is. We may wish to do so, and in times of lesser social discord we may succeed for long periods in devoting our attention primarily to our work and our families and our cultural enjoyments. But we pay a price, if we become so accustomed to such a life that we lose all inclination and capacity to be also active political participants, anticipating and working out on concrete terms the solutions to the great problems of our society. That task, we must then relearn in painful ways, cannot be left to government alone, or to those citizens with a short and narrow view of our law, our culture, and our history.

One other related problem in understanding student activism today seems especially troublesome for many academic people. This problem is the ready willingness of students to take strong actions on the basis of group membership, and to oppose group interests in the rhetoric of debate. Student power, black power, and similar slogans are scare words on many campuses. Some see in such ideas and actions an ominous class conflict theory of all social relations, with demonic Marxian origins. And, again, such an emphasis on inexorable hostilities between groups is one possible version of the argument; it is found, significantly, in the rhetoric of leaders for presently powerless minorities—especially blacks.

But a deeper insight about society is being probed: it is that Americans must come to terms with the fact of group memberships and loyalties, with the realities of subcultural differences, and with the collective bases of political power. Every successful politician knows these facts, and uses them in his campaigns; so do skillful trial lawyers, when choosing juries. Ethnic, economic, educational, and other groupings, while they hold always the danger of dividing us into irreconcilable armed camps, are still realities that cannot be wished away, or obliterated by pretending in our public rhetoric that they do not exist. That is the central fact of modern American public life that gives meaning to the cries for power and solidarity by leaders of status groups scattered throughout the society.

How we will deal with the intergroup conflicts that arise from these attempts, we do not yet know. We must win deserved loyalty for our national life from members of all disparate groups, while we try to repair social injustices. Whether we will see this before armed repression brings armed reprisal, it is not yet clear. But Pandora's box is open; the *group* character of injustices— to blacks, to students, to the poor, and so on—has now become publicly apparent. So has the usefulness of such group member- ship for gaining political power in our system. The choice of *whether* to deal with these things is now out of our hands.

The danger, then, is that we as academic men and women will continue to protest our noninvolvement, our bystander status, the need to get back to our jobs, the separateness of our institu- tions from society. That leaves the political contest to angry student activists and to the backlash of the right that some of us so direly predict. To the extent that we remain uninvolved, we— detached observers of the social scene—may confidently predict that student protest will move farther toward resistance and de- fiance, and that simultaneous movement will occur in the direc- tion of repression of dissent by authoritarians and police.

8

JOHN COTTON, ANNE HUTCHINSON, AND THE STUDENT POWER MOVEMENT

Theodore P. Greene

Any teacher facing with mixed feelings the current movement for student power must—especially if he is a teacher of colonial American history—look back with considerable sympathy upon the dilemma of the Reverend John Cotton three hundred and thirty years ago in the Bible Commonwealth of Massachusetts Bay. For readers who may not know the Antinomian Crisis in 1637, let me sketch briefly the story of John Cotton and his talented, troublesome pupil, Anne Hutchinson.

Within a year after his arrival at the First Church in Boston, John Cotton had proved himself the most effective, the most moving, the most inspiring preacher in the young colony. Better than any of his colleagues Cotton could rouse in his listeners a felt sense of the need for an inner, personal conversion and conviction. He could convince a congregation that dutiful conduct, abiding by the rules, doing what was expected by the authorities could lead only to a meaningless, hypocritical life if these actions did not spring from a deeply personal sense of involvement and sharing in grace.

Under Cotton's preaching, attendance and membership at First Church soared. Never had even this pious people taken their religion so seriously. The authorities were delighted. But within two years the church and the whole colony were brought to the brink of chaos, and nihilism seemed to have been unleashed.

The trouble centered around the most devoted disciple of John Cotton, an extremely able woman, Mistress Anne Hutchinson. Anne began holding meetings in her home to discuss more fully the meaning of the weekly sermons—a practice the authorities had earlier tried to encourage with little success. At these meetings Anne and her adherents, out of genuine concern for the state of grace in their church and their society, began to raise questions about the adequacy of other ministers, began to condemn the authorities for leading hypocritical lives. Finally Anne's group acted to seize power. They tried to dismiss Cotton's colleague in the First Church, since they found his preaching dull and *irrelevant* to their inner spiritual concerns. In a crucial election, they made an unsuccessful bid to win the governor's office and then relapsed sulkily into signing petitions and harassing the authorities. Some of them refused to serve in the war against the Pequot Indians. The climax came when Anne Hutchinson and some of the other leaders were brought to trial for subverting the authority of the ministers and of the magistrates.

What could John Cotton do? He saw in Anne and her followers a group that might revitalize the church. But then he saw them carrying his doctrines to extremes that he could not support. He saw them criticizing his colleagues and the institutions of society in ways that were neither fair nor accurate. He found them claiming that a pure heart required no laws or institutional structures. He heard them condemning as hypocrites all who did not agree with them.

Cotton tried very hard to protect Anne, to support what he saw as true in her position, to explain away her more extreme statements. He testified for Anne at her trial very effectively— and was just on the point of saving her when Anne herself brought destruction down upon her head. She burst out with the claim that no one could question her, no one could successfully oppose her because she was acting on the basis of a direct revelation from God. The judges instantly agreed that only anarchy could result from such a claim, and they sentenced her to banishment from Massachusetts. The final tragedy came when Anne, before the whole congregation of First Church, tried to expound fantastic interpretations of the Bible that no sound scholarship could support. It was John Cotton himself, acting on behalf of the reasoned, disciplined interpretation of Scripture, who delivered the address excommunicating Anne Hutchinson from the church.

In this poignant story of the old Antinomian Crisis I find much of interest for those of us, both teachers and administrators, who have lived through the experiences of the 1950's and the 1960's on college and university campuses. Only a decade ago many of us were deploring the dull dutifulness of students who went through the motions of education apparently bent only upon earning their way into some secure niche of the corporate society. We urged them to take a more active and critical and independent part in the whole educational process. We berated them for an apparent unconcern with the larger issues of society and the more immediate apathy of student life.

But now administrators are battered and bruised from the shocks of repeated confrontations while teachers are fearful lest all the intellectual rigors of their disciplines crumble before the demands for independence, relevance, and freedom from formalities like grades and classes. We find students adopting many of the attitudes and practices of Anne Hutchinson. We look upon the dilemma of John Cotton in his relation to the Antinomians with a greater sympathy.

Few will deny that the recent awakening of students has

been the most significant and promising development in higher education during the decade. On campuses where this has not occurred the problem would seem to be to stimulate it. What concerns us, however, is the problem of how to meet constructively the growing student demands for a greater role in determining the conditions of their education. We have been asked whether that role should be viewed as that of an adversary, a legislator, or an adviser. I shall try to suggest how we may avoid the experience of the Antinomian Crisis. In that situation the promising force for regeneration in the church lapsed into nihilism and irrationality while the only response of the society was expulsion and enforcement of orthodoxy.

The first necessity on any campus is to accept honestly and to make possible actually the role of the student as an *adversary*. Making this role possible calls for recognizing the independence of the student, for understanding that his needs, his interests, and his perspective are necessarily and properly different from those held by other members of the college community. It calls not only for tolerating but also for encouraging the means through which he can feel the truth of that independence and clearly express the difference in his point of view. Unless the student has the clear opportunity to act as an adversary on all matters of college policy, his education will be stunted and his roles as a legislator or an adviser will be made a mockery.

The stance of independence required by the adversary role is actually a difficult one for the student to achieve. He feels a loyalty and an identification with his institution, a certain awe for the faculty, a sense of dependence upon the administration. The great contribution of the present student movement is that it has transcended institutional lines, has made it possible to identify with students elsewhere, has encouraged the articulation of distinctive student viewpoints. The result is to create the possibility for students to conceive of themselves as having ideas, philosophies, criticisms, proposals worth developing and asserting in the college community.

It is even more difficult, of course, for administrators and faculty to refrain from undermining the independent adversary position of the student. In small colleges the aura of paternalism endures. The ideal of the harmonious community smothers honest expression of difference. Where personal relations are close, intellectual differences are sometimes taken as personal affronts. And in the large university the necessity to see things in bureaucratic terms, the difficulty of determining or changing any policy, the multiple groups involved—all these reduce the student's identity to that of one minor interest among many.

In this situation, therefore, the student needs all the institutional supports he can get for an independent adversary role. He needs the right to form his own associations without suppression or close supervision. He needs a student newspaper as independent as possible from college control, the right to publish course critiques, to invite outside speakers on his own initiative and responsibility, the right to picket, petition, and demonstrate. He should be allowed to set up institutions paralleling the official institutions of the college: a student curriculum committee to make recommendations, even a free university run by students where voluntary courses will be offered outside the bounds of the regular curriculum. Above all, then, the student should be enabled and encouraged to develop an attitude of critical detachment toward his educational experience and toward the policies of his institution. His role in an adversary position should be respected by all including himself.

Most of the dangers involved in the free exercise of an adversary stance by students are obvious to us all. The public image of the institution may be threatened, and internally feelings will be bruised. But the greatest danger lies in the habit of mind it may cultivate in the student. He may be led into the nihilism, the self-righteousness, the totally irresponsible charges and rhetoric that the Antinomians displayed in 1637. The answer is not to haul students into court on heresy charges but to influence their own style, their own approach, by the nature of our response. Faculty and administrators should on occasion respond publicly, reasonably, seriously, and not always negatively to the criticisms, proposals, and viewpoints put forward by students. If the student is to become a worthy adversary, he is worth the best response we can provide.

To what extent should students be granted a legislative role in the actual decision of major college policies? Amherst College has been relatively conservative in this regard. Only two minor faculty committees have added student members. On the other hand, the independent position of students has been strengthened by giving the student council almost complete responsibility over the chartering, the financial support, and the regulating of all student activities and organizations. This student government is an active, creative body that expresses student views on college policies, administers our honor system, and subsidizes a wide variety of enterprises. Its net effect is to reinforce the role of the student as an independent, adversary voice in college affairs.

The single clearest achievement for student power on our campus during the last three years has been the creation of a college council on which six students sit with four faculty members and two deans. I drew up the charter and am presently its chairman. Obviously, then, the nature of this college council represents my own considered answer to the role students should play in the formation of college or university policy.

The single most important purpose for this council was to introduce more rationality into the continuing adversary debate between the students, the administration, and the faculty. The student power movement had led to a rash of proposals and criticisms from students, which in some cases had at least a germ of creative possibility. Too often, however, this germ was floating in a sea of utopian assumptions, extravagant rhetoric, and petty sniping at authority. The harried administration responded in traditional and somewhat incoherent ways. The busy faculty responded seldom at all. The student sense of frustration grew greater, and their carping grew more bitter.

Our hope was that a council on which students held half the seats could engage in serious dialogue over their concerns, could consider thoughtfully any real difficulties that their proposals raised, and could work out more acceptable, realistic means for achieving some of their ends. The council was given final power to determine policy in only three areas: faculty-student relations, social regulations, and the honor system. The council's decisions in these three areas will be the college policy unless specifically vetoed by the president. The council also was given the formal power to make recommendations on any matter (except individual personnel decisions) to the existing authorities, whether these were faculty or administration in particular cases.

These recommendations obviously would be the joint product of students, faculty, and administration. Their persuasiveness would depend simply upon their inherent reasonableness and upon how thoroughly the members had thought out all the implications of the proposals. They would carry much more weight than the hasty notions previously tossed off by students. If the authorities rejected them, such rejection would require an equally thoughtful rationale. We would have turned the previous *adversary* proceedings into a situation requiring the equivalents of reasoned *judicial* decisions. And, we hoped, the very assurance that any serious student interest would get a full consideration in the college council could elevate the whole tone of student protest.

The result, I think, has been to support most of our hopes. The council has handled all of the hottest topics on campus, has achieved a few major changes, and has issued several reports which won the respectful attention of students and faculty.

Although I still feel at times like John Cotton, we have avoided an Antinomian Crisis. If some students still speak as though the voice of the student was the voice of God, not all faculty members remain convinced that God could never speak at all through a student's voice.

In 1637 Anne Hutchinson was cast out, gave birth to a monstrous baby, and was massacred by the Indians. Massachusetts Bay suffered from her absence by becoming the kind of stiff, moralistic society against which she had protested. And John Cotton, having lost much of the fervor of grace in his preaching, became the official spokesman for the Puritan establishment. Those are fates I trust we all can escape.

9

FACULTY RESPONSE TO STUDENT DISSENT

Richard Axen

Student protests, especially the more vigorous and defiant forms, have destroyed the calm and objectivity of even academic man. One hears him expostulating daily on the campus walks, among the administrators, in the academic senate, or at lunch. If my memory serves me right, his opening gambit goes something like this:

> Now I defer to nobody in my dedication to free speech and the inherent right in a democracy to dissent. I believe my record on this subject speaks for itself. But the current dedication of a minority of students to move from this democratic right of dissent to anarchistic de-

fiance and disruption threatens the very essence of both our democratic society and the academic values that you and I hold so dearly. This dedication to coercion and intimidation rather than to reasoned, cooperative problem solving is inimical to all that liberal education stands for, and unless we unite immediately to put a stop to this totalitarian behavior we will be destroyed from within and from without.

That speech, with the proper intonation and timing, is guaranteed in the current febrile atmosphere to make one a prime candidate for a deanship, vice presidency, or maybe even the top job. For many, a man on horseback might not make a bad president at the current moment—especially if he directed his strong-armed activities toward the enemy, not toward us and our incriminating foibles.

Colleagues who see their classroom authority challenged by these militant students, their salaries threatened by an enraged legislature, their two or three day teaching schedules and their research opportunities disrupted by this climate of campus ferment applaud enthusiastically when such a strong leader appears on the scene.

Now, I must admit that the temptation to take such a stand is attractive. As one who has been deeply involved on a campus where dissent, among both the black and white students, has escalated to defiance, intimidation, and disruptive behavior, I know all too well the deep threat such behavior poses for much that we all cherish and deem essential to our academic enterprise. I have witnessed the mob scene and some destruction of property, I have felt the hostility and intimidation of an almost totally black audience while I voted negatively in the senate on a resolution to grant amnesty to suspended black students, and I have seen bullets shoved threateningly under the door to the president's office. The atmosphere is indeed not conducive to the pursuit of the fundamental values that we all hold in common. Were these tactics and values to become paramount, higher education as we desire it would disappear. And, in passing, let me say that those who have only struggled with white militantism have only glimpsed the tip of the iceberg. Black anger directed in black nationalistic ways toward college policies that frustrate their black ambitions is a threat far more ominous—and far more fearsome.

I have also observed at close hand the increasing political knee-jerk reaction to this disruptive student behavior on tax-supported facilities: last year my sabbatical was spent in California's capitol pursuing the prescient topic, The Politics of California Higher Education. What with such politicians as our Governor Ronald Reagan, Max Rafferty, and Jesse Unruh eagerly seeking such popular issues as student defiance in order to gain political mileage, the external political threat to higher education produced by student activism is deeply felt in California. We have a myriad of threatening pieces of legislation already introduced—including one that would create a campus police force directly responsible to the governor's agent and another directing our Board to fire two faculty members accused of responsibility for a pornographic play. We have serious budgetary reprisals, and we have lost a number of good college presidents, including, most recently, John Summerskill.

But as attractive as it might be to dwell upon the threat to our open academic society posed by the change of mood and action among militant students, I think I can put these pages to better use. The threat that I find most disturbing is not the defiant behavior of our students but the emotional, irrational, authoritarian overreaction to this behavior by many of our faculty, administrators, politicians, and community leaders. In essence, I see this student militancy exposing many fundamental flaws in our academic establishment and our broader society, flaws we have all been aware of but have blithely condoned because corrective action threatened our status quo and its accompanying prerogatives. So, instead of moving painfully to modify our comfortable operations, we have projected all blame on these anarchistic students. Excoriating these students, throwing them off the campus, insuring "law and order" and a return to antebellum modes, will simply not solve the fundamental problems. As one student at our college said, after revealing his frankly revolutionary goals in a faculty-student departmental meeting and then listening to the expected faculty diatribe: "Listen, if you really want to stop my revolution all you have to do is correct some of the obvious conditions that breed converts to my cause."

But correcting these conditions is a vastly more onerous, soul-searching task than getting rid of the troublemakers. Yet, in the long run, it is the only productive approach. At the heart of the Student Movement, the New Left Politics, Students for a Democratic Society, or the Black Students Union is an essential condition of impotency, of powerlessness. The reverse of Lord Acton's famous truism—in this case, "Powerlessness corrupts, and absolute powerlessness corrupts absolutely"—presents the essential insight for understanding modern student militancy and for charting corrective action. Essentially the student in American higher education, like the black person in white society and the draftee caught in the midst of American foreign policy, is simply that: powerless. And this is a condition seemingly desired by those of us who stand to profit by his servility and emasculation. Jerry Farber, a former professor at California State College at Los Angeles, wrote an intriguing essay, "The Student As Nigger," that captures the basic similarity between student servitude and Negro servitude. He sees the student shuffling before his all-powerful professor and saying, "Yes, Massa, now just how do you want that footnote?" in a fair burlesque of the Southern Negro ingratiating himself with his plantation master.

As a placebo to make his impotency more palatable, we have told the student and we have told the black person that in America he is free to express his dissent—in peaceful, powerless ways. The student has feebly expressed his dissent with the modern trends in our society and the prevalent conditions of teaching and learning on the American campus through an occasional student newspaper article or through his student government machinery or, more recently, through his bullhorn at a student protest rally. For those who take an historical view of American higher education, it is all too obvious that the privilege of dissent has not produced anything approximating desired change. The issue of the relevancy of the curriculum has been a running issue for more than a century, yet it is now regarded as a *new* problem. Reform of the graduate school so that it might produce more competent college teachers has been a standard topic on the agenda of meetings of graduate school deans for many years; ACE and AAHE committees, Hazen and Danforth and other projects have been devoted to it; yet the Berkeley faculty response to the

FSM rebellion unearths a doctorate in arts in its Muscatine Report as though a new element had been discovered.[1]

The impotency of dissent as a vehicle for improving the status of the black person for the past four hundred years is too clear to require comment. And peaceful, democratic dissent has not noticeably changed the military posture of this country in the Vietnam War or U.S. Selective Service policies.

And so the modern college student has good reason to wonder whether our reverence for peaceful dissent is a deep, philosophical conviction appropriate to the complex problem of urban America or is, rather, liberal rhetoric aimed at preserving conditions as those in power desire them while siphoning off the frustrations and hostility of those without power. Many of these students are wondering no longer; they are instead experimenting with new styles of protest, styles that disturb the tranquility of the groves of academe, and styles that have all too often produced a faculty-administrator-politician overreaction, an overreaction that might be even more destructive than the original grave disturbances.

I propose that we spend our energies correcting the conditions on our campuses that have fostered legitimate student grievances. We all know that much of our lower-division required curriculum is the sterile product of graduate school research and training and has little relevance to the modern world; yet we refuse to change it. We all know that much college financing and energies are siphoned off into research pursuits at the expense of teaching and student learning; yet we gladly tolerate this state of affairs. We all know that one of the essential conditions for student intellectual and personality growth in college is honest freedom and independence; yet we keep him in bondage "for his own good" and also because it makes our life more comfortable. And we all know that many of our modern colleges are growing at a rate that makes a true community of scholars, dialogue, and shared responsibility impossible; yet we obdurately refuse to decentralize or create smaller administrative units that might offer

---

[1] *Education at Berkeley,* Report of the Select Committee on Education of the Academic Senate (Berkeley: University of California Press, 1968).

a truly productive learning atmosphere. Another Berkeley report, the result, this time, of a joint faculty-student committee, *The Culture of the University: Governance and Education,* addresses itself most convincingly to these urgent needs for fundamental restructuring.[2] Whether the Berkeley faculty can match the creative insights and erudition of its reports with corresponding reforms remains to be seen.

Were we to move on these fronts, as we certainly have the wisdom and the power to do, and were we to take seriously the complaints of the black students that admissions policies discriminate against them and curricular policies frustrate them, it is my conviction that the radical student would have considerably less cause for defiance and his organizations an even smaller constituency than at present.

But such constructive reactions to improve higher education and minimize students' tensions are not making much headway on our campuses, especially on our more troubled ones. Forward-looking solutions to complex problems are a product of reason, commitment, effort, and faith. These qualities do not seem to be thriving on campuses plagued with student rebellion. Instead, it has been my observation that the atmosphere seethes with the polarization of faculty into enemy camps and with the projection of blame on such convenient scapegoats as vulnerable president, radical faculty, budgets, the Students for a Democratic Society, or the legislature. Scratch the surface of the collective faculty and it would appear you reach a substratum of authoritarianism only slightly disguised in moments of noncrisis by a thin patina of liberalism and intellectualism. In this new atmosphere of student challenges to cherished faculty prerogatives, these authoritarian tendencies are blooming. When it comes to the crux of the matter, reformed higher education will require a radically changed faculty role—a role more open, less status-bound, less authoritative, and less self-centered—but such a redefinition of role we shun like the plague.

The inevitable result is a campus climate of mistrust and

---

[2] Caleb Foote, Henry Mayer, and Associates, *The Culture of the University: Governance and Education* (San Francisco: Jossey-Bass, 1968).

suspicion among and between faculty, administrators, and students, and a yearning for a return to the good old days of faculty hegemony, acquiescent students, and pacified legislators. Such a climate does not provide a fertile environment for the cooperative activities absolutely necessary to move our institutions in the directions that would minimize legitimate student discontent. It is, however, a climate almost guaranteeing that some of the exciting educational innovations influenced by this new student activism will quietly fade away—with both their hopes and their threats.

The concept of student power has brought with it a sense of commitment and dignity for the student. The emphasis upon relevance might well resurrect the hopes of a century for curricular reform; the linkage of learning with living and feeling and acting might hold forth promise that liberal education can really liberate people, not merely confirm predispositions, and that lasting intellectual and personality change might actually occur at college. And student insistence that colleges reassert their traditional idealism but express it in the form of an active role in social reform might offer our troubled society a new power base for making inroads on the solution of its vexing problems.

These tender beginnings are certain to be stunted if we continue to polarize, project blame, and react in authoritarian ways—just as they will surely be stunted if we cannot assure the public that, with time, patience, and good will, we can meet new threats of disruptive behavior. With the withering of these constructive reforms, the vicious cycle of rebellion and repression, more powerful and hateful rebellion followed by more powerful and hateful repression, renews itself once more. For those who find the vision of liberal education as basically threatening to their conception of a closed, conservative society, this recycling of rebellion and repression is a goal that is desired and encouraged. For those of us who believe we can never have a free, open society unless our educational system fulfills its promise and liberates the mind, feelings, and will of our young people, such a cyclic train of events borders on stark tragedy. The next decade and our actions in response to student defiance during this period will most likely decide this course of events.

Section V

Explanation and Judgment

～ 10 ～

TWELVE HYPOTHESES OF STUDENT UNREST

S. L. Halleck

Students can no longer be taken for granted. It does not matter that a great majority of students remain largely content, conservative, and apathetic. A determined minority of restless college students have forced us to examine and sometimes change institutions, rules, and values that were once considered inviolate. The most significant aspects of student unrest can be described as follows:

1. Some students reject the political and economic status quo and are making vigorous attempts to change the structure of our society. These are the student activists.

2. Some students reject the values of their society as well as the values of their own past and are developing a style of life that is contradictory to the Western ethics of hard work, self-denial, success, and responsibility. These students sometimes participate in efforts to change the society but for the most part they

are withdrawn and passive. They can be described as alienated.

3. Both activist and alienated students tend to come from affluent middle- or upper-class homes. They are sensitive and perceptive individuals. They are also highly intelligent.

4. Both activist and alienated students have difficulty in relating to the adult generation. They are articulate, irreverent, humorless, and relentless in their contempt for what they view as adult hypocrisy. Such youth are highly peer-oriented. They turn to one another rather than to their parents when shaping their belief systems or when seeking emotional support.

5. Alienated students and, to a less extent, activist students find it difficult to sustain goal-directed activity. Their capacity to organize for any kind of action is limited. They often fail at work or school. Even their political efforts seem highly disorganized.

6. Alienated students live at the edge of despair. Although they seem at times to be enjoying life, there is always a sense of foreboding about them. Often they become depressed and suicidal. Activist students are more emotionally stable but are also prone to deep feelings of helplessness and self-pity.

There is no dearth of explanations of the above phenomena. Some explanations seem to be based on opinions that support the prejudices of differing political viewpoints. Others are more scientific and are presented with analytic objectivity. No hypothesis thus far advanced can be considered a sufficient explanation of student unrest. At best, each is only a partial explanation.

Certain propositions often made about students are not hypotheses but value judgments. The unsupported statement that the behavior of our restless youth represents a healthy and sensible response to the corruptions of our world is exhortative rather than explanatory. Such a position is embraced by those who are discontent with the status quo, and wish to emphasize and exploit student restlessness as a phenomenon that justifies their own grievances. Similarly exhortative are unsupported statements that students are more emotionally disturbed than they used to be. Implying that students act as they do because they are mentally ill serves to demean their behavior by casting doubts upon the validity of the messages that behavior is designed to communicate.

A more interesting proposition concerning student unrest is that it is neither new nor exceptional. Precedents can be cited in our history when students were even more restless than they are now. Periods of unrest do seem to run in cycles, and it is conceivable that we happen to be in an active phase of a predictable cycle. This proposition is reassuring to those who look forward to a quiet future. Its weakness, however, is that it assumes that those forces that make for cyclical behavior will remain relatively constant. My own opinion is that the world is changing so rapidly that using historical precedents to predict future behavior is a risky business. We can deplore student unrest or we can welcome it, but we cannot ignore it or simply wait for it to go away.

Those who are critical of student activism and alienation are most likely to seek its causes in factors that they believe have created a moral weakness in our youth. They believe students are restless because they lack discipline, values, or purpose. These deficiencies are believed to originate within the disturbed family, particularly that family which has been influenced by affluence, liberal thinking, and modern psychological notions of child rearing. While these hypotheses may also appeal to those who are sympathetic toward students, they are primarily critical in the sense that they imply that something is wrong with those students who protest or withdraw.

Perhaps the commonest explanation of student unrest is that it is the result of too much permissiveness in rearing children. The proponents of this view argue that some parents have, through painstaking efforts to avoid creating neuroses in their children, abdicated their responsibility to teach and discipline their children. In doing so they have reared a generation of spoiled, greedy youth who are unable to tolerate the slightest frustration without showing an angry or infantile response.

Although the permissiveness hypothesis has been used in the crudest manner to berate and deplore the behavior of youth, it cannot be lightly dismissed. There is considerable evidence that activist and alienated students are members of well-educated families, deeply committed to liberal doctrines. In such homes children are given unusual freedom to criticize, debate, and question. Restless students also have frequently attended primary and secondary schools dedicated to the ideal of progressive education, schools that, in their efforts to maximize freedom and creativity, seek to minimize discipline and frustration.

It can, of course, be argued that children raised in permissive homes will be better citizens than those raised in stricter homes. Restless students do seem to be more open to ideas, more involved with social issues, and more flexible than their peers. The critics, however, can point to other characteristics of restless students that seem to be related to their permissive upbringing, and that are not so salutary. The response of such students to discipline, for example, is, in no useful sense, adaptive. Arbitrary regulations enrage them. Even rational forms of discipline, such as the need to master basic concepts before moving on to more abstract ideas, bother them. Restless students also react inappropriately when their demands are not immediately accepted. They are prone at such moments to protest violently, to give up and withdraw, or to wrap themselves in a cloak of despair. Much of their abrasiveness and much of their ineffectiveness can be explained by their uncompromising demands for immediate gratification. This inability to tolerate frustration or delay must be considered a weakness or defect.

A second hypothesis focuses on the concept of responsibility. Many who are concerned about the dangers of permissiveness also believe that our culture has been "psychologized" to the extent that youth become unwilling to assume responsibility for their own behavior. The expansion of the social and psychological sciences has confronted the public with elaborate deterministic explanations of behavior. When a behavior is totally explained, there is a tendency for people to act as though they are no longer responsible for that behavior. They confuse the theoretical issue of scientific determinism with the society's practical needs to have its citizens remain accountable for their own actions.

When the sociologist documents the impact of poverty and discrimination upon Negro youth, he is conducting a logical and scientific exercise. The subjects of his research, however, are tempted to utilize his findings to support an individual and collective feeling of responsibility. The Negro adolescent who participates in a riot, for example, might sincerely believe he could not do otherwise, being moved by forces over which he has no control. Psychological explanations are also utilized to avoid accountability. It is becoming more common to hear criminals say, "I should not be held responsible for what I have done because I am neurotic or mentally ill."

Psychiatry, particularly Freudian psychiatry, has been maligned as a critical agent in producing a climate of nonresponsibility. While there is nothing in the theoretical doctrines of psychoanalysis that favors abdicating personal responsibility, it does seem that the psychiatrist's ability to expand and legitimize the mental illness role has had an impact on the manner in which people view the question of responsibility. Behavior once considered bad is now considered sick. Sickness implies that one cannot help himself or that one is not responsible for his actions. The proponents of the nonresponsibility hypothesis would argue that by expanding the sick role to include forms of behavior that were once considered in terms of good or bad, the healing professions have helped create a social climate in which more people manage to avoid accountability for their actions. Youth growing up in such a society are tempted to behave in a pleasure-seeking, antisocial, and irresponsible manner. Many feel that this is exactly what restless students are doing.

The evidence that activist and alienated youth are deeply influenced by a climate of irresponsibility is inconclusive. Some activist students are often impressively willing to hold themselves accountable for their actions. On the other hand, most alienated students are not. They tend to seek medical or psychiatric excuses from their obligations at the first sign of stress. They also have a discouraging tendency to break laws and to insist that their own personal needs and problems are such that they should not be held accountable for these actions.

The situation with regard to use of marijuana is a case in point. Thousands of students use this drug illegally yet it is practically impossible to organize students to do anything to legalize the sale of marijuana. When students are occasionally arrested for smoking marijuana, they almost always avoid punishment by becoming informants and thus not only avoid legal accountability but seem unable to adhere to their perceived obligations toward their deviant subcultures.

It is almost as if they say, "Because the world is so bad and because it has treated me so badly, I cannot be blamed for my actions. There is no point in holding me accountable for things I cannot help doing anyway."

A third hypothesis that appeals to critics of student unrest is based on the alleged hazards of growing up in an affluent society. It is sometimes argued that affluence that is unearned, and that is unaccompanied by a tradition of service and commitment, creates a sense of restlessness, boredom, and meaninglessness in our youth. The child raised in an affluent society has difficulty finding useful goals. He does not learn to use work or creativity as a means of mastering some aspect of the world. He therefore, according to this argument, is trapped in a never-ending search for new diversions and new freedoms, which sooner or later begin to feel sterile and ungratifying.

Man seems less likely to be troubled if he is distracted by some monumental task that dominates his life goals. In a relatively poor society, the very need for survival creates a structured and seemingly purposeful life. In an affluent society, man has the time and freedom to contemplate the meaning of his existence. Many restless students do come from affluent homes and many have decided that their lives are devoid of meaning. Sometimes it seems that their provocative behavior is designed primarily to invent new struggles and even imaginary hardships that will free them from their lethargy and help them atone for their guilt over having it so good.

The affluence hypothesis has certain undertones of criticism directed toward the parents of restless students. Affluence, after all, does not always produce protest or indolence. Traditionally, many of our most useful public servants have been products of wealthy homes. The critics of student unrest would reserve their harshest barbs for those newly affluent parents who have themselves become so caught up in materialistic pleasure-seeking life that they have failed to meet their responsibility of teaching children the kinds of values that would lend meaning to a young person's existence.

A number of explanations of student unrest focus upon the disturbed family. According to this hypothesis, activist and alienated students behave as they do because they are responding to an unresolved conflict within the family unit. It is usually suggested that the restless student has been subjected to too much pressure by his parents or is "acting out" a need of his parents. A more general approach to the problem focuses on a family structure in which the father is a weak or shadowy figure. This approach emphasizes the breakdown in authority of the paternal figure, the confusion of sexual roles in our society, and the break with tradition that such confusion produces.

The evidence for the existence of a high degree of pathology in the families of restless students is inconclusive. Sociological studies of students and their families do not support any family pathology hypothesis. In fact, such studies suggest that activist students, at least, come from rather stable families. Psychiatrists, on the other hand, find some evidence of serious familial conflict in most of the families of restless students they treat. It must be emphasized, however, that the psychiatrist deals with only a small proportion of such students.

If family disorganization is an important cause of student unrest, the manner in which it exerts its influence must be complex and subtle. Sociological techniques are simply too superficial to get at the complexities of the problem. The findings of psychiatrists are based on depth explorations, which may be valid for some families but which cannot be generalized. Neither sociologists nor psychiatrists can provide valid answers. The most we can say is that some aspects of student restlessness may be directly related to family pathology. Certainly, it is conceivable that in today's highly charged social climate, even minimal family disturbance may be translated into highly provocative behavior.

The next group of hypotheses place the student in a favorable light. They view him as a victim of man-made circumstances and maintain that student unrest is a legitimate and rational effort to change these circumstances. The student is viewed as either a helpless victim of a world he never created, or as a hero seeking to cleanse the world of the evils of previous generations. To be useful, these hypotheses must not simply define what is wrong with the world, but must suggest how various factors have made students more capable of perceiving and acting upon the injustices and irrationalities of our world.

The first of these "favorable" hypotheses focuses on the cold war. This generation of students has grown in an age when the world has been divided into two large camps that have been competing with each other ideologically and politically; and since the Russians launched their first satellite, the competition has also been educational. Students today are trained in a school system that emphasizes the competitive acquisition of knowledge as a source of power and stability. By the time they leave high school they are better educated than any previous generation of students; but they are also more overworked.

All of this emphasis on education and competition is not easily sustained after the student arrives at the university. By this time he is at least partially burned out. The personal benefits of intensive studying and searching for a profitable career begin to appear less attractive in an affluent world and particularly in a world that seems to be making it increasingly difficult for a young person to become an integral part of the economic system. As the student comes to view the implications of our competitiveness with Communism as a never-ending phenomenon, he also begins to question the social value of his efforts. Even if he maintains his enthusiasm for academic work through the undergraduate years, by the time the student reaches graduate school, he increasingly asks himself whether the competitive search for knowledge is worth it. At this point he begins to view our competition with the Communist world (and sometimes competitiveness itself) as a form of mass paranoia and he views the university as an agent of the government that contributes to the perpetuation of the paranoid system. He reacts by protest or withdrawal.

The second "favorable" hypothesis focuses on the war in Vietnam. Although student unrest began long before the war in Vietnam ever escalated to massive proportions, there can be little doubt that in the past few years this conflict has been the major factor influencing the behavior of students. The war is particularly unpopular on our campuses. A large proportion of students, perhaps the majority, see it as a misguided effort. A significant minority see it as wholly immoral. Much of the restless behavior of students can be directly related to their efforts to do something to stop the war or to their sense of total frustration when they feel powerless to stop it.

The draft and the inequities engendered by the II-S deferment also contribute to unrest. The major issue here is fear. The average male student is plagued with fears that he will fail in school, will be drafted, and will run the risks of being killed in a conflict he may not consider vital to our interests. A second issue is guilt. The university student knows that he is spared from military service only because he is richer or smarter than someone else. While he may believe that the war is immoral, he also knows that his privileged status is immoral. When he accepts the II-S status he suffers guilt. Much of the activism on our campuses is a means of atoning for that guilt. Much of the alienation on our campuses is a means of denying the relevance of the society that created such guilt.

Students also feel some shame in not participating in those aspects of military service that might make them feel more masculine. It is rare for anyone even in peacetime to embrace military service eagerly, and a normal late adolescent has justifiable concern with interrupting his career to face the harshness of life in the service. The unpopularity of this war gives the student a cogent reason for avoiding military service; but it does not resolve his nagging fears that he is somehow or other being cowardly or less masculine by being treated specially.

It is also true that the antiwar climate on our campuses makes the student progressively more disinclined to serve in this war the longer he remains on campus. Education breeds a dislike of violence. Furthermore, whatever romantic thoughts a young man may have about the war at the age of eighteen are somewhat attenuated with a year or two of maturation. Students spend many hours arguing about the war, the draft, and means of avoiding the draft. This preoccupation creates a highly tense situation in which the student feels supported only by his peer group. He begins to relate to subcultures that become progressively more separated from the rest of the nation and particularly from the adult generation.

A third hypothesis favorable to students is offered by those who believe that student unrest is an appropriate response to the deterioration of the quality of life in America. Overpopulation, which results in crowds, traffic jams, and mass-production businesses, has taken much of the joy out of life in our towns and cities. Personal care or service is hard to find in any shop, restaurant, or hotel. People begin to feel faceless and insignificant.

Students, it can be argued, are among the first to sense the painful anonymity associated with bigness. This is a particularly serious problem on overcrowded campuses where students are painfully isolated from their teachers and other adults. A sense of student-faculty intimacy and a sense of scholarly community are sorely lacking on any of our large campuses. Students find it difficult to develop a sense of identification or loyalty toward a monolithic and impersonal university. In their complaints that they are treated like numbers or IBM cards they strike a poignant note for all of us.

Overcrowding is only relative and would not be so destructive were it not for the manner in which we have incredibly neglected the planning and development of town and country. Our cities grow with no respect for the land. Beauty and wilderness are easy prey for the builder and contractor. Clean air and clear streams are almost a thing of the past. An adolescent who grows up in a world in which he must sit back and watch beauty fade while pollution advances comes to despair of the future. One way of looking at student unrest is as a massive reaction to the destruction of that kind of world and way of life that their forebears enjoyed but that will be denied to them. It is not uncommon to hear a student say to an adult, "In your world life had some hope and meaning, but in the world you have left for me, these qualities are gone."

A fourth hypothesis comes out of political hopelessness. Many individuals see our mass society as immutable to change. It has been argued that our society is so complex, our systems of checks and balances so intricate, and our interplay of pressure groups so self-equalizing that really effective change is no longer possible. Our business-oriented economy has so indoctrinated us into the role of credit-bound consumers that we are all beholden to a way of life that may not be in our best interests. An increasing number of radical students are convinced that the forces of government, industry, and education are totally interdependent and allied to one another for the purpose of warding off any reasonable attempts to change the society. They believe that our country has developed a system of life that simply absorbs legal efforts to change our society, even protest, in a manner that ultimately preserves the status quo. In this regard it is somewhat distressing to note the manner in which hippies and protestors have not only been institutionalized as part of our folklore and humor but have been exploited by the advertising industry, an institution they initially intended to destroy.

Guided by the philosophy of Herbert Marcuse, many students are convinced that constructive change within our society is not possible by working through the system. They do not have any sort of vision as to what will replace the old order, but they are convinced that our society is fundamentally irrational and must be destroyed. They do not reject illegal acts or even violence as agents of destruction.

A fifth hypothesis favorable to students centers on civil rights. The civil rights movement not only increased youth's awareness of an historical injustice that made it difficult for them to be proud of this country, but also served as a training ground for future radicals. The new campus protest began at Berkeley when students demanded the right to work freely on their own campuses on behalf of oppressed Negroes. Many campus radicals shaped their images of the Establishment and of unreasonable authority on the basis of their early work in the civil rights movement. Students throughout the country have developed an amazing empathy and identification with Negroes. Their commitment to the Negro cause has taught them the psychological meaning of oppression and has encouraged them to seek out and attack sources of oppression in their own lives.

I should like now to present three hypotheses—or, perhaps, *groups* of hypotheses would be more accurate—which are neither favorable nor unfavorable to students. Some explanations of student unrest focus upon impersonal processes. The causes of unrest, according to these hypotheses, are not to be found in the actions or philosophies of other men, but are believed to reside in changes in our highly complex society, which seem to create the need for new modes of psychological adaptation.

The first of the "neutral" hypotheses focuses on modern technology. Man has always lived with hope, particularly with the hope that his efforts in the present will be rewarded with gratification in the future. A certain degree of predictability in the future enables one to make commitments to goals and to other people. To the extent that we live in a society in which past, present, and future lose their interrelatedness, the power of hope to shape man's behavior is diminished. New means of adapting to the world must then be found and the manner in which people relate to one another must be profoundly altered.

Postwar America has been characterized by a massive and continuous growth of technology. Our society is one in which the conditions of everyday life are constantly changing. Moreover, the rate at which technology changes our lives is itself increasing. No one can predict what life will be like in twenty years, ten years, or even five years. Today's knowledge, today's work skills, and today's values may be totally irrelevant to tomorrow's world. Kenneth Keniston has described the manner in which some youth, who, when exposed to an ever increasing rate of technological growth, come to perceive that the values of the past will be totally inappropriate for the world in which they will be adults. Moreover, they feel powerless to anticipate or direct the future. In this environment, hope no longer sustains. It is adaptive to be cool, to learn to live in the present.

What are the advantages and disadvantages of living in the present? The advantages are more or less obvious. One is more flexible and, superficially at least, more comfortable. It is not necessary to delay gratification nor need one allow himself to be tortured by the mistakes of the past nor to be deluded by unrealistic hopes for the future. The disadvantages of life in the present are more subtle, yet more powerful. To live in the present one must narrow his commitments. He must travel lightly and be ready for anything. More intimate relationships are unlikely since they cannot be sustained by reference to past experience nor to promises of a better future. Passion and romantic longing must be avoided because they may breed pain or impair one's flexibility. In short, if carried to extremes, life in the present is a selfish life incompatible with the growth of that intimacy and passion that man has always found essential to a fulfilled life.

Distrust of the future and a determination to live in the present seem to be characteristic of both activist and alienated. students. The student activist seeks immediate change and has difficulty in developing the patience or optimism for long-term planning. The alienated student adopts the philosophy of the hippie. Believing that the only certainty in life is change, or uncertainty itself, he adapts by "doing his own thing" and behaves as though he is responsible only to himself.

A second group of hypotheses in our "neutral" category attempt to relate the growth of new media, particularly television, to the troubling behavior of students. It can be argued, for example, that simply by being available to publicize the activities of protestors and hippies the media exaggerate the importance of these groups. The television camera forces all of us to take seriously forms of behavior that might have been dismissed lightly in earlier decades. Conceivably, the media may be creating a climate of expectation in which youth are subtly seduced into dissenting roles that may not represent their actual interests.

It is also true that many television commercials, radio ads, and most modern music are directed toward the youth market. The self-consciousness of youth is thereby heightened. They are made more aware of their potentialities and sometimes develop an exaggerated sense of their own power.

Another attempt to relate changing media to student unrest has been implied in the writings of Marshall McLuhan. McLuhan believes that electronic media are bringing us all closer together in a more truly communal and shared society than ever existed. Our youth, who have grown up with the new media, are ready for such a society. Elders, who are committed to sustain the institutions of the past, are not. Much youthful rebellion can then be visualized as an effort to make older people see that the world has changed and that many of the values of the past are now irrelevant.

Although McLuhan's hypothesis has some attractiveness, it does not seem as plausible as those that focus upon the psychological impact of the content of media. Frederic Wertham believes that the massive degree of violence that young people see on television makes them more violent and less responsible. Vance Packard, for example, has argued that chronic exposure to the values implied in TV commercials could create a generation of unrealistic, demanding, and present-oriented youth. I would like to propose my own hypothesis of student unrest based on the manner in which the media influence the character structure of youth by prematurely confronting them with the harsh truths and realities of life.

As an animal whose growth and development requires him to be dependent on others for a long period of time, man learns to rely on others for an optimal amount of structure and order in his life. It is obvious that authority is not always benevolent, not just; and yet it is true that no man can be at ease if he does not commit a part of himself to some authority, whether it be his church, his family, his government, or an ideology. Nor can one come to develop a firm sense of who he is without making such commitments. It is at least partly through experiencing limitations that are imposed by others, by respecting others, and by emulating those who are respected that one finds his own identity. The process by which one comes to terms with authority is not always deliberate nor rational. Sometimes even benevolent authority relies on faith, mystique, or untruth to retain its control.

This is especially relevant to the situation of young people. The most well-meaning parents must on occasion deceive their children because they know that children would find many of the hard and cynical facts of life unbearable. Until recently it was possible for young people to begin to experience the world as adults know it only after they have reached adolescence. Most of the time the adolescent absorbed this new knowledge gradually and painlessly. Even when he did feel that his parents had been hypocritical or had deceived him, his awareness of their dishonesty came so gradually that his resentment and rebelliousness were restrained. Today it is different. One of the significant developments in postwar America has been the influence of mass communication media, particularly television, which are capable of disseminating information to all age groups immediately.

Even before adolescence, television acquaints youth with the cynical facts of life at a time when such truths may be indigestible. Other media communicate knowledge so quickly now that there is little opportunity for anyone to live comfortably with myth or self-delusion. Beliefs that were once casually accepted are vigorously scrutinized. The belief that there is equality for all Americans can hardly be sustained when one has a front row seat from which he can observe the Negro's unsuccessful struggle to maintain a decent life in this country. Blind faith in the veracity of leaders of nations is quickly lost when one can watch the proceedings of an organization such as the United Nations in his own living room. I have no doubt that diplomats have always lied to one another, but what is new about this world is that children can now watch them lie in living color.

The hypocrisies of older generations have always been with us. What is new today is that it is ridiculously easy to expose them. The effect on our youth of premature emergence of truth has been to create a deep skepticism as to validity of authority. Neither the family, the church, the law, nor any institution demands the automatic respect it once did. There may be other factors contributing to this decline in respect for authority, but in my opinion it is best understood in terms of the psychological impact of our new media.

A third "neutral" hypothesis has to do with the reliance on scientism. Today's restless youth have grown up in a world that has sought answers to the questions of life not in religious faith but in science. Many of us believe that science can provide all the answers. We ask that the speculations and opinions of the social sciences contain the same hard truths as more rigorous findings in the physical and biological sciences. In my work with students, I am often impressed to find how easily they believe or once believed in the perfectibility of man. Hostility is seen not as an innate quality of man but as a response to frustration. The teachings of the social psychologist that aggression is a learned phenomenon have gained prominence over Freud's more ominous warnings that aggression is innate.

This generation of students seems to have grown up with the belief that original sin, in the religious sense, or Thanatos, in the psychoanalytic sense, does not exist. Much of this belief has been reinforced by the mode of their existence. Many are affluent and have grown up in suburban communities where, except for what they see on television, they are shielded from the tragedies of life. The realities of their own lives convince them that whatever calamities are imposed upon others are not inevitable. Statements such as "life is a vale of tears" or "the mass of men lead lives of quiet desperation" seem absurd to them. In their adherence to scientific rationality they also cannot accept guilt. They are convinced that in a perfectible world man should be joyful and guiltless.

When a person raised with such beliefs encounters the harsh realities of life, he has little to fall back upon. If he perceives his own aggressive tendencies, he is frightened by them and attempts to deny them. He may project his anger upon those whom he feels are frustrating him or he may simply deny that such anger exists. When he perceives the evil of others he is mortified. In his conviction that there are rational solutions to any problem, he cannot help but be intolerant of the irrationalities of those who prevent progress. In his belief that life and especially the sexual aspects of life can be enjoyed without guilt, he becomes highly disturbed when he discovers that he cannot escape his past and that a certain amount of guilt is inevitable. He even becomes plagued with additional guilt over the realization that he is guilty.

The restless student is one who has taken literally the message of science, rationality, and perfection. He is more open to action and change than were earlier generations of students. At the same time, however, he is not equipped to understand or deal with the depth of that irrationality in man that resists change and leads man to seek his own destruction. Too often such a student finds it necessary to construct devil theories of history, in which the existence of evil is attributed to only a few who block the progress of the many. He has sacrificed the comfort and patience that come with the idea of accepting original sin. Sometimes the student becomes totally overwhelmed with the irrational aspects of the world and reacts by totally abandoning his earlier beliefs. In their disillusionment some alienated students seem to be turning away from the promises of scientism and searching for solace in the most dubious forms of mysticism, magic, and astrology.

Hopefully this review of twelve hypotheses—or, rather, groups of hypotheses—has been more than an exercise in cataloging. By emphasizing the diversity of explanations of student unrest, I have attempted to demonstrate the intellectual futility of searching for simple explanations of highly complex phenomena. As citizens, we may wish either to support or to attack the causes that the restless students have dramatized. But as scholars concerned with educating and understanding and helping students, we need a more objective approach. We must recognize that there is some truth to the most critical as well as the most sympathetic hypotheses.

Some of the hypotheses suggest guidelines for action. The critical hypotheses remind us that youth are not always as wise or powerful as we might suspect. Like adults, their actions are determined as much by personal weaknesses and selfishness as by sensitivity or idealism. While youth certainly do not need more paternalism and coddling, they still need our understanding and guidance. They can still learn much from adults who are committed to the pursuit of ideals in a climate of tolerance, compassion, and responsibility. The critical hypotheses need not be used only to berate students. If their validity is appreciated they can be helpful in freeing adults from that unreasonable guilt that impairs an honest confrontation with the issues the students have raised.

The sympathetic hypotheses emphasize the unusual degree of stress this generation of students has experienced. Those hypotheses that invoke the war, overpopulation, and pollution as sources of stress forcefully remind us that student unrest is often an appropriate response to what sometimes seems to be a hopelessly troubled world. Other hypotheses raise many questions for those entrusted with the management of our universities. Does the emphasis on education as a means rather than an end have any meaning in an affluent society? Should youth be encouraged to remain in a passive role as students throughout the first third of their lives? Are there means of bringing young people into important roles in the power structure of our universities and our social system before they reach the age of twenty-five or thirty? Is the II-S classification anything more than a bribe that weakens the moral position of dissenting students and creates havoc on our campuses? Should it be abolished? To what extent can we continue to depersonalize and enlarge our campuses without creating a generation of alienated youth who feel no sense of identity, no sense that they have a voice in what is done to them, and no sense of commitment to anything but their own interests?

It is my belief that the neutral hypotheses are the most intriguing and the most powerful valid explanations of student unrest. At the same time they are the most difficult to live with optimistically. If progress itself, in the form of technology, science, or new media is the most severe stress in the lives of our young people, then we are faced with a seemingly impossible task, namely how to control progress and change rather than allowing these forces to control us.

Students have demonstrated to anyone who is willing to read their message that a complacent drifting into the future, an unchecked growth of technology, science, and media cannot take place without profoundly altering the nature of human existence and the character of man. Some of the behaviors of youth, including many forms of student activism, are efforts to warn us of overwhelming danger. They are adaptive insofar as they seek to ward off social calamity. Other behaviors of our youth, such as profound alienation, are by-products or symbols of a process of social decay that may well be irreversible. They are efforts to live with a calamity that already exists.

Faced with the grim realities of the postwar world, how will man continue to survive with dignity? Most of our counselors, scientists, and theologians have faith in man's infinite capacity to adjust. They seem convinced that man can mold his personality, can adopt new values, and can learn to live in a flexible and uncommitted manner. Some find cause for optimism in the possibility that man might learn new methods of child rearing so that he may overcome the psychological lag between his needs and the demands of the new world. I wish I could share this optimism, but I cannot. It is not likely that child-rearing methods can be changed quickly enough to keep up with the rate of technological change. It is also possible that some of man's psychological needs are immutable. I doubt that man can live without intimacy, without compassion, without ideology, without faith, without autonomy, without privacy, and without beauty, and still be man.

The only effective solution would require a drastic revision of many of the traditions and structures of our society. Our first need is to study and to plan, to determine what kinds of technological progress are consistent with making man a better human being and what kinds are not. The latter must ultimately be rejected. We must find a way to communicate those values that are essential to man's survival to our children in an open and questioning but noncynical manner. We must re-examine our time-honored reverence for affluence, power, and bigness, and face the possibility that affluence bores, that power corrupts, and that big institutions diminish the stature of man. In a nation struggling with an unpalatable war and an excruciating racial problem, these problems may seem premature, vague, and almost grandiose. Where can one begin?

If we do nothing else, we must at least begin to study the impact of technological progress upon man's personality. Only a handful of scientists and philosophers are seriously concerned with the study of man's psychological future. No university or government agency has ever created a department or institute to study this problem. This need is immediate and critical. Only man's intellect and reason can protect him from himself. If we deny the existence of the problem, if we equivocate, or if we merely drift, man's tenure on earth will have been truly absurd and meaningless.

11

THOUGHTS ON THE DECAY OF MORALS

Edward Joseph Shoben, Jr.

For nearly two hundred years, a strongly shared set of values has shaped and given direction to the American dream. Inherited largely from the European Enlightenment and the traditions of Western liberalism, those values have been essentially the ones identified by Max Weber in his classic analysis of the Protestant ethic. At the core have been work, achievement, and security; playing more instrumental roles, self-control, an orientation toward the future, the supremacy of rationality over the impulses and emotions, and the potentially supportive and protective approval of society have all been vitally important. As the United States has grown, this central value-structure has provided room and reinforcement for individuality through frontier-related opportunities and through an enlarging multiplicity of forms, primarily occupational, over which the basic ethic could be effectively stretched.

Currently, the nation is subject to a panoply of forces that challenge that ancient pattern of dominant values. Among these powerful influences are the tempo and massiveness of contemporary social change, the technology of communication and its interaction with a highly literate population, the human crowding that results from population growth and urbanization, and the transformation of the economy from an industrial to what has been called a post-industrial base.[1] It is within this context that one can grasp some of the significance of student unrest and the dissidence of youth. What is crucial about these phenomena is not their greying of administrative heads or their interference with large-scale institutional machinery. Their importance lies, rather, in their strong suggestion of a sharp decline in the potency of traditional values to guide and animate American life.

Born to a time of jet travel and television, with little sense of either the Great Depression or the war against Hitler as much less remote than the Black Plague or the Thirty Years War, and aware from infancy of the near-genocidal weaponry that ironically defines modern man's most creative achievement, today's youth are, in the main, indeed, children of both affluence and anxiety. They are a part of what is most novel in our rapidly and radically changing age; and what is now most novel is what is least familiar to those with longer memories and more antique arteries.

It follows, then, that if there has always been a "generational gap" of some kind or other, the conditions for the gap's widening are presently particularly acute, and the magnitude of that gulf is lent special meaning by population projections. Almost half the American people are currently under twenty-five years of age. By 1972, a majority will be under twenty-one, and the median age of the American voter in that year should be about twenty-six. Beyond their increase in numbers, youth have attained a kind of solidarity by virtue of college attendance. Now enrolled in excess of six million on campuses across the country, students have been recognized as something roughly analogous to a social class. Selective Service deals with them on special terms; advertising identifies them as a distinctive and important "target public"; they are

---

[1] Daniel Bell, "Notes on the Post-Industrial Society," *Public Interest* (Winter 1967), pp. 24–35, (Spring 1967), pp. 102–118.

courted politically, and their mores are acknowledged, sometimes with acceptance and sometimes with retributive outrage, as different from those of older generations.

Numbers and a kind of corporate identity imply potential power. For potential power to become manifest, spokesmen are needed to give leadership and focus to size and membership; and spokesmen are now available among student activists who, even though they represent a minority of youth, still compose a considerable group. If only 3 per cent of current college students can be called activists, they yet number in excess of 180,000, and they appear, in one way or another, to voice the sentiments of from one-fifth to one-third of their less directly involved peers.

Both intrinsically, therefore, and as the heirs apparent of American destiny, contemporary college students can hardly be ignored. And whatever one may say—and a good deal of importance *can* be said—about their style and manners, their primary concerns hardly merit neglect among thoughtful and goodwilled men.

In a complex fashion, four major themes have underlain student unrest as we have known it since 1960. One is civil justice. A second is the humanization and personalization of international relations, expressed basically in vigorous opposition to the American posture in Vietnam and in the endorsement of such person-to-person ventures as the Peace Corps. The third is the modernization of the university and its relationship to society. And the fourth, cutting across the other three, is an emphasis on individual freedom and self-determination, on the existential primacy of the present and of experience in contrast to the traditional dominance of the future or of either authority or the accumulated wisdom associated with guiding conventions.

In pressing for a hearing in the prosecution of these broad and humane interests, students have typically assumed a stance that is political and tactical, but their energizing convictions have been profoundly moral. Active and often risky involvement in the fight for civil rights, in opposition to the war in southeast Asia, and in battles for educational reform grow basically out of beliefs about the right way a man should live and commitments to the principle that individuals must contribute actively to the attainment of a more generous and decent world. Indeed, these involvements primarily reflect the social implementation of the ethic of individual freedom in the existential present: at their richest, freedom and authenticity of experience must be widely shared. Civil justice, peace, and more relevant forms of educational opportunity are, on the one hand, the conditions under which such a sharing can be most significantly achieved and enjoyed; on the other hand, the vigorous pursuit of these social goals makes possible the experience of meaningfulness and freedom that is the touchstone of the moral life.

Such an experiential and existential touchstone contrasts sharply with the traditional moral criterion of how well behavior accords with conventions or time-established rules. It has little to do with work and earned security as our civilization has enshrined them, and it often flies in the face of a prudent self-control or cultivation of social approval. When applied to such affairs as sexual conduct, the use of marijuana, and personal appearance, the existential test can too readily be misunderstood as a legitimizing of license, an escape from the harsh realities that a truly moral man faces, and an unsocialized sloppiness. Although the way of wisdom with respect to sex, drugs, and dress is more than merely moot, and although one need not be at all convinced that the advocates of the New Left or of the hippie mode are within gunshot of newly persuasive and genuinely humane insights, the basic issues here are very different. They concern such matters as the right of privacy in an era when that right is subject to subtle but enormous and debilitating erosion. They concern the question of the extent to which pharmacological agents can be employed for the improvement of the human condition and for the enlargement of personal experience in a time when psychoactive drugs have become commonplace in the adult community—witness the huge annual bills paid for caffeine, nicotine, alcohol, and a startling variety of tranquilizers by the most stable and conventionally contributive members of our middle class. They concern the question of the degree to which contemporary life has come to focus on traditional forms and the externals of social interchange as against the experience of pleasure and the real substance of personal relationships. Such matters have always been of moment to civilized men, and history has consistently recorded the indebtedness of cultures to those who, by searching out the elements of hypocrisy and decadence and self-delusion in them, have helped to revitalize them.

But the thoroughly appropriate debates that can be held

about the specific positions of activist students on particular problems is not our business here. The present thesis is a twofold one: First, the confrontation that has been shaping up between the student sector and traditional society is an authentically moral one, fundamental and serious in tone and implications, generative of a healthy rethinking of ethical ideas and the ways in which they can be made manifest in social policy, and a decided aid in helping America gear itself to the pace and pattern of the changes that are the hallmark of the age. Second, insofar as it has accepted the slogan of "from dissent to resistance," the moral force of student activism has become corrupt and subject to decay.

It is not that the escalation of criticism and protest to disobedience and disruption is hard to understand. In many instances, youth have found it difficult to obtain more than a *pro forma* hearing for their grievances and their recommendations in the corridors of institutional or national power. A highly relevant illustration is the lack of response to the two very moderate letters on Vietnam and the draft adressed to the White House at Christmas time in 1966 and in June of 1967 by the student body presidents of two hundred extremely varied colleges and universities. Conscious of their numbers and their college-based corporate solidarity, informed and concerned students are unlikely to be put off for very long by silence, a figurative pat on the head, or mere access to a patient but inattentive ear of authority. The point holds in spite of the discourtesy, disrespect, and deliberately provocative style of which students have frequently been guilty in their search for a proper forum in which to make their case. Youthful bad manners have often been not only tactically stupid; they have contravened the argument for increased humanization that has been the main and most convincing tenet in their pressure for reform in both the university and the larger society. Nevertheless, their sins have sometimes been less objectionable—on the grounds, by the way, of quite traditional concepts of civility and wisdom— than the neglectful, patronizing, or intransigent reaction from responsible and established seats of power.

If, however, this state of affairs helps to explain, it in no way justifies the move from dissent to resistance, from a vigorous competition among moral ideas and ethical models to a clash in which raw might is the only determiner of the outcome. Almost by definition, this shift in the character of the confrontation removes it from the moral domain. When contending parties attempt to settle their differences by weapons alone, one side always considers the other to be illegitimate, unredeemable in its villainy, and inaccessible to either reason or moral suasion. It is for this reason that war is so typically callousing to the human spirit. Because of the imperfections that so mark man's condition, resorts to warfare may be comprehensible, but they give no warrant to anyone to engage in organized violence in the name of an unsullied morality.

Clarifying this position in the context of student unrest today requires an examination of the notion of civil disobedience with respect both to violating the law and the deliberate breaking of institutional rules. The flouting of duly adopted social regulations is dangerous, of course, on two scores. On the one hand, it rends the fabric of community, opening the doors to anarchy and disorder. On the other hand, because the basic reason for laws in the traditions of the West is to protect society against the tyranny of men, civil disobedience always carries with it the risk of the rise to power of a charismatic dictator or an authoritarian junta; the restoration of social stability and the achievement of some regularity in the community's operations have often provided the road over which a Führer has traveled to prominence. At the same time, experience suggests certain circumstances under which the systematic and planned violation of social rules may be looked upon as acceptable, justified, and beneficial:

(1) The existence of a societal state of affairs so inhumane and indefensible as to demand extreme corrective measures. This condition is adequately fulfilled only when (a) no mode of appropriate redress is available through law or the usual political machinery and (b) the moral or political principles by which the existing state of affairs is judged intolerable are articulate, explicitly formulated, and supported on behalf of the *total* community.

(2) Techniques of civil disobedience that entail minimal or no risk of injury to others.

(3) Minimal or no infringement of the legal rights of others, including those against whose interests the disobedience is aimed.

(4) The avoidance of violence.

(5) The acceptance of the consequences of civil disobedience. By definition, civil disobedience involves not opposition to law but breaking a particular and offensive law in support of a "higher" moral or social principle. Attempts to escape the penalties imply both that no offensive law has been broken and that the higher principle is not worth the sacrifice.

(6) Clear support of the justifying principle by a substantial minority of the population subject to the rule which has been attacked. Because the violation of regulations is a community affair, it cannot properly and on principle be acted out unless both the basic grievances and the justifying principle have a base in significant community endorsement.

(7) Some probability that disobedience will achieve a remedy to the ill that initiated it.

Unless these conditions are met, civil disobedience can readily degenerate into indiscriminate rioting, a technique for serving selfish interests, and a route to one brand or another of fascism. Despite the strength of the instigations and the desperation that may lie at the roots of civil resistance, the resistance movement itself is likely to prove, in such a case, self-defeating. Social action not infrequently has consequences unforeseen by those committed to it, and totalitarian outcomes are rarely the aim of civil disobedience. In any event, without full regard for the justifying circumstances, civil disobedience can lose its moral base and slide rapidly into mob violence, the venting of miscellaneous frustrations, and the ugly expression of a variety of doubtfully relevant hostilities.

In any context, then, a progression from dissent and protest to resistance and disobedience must prove its moral validity by adherence to the conditions set out here. In a university, this kind of proof is particularly difficult to attain. Among its central functions, the university must give a high place to serving as a forum for the exploration and debating of significant ideas. The processes of exploration and debate can be abridged or stifled in many ways, and this kind of interference is no less objectionable when students are responsible for it than when a legislature or an administrative officer is at fault.

To provide a meaningful forum, a college campus must be

thoroughly open,[2] offering hospitality to speakers who attempt to recruit minds and to officials from government and business who attempt to recruit talents. To demonstrate against the ideas and practices that an agent of the Department of Defense or the Dow Chemical Company may represent is quite legitimate; to capture him, to prevent his doing his lawful job, and to interfere with access to him on the part of other possibly interested students— such activities have too much in common with a ban on speakers, the censorship of the college newspaper, or restrictions on the circulation of "dangerous" library books. In all these instances, a fundamental purpose of the university is subverted, and the morality of the subversion is hard to find and harder still to justify.

There is another ground on which the dissent-to-resistance notion seems questionable. Any morality, including an ethic of immediate experience, gives some attention to the consequences of acts and to the future entailments of conduct. In the case of contemporary student activism—particularly those aspects of it concerned with Black Power, nihilistic efforts to overthrow the entire educational and social system, and some of the most extreme protestations against the war in Vietnam—it seems probable that the advocates of disobedience are breeding a backlash that could make the McCarthyism of the early 1950's seem tame and generous. John Fischer [3] has rceently pointed out this very real danger:

> . . . Some members of the New Left . . . have openly proclaimed their allegiance to Mao or Castro . . . and their hopes of destroying or at least "dislocating" American society. Others have engaged in what now can be excused as idealistic gestures—burning draft cards, assaults on induction centers, blocking of troop trains, mobbing Cabinet officers. Tomorrow, in the hot glare of a Senate investigating chamber, a skillful dema-

---

[2] See the memorandum of 30 October 1967, by President Martin Meyerson to all members of the academic community at SUNY-Buffalo. The statement was drafted immediately after an episode of interference with the activity of a Dow Chemical recruiter.

[3] John Fischer, "The Consequences of Peace," *Harper's Magazine* (February 1968), p. 18.

gogue could easily make such behavior look like giving aid and comfort to the enemy.

Moreover, the New Leftists are busily undermining their own best defense: the American traditions of free speech and tolerance. Increasingly, they are taking the position: "I'm right. You are wrong. Therefore I cannot permit you to be heard." So, in the name of morality, they are stoning and howling down anyone who might disagree with them. . . .

The saddest prospect is that the coming reaction will fall not only on these [New Leftists] but also on . . . a good many students of the kind described by Nan Robertson of the *New York Times* as "intellectual hobbits—warm, lovable, and a little furry-minded." Among them, too . . . will be people like Mr. Rovere and myself, who still believe in the old-fashioned virtues of free speech and fair trial—and who will feel compelled, therefore, to oppose the new crop of witch-hunters as we opposed McCarthy. . . .

Unless there is evidence of some appropriate concern for this disturbing possibility, it seems only accurate to read the morality of student radicalism, recently so promising and so vital, as decaying at its center and as far less humane than many of us would prefer to believe.

Finally, there is another problem that must be considered in evaluating the new morality that has found its voice in youth— particularly in college youth. Throughout the history of man, his communities have had to steer between the Scylla of ossification through too much discipline and too slavish a reverence for tradition and convention and the Charybdis of dissolution or conquest because of an efflorescence of individualism and privatism that makes cooperation impossible. Many civilizations have failed, foundering on the rocks of either overorganization or anarchy. Because extremes tend to beget extremes, and because ours is an age in which the bureaucratization, systematization, rationalization, and routinization of life proceed at a subtle but startling pace, it may be well to remember that the correctives, deeply desirable as they may be, hold their dangers, too. The existentialist, highly personal moral stance of many contemporary young people, despite its considerable virtues, recalls Bertrand Russell's observation [4] that "with subjectivism in philosophy, anarchism in politics goes hand in hand." If we are to achieve both authentic personhood and a genuine sense of community in the modern world, and if the university is to play its significant part in the quest for that achievement, then the emerging power of contemporary youth must be disciplined by an awareness of the moral vulnerability common to all men. That vulnerability is currently italicized by the attractiveness of the dissent-to-resistance slogan, and a major question before us all is whether students will display the sensitivity of the genuinely educated in responding to it.

---

[4] In *A History of Western Philosophy* (New York: Simon and Schuster, 1945), p. xi.

12

A RENDERING
OF
ACCOUNTS

Lewis B. Mayhew

At the acme of success, American higher education stands on the verge of imminent impotency unless new ways of dealing with restless students are discovered. The litany from 1964 to 1968 is well known. The movement begins when the University of California is brought to its knees. As aftermath a talented president is let go, a conservative governor elected, and a new term (Berkeley) added to the language. A liberal president of the University of Colorado, seeking to make his institution a bastion of academic freedom, is forced to recant and then is deposed. A university that has shown it could grow great by welcoming talented children of immigrants—Columbia—is forced to close its doors and is made to appear as an oppressor of minority groups. A sensitive psychologist, tuned to the liberal cause, is pilloried in the public press and by members of his own board of trustees because he was forced to extreme lengths in order to avoid bloodshed on the campus of San Francisco State College. And a wise, experienced administrator is told by a student at his inauguration that only time will tell whether he has the wisdom to preside over the University of Michigan.

In the midst of national material prosperity, relative psychological sophistication, and expanding frontiers of thought and opportunity is a student generation best characterized as restless and disenchanted. Its spokesmen, if not its leaders, reject the political and economic status quo and wish to change the entire social structure. They have rejected the values of their society and tradition and have retreated from an ethic of work, rationality, and responsibility. They have widened the historic gulf between generations and are irreverent, humorless, and relentless in their contempt for adults, especially their own parents. Although dissatisfied with the goals of their society and of their parents, they are generally unable to set goals for themselves or to sustain goal directed activities. And they seem constantly on the brink of despair in spite of moments when they seem to be enjoying themselves. There is always a sense of foreboding about them so that depressed and suicidal feelings are not at all uncommon.[1]

In a nation whose form, structure, and ideology are rationalistic, optimistic, and rooted in a belief in the perfectibility of man, pure nihilism has been elevated to one of the prevailing styles of thought. Much of student rhetoric echoes Nietzsche's belief that the will to power begets nihilism. If man becomes the master of his planet, then his universe, then galaxy, then what? Power for power's sake, no matter how far extended, leaves the dread of a void. Nihilism seems the only possible response to that void since God is dead, God in the sense of a supersensible reality.[2] Hear the overtones in excerpts from the Port Huron statement of the Students for a Democratic Society: "Our work is guided by the sense that we may be the last generation in the experiment with living.

---

[1] See the paper by Seymour L. Halleck in this volume.

[2] William Barrett, *Irrational Man: A Study in Existential Philosophy* (New York: Doubleday Anchor Books, 1958).

. . . Beneath . . . is the pervading feeling that there simply are no alternatives, that our times have witnessed the exhaustion not only of Utopias, but of any new departures as well. Feeling the press of complexity upon the emptiness of life, people are fearful of the thought that at any moment things might thrust out of control. . . ." [3]

At a time when more and more of the nation's youth are led to aspire to higher education, the most revered institutions are respected for limiting access and for encouraging professors to eliminate concern for students as a viable or desirable ethic. In prestige institutions undergraduate students are tolerated as a financial base, through tuition or full-time equivalent appropriations, for the support of professors' real work, and as a large source from which a few new recruits for the priesthood of scholarship may be chosen. The university, claimed to be the focus of the creative energies of the society, thus seeks to alienate itself from those whom society wishes served, and, in some of the most highly financed and selective institutions, it seems determined to alienate itself from all other professions and callings. The preparation of future scholars, whether they be in history, medicine, law, education, physics, or sociology, is judged of infinitely greater worth than producing those who would practice in the service of man.

Although apologists for higher education have canonized the role of higher education as properly a critic of society, free from the political restraints placed on other institutions and offices, it is increasingly being made an object of political concern partly through its own artlessness and partly through the efforts of nihilistic youth. States, private donors and parents have been persuaded to support colleges and universities to do as they pleased. But the bills have become so large and the evidence of social utility so lacking that a rendering of accounts, long overdue, is likely to be demanded by political forces. These forces are strengthened in their resolve by the one tangible evidence of the outcomes of higher education blazoned on television screens and newspapers—the facts of student revolt, radicalism, and challenge of the conventional wisdom.

---

[3] Mitchell Cohen and Dennis Hall, *The New Student Left* (Boston: Beacon Press, 1966).

The combined influence of continued student protest and disorder in urban streets will at least bring greater political scrutiny of the operations of colleges and universities and could hasten a conservative or even fascist government to preserve order even —or especially—at the expense of law. Make no mistake about this. Students occupying administration buildings, conducting pagan happenings, or stressing the erotic in plays, poems, and publications are directly responsible for cuts in educational appropriations, investigations of academic operations, and overruling by political authorities of decisions and prerogatives of academic administrators.

The power of rampant nihilism encountering intrenched syndicalism of professors within a society of frightened and vengeful people could polarize the society in any of several directions. Youthful intellectuals allied with the poor could confront the establishment as did a similar alliance in France in 1789. One wonders what the twentieth century version of the guillotine would be. Or, youthful intellectuals and their not-so-youthful mentors who decry growing up absurd could force themselves into a cul-de-sac rejecting society and denying it their very considerable talents. Or, the nihilism of youth could so spread to other segments of society that an atomic resolution of the bleak uncertainties of an age would seem a welcome respite. Of course there is always the counterrevolution standing in the wings with its powers of legitimacy and appeal to ordered convention.

But a more creative stance would be to seek a resolution of the conflict now confusing campuses, a resolution that would accommodate to realities and preserve educational energies for the benefit of society. Such a stance rests on the need for thorough diagnosis to determine whether the malaise of higher education is terminally malignant or benign. Since higher education is organically related to the rest of society, it, too, must eventually be scrutinized, but for a beginning some of the roots of dissent within education may be exposed.

Institutions are captives of their histories and nowhere is this more apparent than in dealings with students. The American college lodged considerable power in the hands of its president both to maintain the institution and to mold and shape students, exercising in the process the same prerogatives the law allowed a parent or the master of a slave. A president could dismiss a student from school the day of graduation, could search students' rooms, could punish by lowering grades for crimes against a community or make a matter of college concern acts of students committed while far distant from the campus and under even parental jurisdiction. Such powers were exercised in the belief that students were indulged, petted, and uncontrolled at home and allowed to trample upon all laws human and divine, that they came to college with undisciplined minds, uncultivated hearts but with exalted ideas of personal dignity. It is true that such a belief in the depravity of students gave way but not fast enough. Too many institutions, through their leaders, act as though they still really had the power of a colonial president and that students have no procedural rights nor rights to due process. Thus, one dean cancels, without consultation with students, their time-honored right to assemble in a space next to the campus. Still another official acts to suppress an article proposed for a student magazine, while another suspends a student for alleged violations of college rules— without a hearing. Now many such actions would make sense to outraged adults but are indefensible in the light of the American judicial tradition. Hence one angry reaction on the part of a university official to vexing problems of students provides the legitimate focus for many not so legitimate student protests. Virtually every major student uprising was made possible because at some point some college official made the institution vulnerable through denying generally recognized procedural rights. Behind every successful student outbreak stands some administrator who exercised discretion without legitimacy.

Institutions have been unable to take and maintain a strong moral stand against student destruction of property or violation of the rights of others partly because their own moral position was assailable—and bright militant students quickly recognize tarnished values. Thus, lurking in the background of presidential recanting in confrontations with students stand examples of arbitrary action, double standards, and even some examples of dishonesty. The dean of students who denies a white girl the right to bring a Negro date to a dance in the 1960's is not really in a position to face militant students sitting in an administration building in protest over Dow recruiters on the campus, even granted that the student technique and concern were inappropriate to the mission of the university. The institution that, through the unconcerned operation of its recruitment policies, allowed itself to become "lily white" is not really in a position to dispute charges that its athletic department had practiced racism. Or, the institution that acts out of anger or petulance in dealing with a difficult faculty member in violation of the spirit, if not the letter, of the law regarding tenure and the like, can scarcely confront students who similarly violate the spirit if not the letter of the law of a collegiate community.

Of a different order is the failure of institutions to recognize the fact that in many respects college students represent a new kind of adolescence, requiring a special kind of response. Of course, there is the counterpoint that students have not faced the fact that they are not yet full adults. Adolescence is that period between childhood and adult responsibility for oneself, one's mate, children, and society. It is as well a biological phenomenon involving the advent of puberty; but in an even more significant sense, it is a cultural phenomenon involving both status and function. Now within American middle-class society there has always been some dysfunction between various adult statuses and adult functions. One can drive at sixteen, kill at eighteen, drink at twenty-one, all adult statuses but not adult functions, in the sense of economic self-sufficiency, until one is twenty-five. In the past biological, status, and functioning adulthood were achieved within a relatively short span of time. Puberty would come at fourteen or sixteen, end of schooling at sixteen or eighteen, marriage at nineteen or twenty, franchise at twenty-one, and a full-time job at about the same time. During that five-year period, the characteristics of self-consciousness, exclusive allegiance to peer groups, irresponsible criticism of adults and adult values, and the hiatus status (neither children nor adults) could be tolerated; and ways could be worked out within the family to contain extreme manifestations.

At present, however, a number of forces have operated to extend the period of at least cultural adolescence to even before puberty. The early teen-ager has achieved economic power, yet by his late twenties he is not yet responsible for himself as an economic unit. Puberty may come slightly earlier and the opportunity for the killing or marrying prerogatives occur more frequently, but the *rite de passage* of formally ending education comes a great deal later. Thus, the time span of incomplete adulthood has been extended from perhaps five years to ten or fifteen years, and at the same time institutions other than the family, church, and high school are now required to deal with large numbers of adolescents. Thus, the contemporary university is faced with finding ways of dealing with large numbers of students who have achieved biological adulthood and many, if not most, of the statuses of adulthood, yet who cannot really be responsible for themselves, mates, children, or society in any save limited ways. Until the present the attempt was made to deal with these students in ways similar to those appropriate for those adolescents with fewer of the attributes of adulthood. And, of course, it doesn't work. Some of the struggles of college students in their middle twenties to obtain a share in the governance of a college may in reality be an effort to simulate a part of adulthood that their economic condition denies them. In earlier times a twenty-five-year-old man was responsible for himself and family and felt responsible for a part of society. The modern twenty-five-year-old college student probably labors with considerable guilt because he is not similarly placed, hence his drive to campus power sublimates guilt.

There are, of course, a number of other explanations or hypotheses as to why students, especially the restless or militant ones, seek confrontations. One is that the permissiveness of liberal parents has resulted in children who, wanting immediate gratification of desires and not gaining their ends, protest violently, give up, or descend into despair. Related is the theory that students have been so led to underlying psychological bases for behavior that they are unwilling to assume responsibility for their own conduct. If blame for problems can be placed on parental conduct as recalled in an analytic session, the student is thereby relieved of responsibility or guilt over lack of responsibility. Then, too, there is the belief that affluence has taken from the young the need to earn things for themselves. Boredom and restlessness come when the spirit of service goes. Some have thought, but without much clinical evidence, that restless students are merely reflecting family pathology and disorganization. It may be, however, that in a highly charged society even minor family disturbances could be operative. Then, a series of other explanations are advanced. The fact of impersonality of life in a complex society is seen as a stimulus to protest. The despair that comes when students see the difficulty of acting in the political sphere is suggested as the reason radicals prefer direct action. And feelings of powerlessness in the face of the inexorable advance of technology are said to be involved in feelings of determinism tending toward nihilism. Then, there is the opposite force. College youth have been bred on lessons of the power of science and the perfectibility of man. When they experience the spotted reality, they are shattered.[4]

At least two other factors must be mentioned. The first is the general affluence of middle-class white America existing as it does beside a tradition rooted in Calvinism and the rejection of pleasure. Somehow both adults and students in American colleges display considerable guilt over "never having it so good," with restless students opting for the poverty of dropping out and faculty opting for extending the work day and week into times once reserved for recreation as a means of alleviating guilt. Somehow the student who can wear old clothes, eat simple fare, and scorn the "fat cats" eases the guilt that comes from knowing he has had a life of luxury. Equally the professor who flies at night to avoid losing a day of work and who carries his "own" work into the weekends is coping with the problems of affluence.

This problem of affluence is intensified by the twin issues of the plight of minority groups in America and the war now in Vietnam; but who can tell where next? With respect to the war, there is more than a small suspicion that at least part of present affluence is war based. Hence to enjoy affluence is to condone a war the justice of which is in considerable doubt. In a very real sense the protesting college student may be covering the guilt he feels because he knows had his parents not been war-based affluent, he might be fighting the war instead of in college. Police billy clubs are still safer than Viet grenades and he knows it and feels guilty about it. Of course, the moral dilemma of affluent America over the plight of the Negro is the most divisive force in the society.

---

[4] Halleck's essay presents these positions in greater detail.

The guilt and grief that white America evidenced on the death of Martin Luther King is just illustrative of the subterranean feeling there before his death. It is no accident that the student protest derived from the civil rights movement. When it ceased to attract, other protest activity could be used to sublimate the guilt of over three hundred years of injustice.

If this analysis has even limited validity then some possible solutions to the problems dealing with restless students are suggested. The first is really just a palliative, although a not insignificant one. It is to put the problem in some kind of historical perspective. Students have always been difficult to live with and have frequently assumed postures that bothered adults and disturbed institutions. Medieval students rioted, dumped garbage on passersby, wrote erotic or ribald poems and read them on church steps and in other sanctuaries of the establishment, coerced their professors, and, on occasion, killed one. Colonial college students rioted about food, stole, took pot shots at university presidents, protested infringement of their private lives, and gradually forced colleges to modify stringent rules regarding personal conduct. Nineteenth-century students took sides over the Civil War and demanded a voice in academic governance. Twentieth-century students signed the Oxford Peace Pledge, joined in the Spanish Civil War, rioted over food, violated the Eighteenth Amendment, and experimented with sex. There is probably good reason to believe that the present wave of student unrest may be qualitatively different from those earlier times. However, at least an important portion of student protest replicates those of the past simply because the process of growing up is after all a human process and human life has really not changed much in quite a few years. If somehow the embattled administrator could with some humor reflect on the past, and perhaps even learn from the past, his feelings, if not his plight, might be helped. Especially is learning from the past important. Students, when they have protested, have on occasion been trying to say something. Student riots over the quality of food in the commons and the subsequent organization of fraternities and eating clubs were real responses to bad conditions. A confrontation between Princeton students of different persuasions indicated that there were serious moral questions as to whether justice lay with the North or the South. Student agitation over strict rules of conduct was sparked by an overzealous desire on the part of faculty to impose a Puritan ideal of conduct that simply could not work in a changing society. Perhaps historical reflection might suggest that old standards can be changed and still the world turns.

But there are other more direct ways that might be attempted. In virtually every major campus upset from 1964 on, involved was a lack of procedures and procedural rights that could have kept grievances within legitimate bounds. The technique of direct administrative handling of disciplinary matters has lost its legitimacy in the eyes of students and of many faculty and this should be recognized and changes made. The nature of these changes seems reasonably clear. First, there should be only a limited number of offenses over which the university should assume jurisdiction. This would include such academic offenses as cheating and plagiarism and such violations against persons and property as misusing equipment, damage to university property, or interference with the legitimate rights of others to use institutional facilities. These, codified, should then be the responsibility of a campus judicial system with procedures for indictment, hearings and appeals made explicit. As a general rule no administrator should have the right to assess guilt or to assign punishment, nor should he have the right to make administrative rulings without the option of a review of both policy and specific substance. Also generally the campus judicial body should be elected from faculty, students, and administration, but administrative officers charged with administering regulations regarding conduct should be barred from membership and even presence during deliberations. Very likely this campus judicial body might have original jurisdiction over offenses regarding the code of behavior and an appeals function for major controversy over other matters. For example, if a student editor and faculty advisor of a student publication disagreed over whether or not an item should be published and the campus editorial board could not resolve the matter, appeal to the campus judicial should be an option, with its ruling final, unless overturned by the institution's Board of Trustees. Within such a structure even the most vexing of campus issues could be resolved and the administration not placed in a vulnerable position. Student sit-ins of university property, obstruction of on-campus recruitment, and student destruction of university property all could be handled if the campus judicial body is allowed to act responsibly.

Then, too, institutions ought to be more parsimonious in their claimed objectives. Colleges and universities are not churches, clinics, nor even parents. They are devices by which a limited number of skills, insights, and points of view are communicated to the young in the belief that possession of these somehow aids the individual to become a more skilled worker. It is true that the implements to achieve these limited goals are many and varied. Thus, residence halls and lectures, participation in faculty committees and discussions, symbols of institutional loyalty and libraries and laboratories are properly viewed as techniques of instruction and should be used in a professional manner much as the medical profession uses x-ray, medicine, or splints. University regulation of the professional uses of its technical resources seems quite appropriate and if regulations were so limited, few students could legitimately protest. Setting library or laboratory hours, establishing safety requirements for residence halls, or requiring conditions of quiet in classrooms or lecture halls do not seem to become issues in campus controversy except when drawn in the wake of a more central issue. It is when the institution claims too much that it becomes suspect. And it is when an institution attempts to regulate beyond what is necessary to achieve its limited educational goals that it becomes vulnerable. Whether or not a student burns a draft card, participates in a civil rights march, engages in premarital or extramarital sexual activity, becomes pregnant, attends church, sleeps all day, drinks all night is not really the concern of a collegiate institution as an educational institution. When colleges regulate such behavior, as many do, they are by implication taking responsibility for developing patriotism, one system of several standards, one system of health standards and one religious stance—activities that are more properly the province of other social institutions. This is not to say that such matters may not be of concern to an institution or that it cannot deal with them. But if they be of concern, it should be an educational—even a curricular one. Instruction in sex hygiene, ethics, law, or health is appropriate. Requiring a specific kind of behavior is no more appropriate than a requirement that all who finish a course in American government vote Democratic.

This is stark doctrine and will bother many. A religiously related school may feel that compulsory chapel is necessary. A girls' school may feel that pregnancy is something it cannot condone. But in each situation the college is acting the role of some other agency. Now many institutions are able to get away with appearing in these many different roles and to regulate a wide variety of conduct because of the kinds of students they attract, its traditions and the like. But such institutions are always open to attack whereas if they kept regulation limited to what is relevant for limited purposes, they would not be.

An even more significant reform involves the assertion or reassertion of administrative prerogative in relevant domains. For better or for worse, American higher education is and has been administrator centered. It is the president or central administration who brings about innovation when it does happen. It is the president or administrator whose goals are most close to those of students who want a better education. Actually the militant students who want to join with the faculty are in a sense allying themselves to the greatest danger, for it is the American college faculty that has so professionalized itself that it can disregard demands from its clients—the students. And it is the president, who if he errs, brings about confrontation and on occasion collapse. In each of the most widely publicized campus upheavals it was administrative failure that led to trouble. Administrative failure in the sense that the chief executive or an associate used his powers on inappropriate problems.

The American college president should have control of the finances of the institution, certain veto powers, certain appointive powers, and, of course, the powers that attend possession of information. These he is expected to use in the exercise of educational leadership but in procedurally established ways and in the light of other powers belonging to other campus elements. The faculty quite properly should have control over the curriculum, its own membership, and the conditions of student entrance and exit. Students also should have the power of self-determination over their private lives and the conduct of their own group living, but with a number of procedural rights guaranteed. To illustrate how these powers might operate in potentially controversial situations, several examples are suggested. A president should have a voice in faculty appointment and tenure because of the financial commitment. A president should not be able to decree a new program, for that is the concern of the faculty, but he should be able to determine whether or not it will be financed. A president should not have the power to expel a student for misconduct but should have the power to veto a decision of the campus judicial body and the obligation to refer the matter to the Board of Trustees.

What all of this adds up to is a formulation involving delegation of powers and authority, the establishment of procedures and due process, and a concern for a limited number of purposes and objectives. It is a tight constructionist interpretation based on the belief that loose constructionism has really brought about the crisis sorts of confrontations. If college officials concern themselves with defensible educational matters through use of clearly defined powers and recognized procedures, leaving all other matters to individuals, order yet may be restored and accounts finally settled.

PART THREE

Organization and Governance

The five essays of Part Three are devoted to problems of institutional organization. They focus on changes that take place—or do not take place—in academic structures as colleges and universities respond to stress.

The authors represent a wide variety of knowledge and experience with social organization. Roger Heyns is the chancellor of the University of California at Berkeley, William L. Kolb is dean at Beloit College, and Frederick deW. Bolman is associate director of the Esso Education Foundation. Essays by these three men appear in Section Six, entitled "The Creation of Leaders." The second section of Part Three, Section Seven, has as its focus the faculty role in governance, and the two authors represented here are Burton R. Clark, professor of sociology at Yale University, and John C. Livingston, professor of government at Sacramento State College.

Roger Heyns' essay, entitled "Stress and Administrative Authority," sets the stage for the entire part. The Berkeley chancellor first outlines the basic causes of stress on American campuses and then analyzes the obstacles that stand in the way of the changes in organization that must come if long-range decisions are to be made. His analysis shows that most campuses are caught in a web that permits only short-run adjustments. Heyns has a solution for preventing the "mindless and inefficient stumbling from crisis to crisis" that is so characteristic of colleges and universities today. Let the members of the university community voluntarily give administrators increased power and responsibility, he says. Only then can they become real leaders rather than consensus seekers and mediators.

It is certain that every category of reader—regent, president, or dean, faculty member, student, or general layman—will find that Heyns' carefully reasoned and low-key essay illuminates what is clearly the overwhelming problem in the organization of colleges and universities. But not every reader will agree with Heyns' radical (or some, we suppose, would say "reactionary") proposal.

Section Six continues with William L. Kolb's brief essay, "The College Teacher as Professional Man Plus," which directs the spotlight away from the administrator and aims it at the undergraduate teacher. And it is appropriate to make this shift at this point, for the college teacher must be a leader, too. Kolb is not presenting his thesis here for the first time, but his presentation of it is always vital; moreover, the persistence of myth being what it is, the argument cannot be restated too often. Kolb's central idea is this: We raise a *false* issue when we oppose knowledge that is "professional" or "specialized" to knowledge that leads to moral choice or to an education that is relevant to the urgent problems of our time. When we abandon this false distinction, we are able to move to a truer conception of the excellent undergraduate teacher.

The third essay in Section Six, "The Administrator as Leader and Statesman," by Frederick Bolman, opens with an interesting and controversial question: Is professional "training" for college or university administration possible through a graduate program? Brief descriptions are given of such programs. Bolman goes on to analyze four problems that every administrator who hopes to be a leader and a statesman must be prepared to deal with; these are the new student ethos, the new demands of faculty, the requirements of inter-institutional planning, and cost-benefit controls. The final portion of the essay, which takes us forward to the year 2000, suggests that any young man whom our present system of training might prepare specifically for current day-by-day tasks of administration would find himself utterly unable to meet the "large doses of change" in store for him during the next thirty-two years.

Section Seven, dealing with various facets of faculty participation in governance, begins with John Livingston's essay, "Faculty and Administrative Roles in Decision Making." The author believes that the traditional *language* with which we discuss power might be a key to the trouble. A moment's reflection convinces the reader of this essay that the very words in which we conceive of power and describe it—the "struggles" for it, the "balance" of it, the "blocks" and "grabs," the "conflicts" and "shifts" in it—severely limit the alternatives open for solution. Such an "outmoded and irrelevant but persistent way of looking at the world" must be abandoned, Livingston maintains. In his view, what we need is a new, viable language with which to analyze the current crisis in governance occurring on scores of American campuses. Livingston's concluding image is arresting: Power politics on the campus leaves no one holding the reins and the enormous beast simply takes its own course, disregarding as best it can the ambiguous and contradictory commands it receives from its several riders.

Burton Clark's essay, which concludes the section, presents a solution to the problem Livingston's paper so nicely defines. His title, "The Alternatives: Paranoia or Decentralization," suggests the progression of his argument. The key to the problem, Clark demonstrates, is to find the organizational structures that promote collegial authority. The present structures, he asserts, do just the opposite—they are perfect for promoting political paranoia. It is not useful, he says, to argue whether faculty involvement should be advisory or adversary or legislative or whatever else; it is a change in structure that is needed. What Clark recommends is decentralization of governance to small units of the campus.

All five essays in Part Three move in the same direction:

new organizational structures are needed. Where there is severe dysfunction (and all of the authors agree that this exists on every campus), there is little point in devising more efficient *modes of functioning* as long as the organizational *structures* remain unchanged. The reason is simple. The old structures demand, going on inside and among them, the kind of functions that are appropriate to *them*. And they will reject other functions that might be imposed upon them. But the old modes of functioning, unfortunately, make meaningful institutional adaptation to our newly developing needs all but impossible.

Joseph Axelrod

Section VI

The Creation of Leaders

~ 13 ~

STRESS AND ADMINISTRATIVE AUTHORITY

Roger W. Heyns

The stresses weighing upon institutions of higher learning are multiple and subtle; they extend through the entire educational structure, affecting each part in different ways. Our resources to cope with the stresses are sometimes nonexistent or archaic. And the social environment of higher education is as likely to be hostile or indifferent as it is to be friendly or supportive. The upshot of this complexity is that people in positions of responsibility and leadership in higher education have been subjected to the greatest challenge in their history, and a correspondingly enormous amount of inventiveness and creative leadership is now being demanded of them.

Let me sketch some of the kinds of stress that institutions of higher education are now facing. Some of its stresses, to be sure, are old ones that are inherent in the nature of higher education. In one of its functions, education serves to bolster the political, economic, and social institutions of society because it trains men and women to assume positions of responsibility in these institutions. Yet in a society like ours, which is built on a principle of rapid and continuous change, higher education must assume the role of continuous irritant to the outside society, if it is to do its job effectively. It must continue to generate new knowledge, which in the nature of the case must erode comfortable traditions and myths. And, in training new generations for the future world, it must infuse the young with ideas that will necessarily disappoint and irritate their elders, who, being of another generation, have their own, differing notions as to what is good for young people to know and do. In short, effective higher education fosters both a continuous, disturbing revolution in knowledge and a degree of conflict between generations. These characteristics are inherent in a dynamic society.

Superimposed on these innate sources of tension, however, are a number of new stresses, which, though they have been a long time in the making, have become increasingly evident in the explosive period of development in higher education since World War II. Most of these stresses stem from the fact that higher education is being asked to do much more than it has done before. Its faculty members and administrators are being asked to educate millions more each decade, so that the size and number of institutions have had to increase dramatically. This growth has imposed a qualitative burden as well as a quantitative one. In the past twenty years, society has become increasingly insistent that the educational process be upgraded all along the educational line. More and more is being demanded of our young people over a longer period of time.

To these demands the young people have responded with their own demands—quite justified, I might add—that if we are going to ask them to take themselves so seriously, then we too, as educators, should be prepared to take our own responsibilities to them more seriously than we have ever done before. And because the current generation of young people is perhaps best known for its idealism and impatience, these demands are more than vague sentiments; they are demands for action and reform, now. Yet, for many reasons, we are not able to respond to these demands with nearly the speed or the effectiveness that they desire. Institutions of higher education are being asked to become increasingly involved in the larger society—in government service, in professional life, in community problem solving, in the international relations. And if the list of new responsibilities is not already impressive enough, let me mention only the increasing demands and opportunities for expanding research in higher education, and the increasing demands on educators' time that arise from more complex administrative needs that accompany rapid growth. In short, institutions of higher education are being asked simultaneously to perform all the traditional functions they have ever performed, to perform these better than ever before, and to perform many new functions more effectively and quickly.

One of the consequences of the fact that society is demanding so much more of higher education is that those within the educational system are demanding correspondingly more of one another—faculty ask that students work harder and require higher standards than ever before; students ask that faculty devote a corresponding amount of commitment and labor to their teaching; faculty ask that administrators assume a much greater burden of administrative responsibility than was required in the days of smaller and simpler educational institutions; administrators ask faculty to involve themselves more and more in administration; and so on down the line. External stress thus becomes converted into internal stress, and the result is a heightened tension and ambivalence in the relations among constituent groups in institutions of higher education.

What are the organizational capacities of higher education to absorb these new and demanding stresses? In many respects it is miraculous that institutions of higher education have been able to continue to do their jobs as effectively as they have, given what has been asked of them. They have readily opened their doors to a flood of new students, expanded their facilities and organizational facilities, and contributed as best they could to the increasing demands emanating from business, government, and the professions. I do not want to minimize this accomplishment. Yet a number of sources of resistance and sluggishness in academic institutions operate to retard efforts to reform as rapidly as is necessary in times of chronic stress.

I must be very speculative about the first obstacle to change, because it is a kind of intangible frame of mind. I refer to a kind of mental set of academics, inherited from the ages, that defines an educational institution as a place that *ought not* be subjected to stress. I suppose that this is our legacy from the monastery and the ancient university, which were conceived—at least in principle —to be isolated and protected from the buffetings of the larger society. It is, I suppose, what we sometimes refer to, with mixed feelings, as the ivory tower complex. At any rate, this mental set, which is quite pervasive, leads many academics to react with denial or moral outrage when situations of stress arise. In many respects our capacity to respond creatively to stress is inhibited by this mental set, for if it leads mainly to reactions of denial, moral indignation, or feelings of being picked on, these reactions are likely to divert us from the proper task of forging new organizational forms to deal with new historical situations.

It is also important to note that a college or university is a kind of organization that does not lend itself readily to mobilization for change. In one respect, it is an organization devoted to nonorganization: to protect the individual faculty member and researcher from organizational involvements, so he can pursue his principal business of teaching and learning in the world of ideas. I need only to point out that the traditionally loose and unencumbered structure of the academic senate, the academic department, and the classroom has been very conducive to this kind of freedom. Though it may sound paradoxical, it seems to me that one of the main functions of academic administration is to protect the citizens of the academy from organizational involvement. (I realize that many readers must find this impossible to believe, but I assert it anyway.)

In addition, the involvement of the student in the academic organization has also been loose, probably for the same reasons— to augment his freedom and maneuverability. And since another purpose of the institution is periodically to graduate students— honorably and with proper training and credentials—they are institutionally defined as temporary citizens. What I want to emphasize is that the loose structure of the college and university, while essential to its central and vital educational functions, does not prove to be a valuable resource when crisis situations arise and the college or university community must be mobilized for collective planning and action. The organizational looseness of academic life inhibits its ability to respond to stress.

The same point may be made with respect to the distribution of power and authority in a college or university. Within the institution, the chief campus officer must work within a system that is characterized by a multiplicity of types of authority, some of them either very weak or greatly diffused by a long-standing delegation that is, for all intents and purposes, irrevocable. The chief campus officer's clearest type of authority is, through his service staff, over the service employees of the university—the clerical workers, the administrative staff, the buildings and grounds keepers, the mailing division, and so on. This is the kind of authority-relations one finds in any kind of organization, such as a business firm or a hospital. Yet with respect to the faculty and students, the chief campus officer's authority is more narrowly defined, and generally weaker. By long tradition, faculties have evolved various principles of academic freedom, of which the most central is the principle of tenure. While tenure has proved to be of tremendous value in securing the conditions necessary for the free pursuit of knowledge in the academy, one of its by-products is that it has taken from the administrative officer perhaps the most fundamental level of authority—direct control over the conditions of employment. In addition, most of the authority over academic matters has been delegated as a matter of course to faculty committees. Individual faculty members have considerable authority, especially with regard to curriculum and course design, and in the evaluation of students, but this authority is highly segmental.

The authority of the administration over the students is also constrained by various traditions, and in modern times has been further pared back. The picture I am trying to paint here is of the college or university as a system of multiple, crisscrossing authority-relations of differing types and strengths. It is enormously more complex than many other types of organization. Viewing it this way, moreover, leads me to a conclusion that I need not belabor: when decisive mobilization for collective action is required by the organization, its authority structure—so valuable for the pursuit of the central goals of the organization—constitutes a serious impediment to effective change.

The internal complexity of the power, authority, and influence structures is matched by an external complexity. In most cases, the chief campus officer and the administration in general receive their authority by delegation from a board of trustees or regents—authority that is revocable at any time. In public institutions, the trustees themselves have been delegated power by the state. In addition, most colleges and universities have an alumni association, the leaders of which often have many views as to what kind of place the alma mater should be and how it should operate. Furthermore, all institutions are located in some type of residential community, with which at least a minimum of tensions and abrasions is inevitable. And, finally, the college or university finds in its environment two especially volatile but nonetheless formidable forces—the mass media, which now look at educational institutions more closely than ever before; and public opinion (or rather, I suppose, what we imagine public opinion to be).

The academic administrator, caught in this web of internal and external complexity, too often finds himself able to respond to stress only by short-run adjustments, and mainly in response to the various pressures that converge on him from different directions. He has always had to be something of a politician. But in modern times, this aspect of his role has become more dominant. The delicate qualities of negotiating, compromising, mediating, pacifying, soothing, appear to have become, in the minds of some at least, the major desiderata of leadership. I do not mean to debase these political arts, but I do feel constrained to say that to give them the highest priority is not at all conducive to rational and long-term solutions to the grave institutional problems faced by higher education.

Let me now comment briefly on administrative leadership in academic life and its implications for the institutional response to stress. And here I do not want to comment specifically on the calibre of individual leaders. I would imagine that, man for man, leaders in academic organizations are as talented and resourceful as they are in any other kind of organization. Rather, I should like to address myself to the recruitment and continuity of leadership. The traditional assumption in the academic community has been—and still is in many quarters—that administration and policy making are activities that the citizens of the academic community could do in their spare time. Even today, many institutions consider administration something that faculty members will do, perhaps grudgingly, 'for a few years and then return to their regular duties. The result is that the motivation and recruitment of full-time, skilled administrators is difficult in higher education. True, there are full-time administrative careers at the top level, but tenure in these positions is notoriously precarious. Only in some particular areas—such as budgetary affairs, librarianship, and perhaps student affairs—is a definite career ladder observable. Many intermediate and high level deanships, vice-presidencies, and chairmanships are filled on a short-term basis by academics who see their commitment to the position as temporary. Two results follow from these practices: first, it is exceptionally difficult for an educational organization to accumulate an existing reservoir of administrative experience if many of its administrators are faculty members on leave from their academic duties for a short period; and second, recruitment into the lower administrative ranks is difficult, because the career ceiling is lowered by the fact that intermediate and high level positions are filled by rotating faculty members. I need not underscore how difficult it is to plan, initiate, and execute long-term changes under these arrangements.

How have governing boards and public officials responded to the contemporary crisis situation in higher education? In many instances boards of trustees and regents have displayed remarkable generosity and patience, and have given educational leaders that degree of maneuverability that is essential if they are to shoulder the terrific burdens of remolding their institutional structures. Yet too often this requisite of support has not been forthcoming. Many legislators, public officials, trustees, and representatives of the press have intervened directly into the internal, day-by-day affairs of institutions. They have pressed impatiently for short-term solutions that might stem the tide, but not get at the roots of the institutional stress. They often threatened to withhold existing resources as a kind of punishment for apparently ineffective crisis handling, rather than supply the additional resources that are required for innovation and reform. In a few cases, drastic outside intervention is no doubt justified by sheer administrative ineffectiveness—but in all too many cases such intervention serves mainly to make the lives of dedicated and laboring educator more difficult than it is under ordinary circumstances.

My statements may seem too pessimistic. I have intended to convey a realistic, but not a pessimistic, impression. I acknowledge that higher education in the mid-twentieth century is in a period of crisis in its own history. It is under enormous strain, and it is beset both by external harassment and internal dissension. The crisis is aggravated by the fact that, while the historical environment of the educational academy has changed, the academy itself has displayed a sluggishness in responding.

I should like now to suggest a line of educational change that will work toward providing a structural setting in which administrative leadership can operate effectively. To put the matter as bluntly as possible, I feel it is necessary to give more power and effective responsibility to college and university administrators at all levels. I emphasize *at all levels,* lest anyone think I mean centralization of power in a top executive. We must identify the major decision-making points and center responsibility and accountability and authority in specific persons. I see no other way to avoid the pattern of mindless and inefficient stumbling from crisis to crisis than to solidify our leadership base. Authority and responsibility are so diffusely spread that there is no way for those with problems to identify who it is that can help.

I am not suggesting that we should ignore all the data that indicate that organizational effectiveness goes up with broadening the base of leadership. But I think that there is an optimum balance in an organization between corporative and individual decisions and that in the university we are no longer as effective as we could be with a greater centralization of authority in persons. This balance probably changes from time to time, depending on the state of organizational health, and now is the time for a shift toward individual responsibilities.

But what about accountability? Here is where I think universities can and must invent something. I think that much pressure toward group decision, spread of participating, and reluctance to give authority to a person comes from a desire to monitor—a vigilance posture. This can be terribly time-consuming and wasteful. We could and should, on the other hand, develop more sensitive and more serious postaudit procedures. In other words, let's give more individuals a broader area of freedom, authority to move, and then spell out the kind of postaudit we want and what we want to audit. This will make administrative posts more attractive and will make the organization more responsible to internal and external requirements.

A posture of greater individual authority has additional consequences that are fruitful. For one thing, it will provide an impetus to the development of clear policy guidelines. Without such guidelines, the centralization I am writing about is too anxiety producing; but more importantly, without them there can be no real basis for the evaluation and postaudit. For the most part, in most academic situations, policy is made in connection with administrative decisions and often on a piecemeal and ad hoc basis. This is actually a deterrent to sound policy.

This posture also calls for streamlining and improving the devices for faculty consultation and advice. These must be more specifically representative, more committed to homework and preparation. Our town meetings are archaic, altogether too subject to the whims and tensions of the moment, and too subject to political manipulation.

Universities are essentially voluntary organizations; authority by and large is attributed by the members. What I am suggesting is that we voluntarily extend, by convention and understanding, the scope of administrative leadership. It is as if each part of the community were to say to a particular administration: "O.K., you run it for a while in these areas, discuss these things with us for advice, share decision making in this third domain, and we'll be back to see you in three years!"

I am keenly aware that this task of increasing administrative authority and responsibility will sound to some like a return to the days of the famous tyrants of academia. It is also being advanced at a time when there is a great deal of dissension about the purposes of the university. It runs against the grain, in the midst of such serious questioning with so much at stake, to make the suggestions I have made.

Obviously, I believe that even the debate about goals and purposes will be improved if leadership positions have power to go with responsibility. Educational leaders must be more than consensus seekers and mediators. Our problem about goals arises in part from the fact that our educational leaders have not had the authority to go with their ideas, and many of them stopped having any.

It must be obvious also that criteria for evaluation of the performance of this administrator newly endowed with authority would include evaluation of techniques for getting advice and spreading participation through the community when indicated. If anything, this posture of greater authority plus postaudit will improve the process of securing advice and counsel from faculty and students.

In my call for more powerful and authoritative leadership in higher education, I am not advising any inroads whatsoever on the faculty and student freedoms that have accumulated over the centuries; my suggestion is made simply in order to maximize the capacity for authoritative mobilization for change. These freedoms are absolutely essential for the existence of academic life. Rather, I am calling for the creation of a more effective organizational framework for change. We need such a framework to recruit and utilize the very highest quality of skilled administrators; to erect machinery that is specifically geared to introducing deliberate change into the academic apparatus; and to allocate the facilities that are essential to plan and evaluate changes. For many decades we have witnessed an enormous expansion of our educational apparatus. But much of this expansion has simply transpired within existing frameworks, frameworks that are now showing signs of weakening at the seams. It is time for the pendulum to swing, and for us to turn toward the creation of leaders—and a structure for leadership—that can introduce the qualitative changes in higher education that correspond in magnitude to the quantitative revolution we have witnessed in the past quarter of a century.

~ 14 ~

THE COLLEGE TEACHER AS PROFESSIONAL MAN PLUS

William L. Kolb

It is an interesting aspect of the current scene of higher education that at the level of the undergraduate student we are confronted with a variety of life styles, demands for relevance, confusions of educational purpose, and a consensus among psychologists that most of our students are still too conformist; while at the level of knowledge we are confronted with the continuing knowledge explosion, specialism and professionalism, and the dominance of the disciplines. If one compares the pictures of the needs of undergraduate education as portrayed in recent works such as

those of Mervin B. Freedman [1] and Nevitt Sanford [2] with the
realities of graduate school where undergraduate teachers are educated, the gulf seems so wide that there is apparently little hope
of bridging it.

The educational philosophy of authors like those named
above, and their concern for student development, seem to dominate the discussions of many administrators and experts in higher
education; while faculty members educated in the graduate
schools seem in their definitions of undergraduate education to
continue to define their tasks in relation to the responsibilities of
their disciplines. For this reason most meetings on higher education tend to have little impact on the mainstream of what actually
happens on campus and in the classroom. The issue is whether
or not there is some way of bridging this gulf in a manner that
respects both the concerns for persons, expressed by the critics of
higher education, and the devotion to the creation and dissemination of knowledge that characterizes the professors.

We must begin, I think, with the idea that knowledge is
going to continue to explode, professionalism and specialism to
develop, and the disciplines to dominate the undergraduate curriculum. This is not only true, but it is also right, given the
nature of Western society. Clyde Kluckhohn may be correct in
believing that there are certain fundamental shifts in Western
culture toward greater hedonism, and the diffusion of Eastern
forms of sensualism and mysticism is, I think, even more real than
apparent. Yet such cultural shifts cannot sustain an urban, industrial, technical society. It may also be true that leisure may
characterize the majority of people in our urban centers in the
years to come, but work is more likely to be the center of life of
those who occupy the central statuses of Western society.

All this is not to say that the trends of the graduate school
in educating undergraduate teachers are not to be challenged.
Concern for personal identity; the development of character, in
the sense of stressing the responsibility of moral choices made in
deepest connection with all the emotional strata of the person;
relevance of knowledge to the urgent problems of our times con-

---

[1] *The College Experience* (San Francisco: Jossey-Bass, 1967).
[2] *Where Colleges Fail* (San Francisco: Jossey-Bass, 1967).

ceived in the most humane manner possible—all these are still the central items of our agenda in higher education. But to conceive them in opposition to professionalism, specialism, and the centrality of the disciplines is naive and futile, both on the level of pragmatic educational politics and on the level of what is educationally correct.

There is little chance that graduate schools in their educating of undergraduate teachers are going to be much affected by strident cries that what they are doing is without relevance and human significance. Nor is the solution to the education of undergraduate teachers to be found in abandoning the quest for rationality or denying the primacy of the cognitive in its function of relating man to nature and to history. Rather the task is to convince those working in the disciplines—and this may not be impossible to do because, I believe, the motivation is there—that identity, moral responsibility, emotional growth, and relevance to the world are to be found in performance as professionals, working in an old discipline or developing a new one, provided the disciplines themselves are conceived as liberal arts.[3]

This means first of all that the cognitive function, the concern for knowledge, is still the prime function of higher education at both the graduate and undergraduate levels. But it means also that the emphasis on abstractness, empirical verifiability, objectivity, and precision must be held in a constant state of tension and positive relationship with the deepest humane values of the professional, with his deepest levels of feeling, and with his concern for the deepest needs of the contemporary world. It also means that concern for communication with the nonspecialist (popularization, if you will); the use of the discipline for purposes of social, aesthetic, and ethical criticism; the ability to respond to the ethical and aesthetic problems that arise within the disciplines themselves—all these must be considered part of the role of the professional performer.

Despite the emphasis on sheer expertise in the graduate school—and this remains a necessary dimension of professional performance—these other concerns have not died out. They have

---

[3] William L. Kolb, "The Disciplines in Liberal Arts Education," *Educational Record*, Spring, 1967.

been overlaid in the graduate school curriculum with the stress on sheer knowledge and research; and in the personality of the graduate and undergraduate school teacher by the institutional forms that shape the demands upon his time. But they are still present. If we are concerned with identity, moral responsibility, and with feeling, we can, I believe, get much farther if we recognize that they are still implicit in the idea of the professional man, and thus not attempt to place them in implacable opposition to professionalism and specialism. It may still be possible for educated man to become human and humane within the context of his work, and for undergraduate teachers still with the Ph.D. and educated in the graduate schools to themselves be human and contribute to this humaneness in their undergraduate students, if we stop separating feeling, criticism, and identity from the realm of work, and return once again to the concept of "vocation" in its fullest dimensions.

~⊰ 15 ⊱~

THE ADMINISTRATOR AS LEADER AND STATESMAN

Frederick deW. Bolman

In the last few years statewide committees, such as exist in New York, and regional groups, such as the Southern Regional Education Board, have expressed great concern over the proper background and preparation of college and university administrators. Large state systems—California is one—will probably often have two or more presidential vacancies in any one year, not to mention many deanships and other administrative officers. Obviously, spotting potential talent for these posts is the first and critical task. Regardless of the kinds of preparation we may seek or introduce for potential administrators, if the right kinds of persons are not tapped for the jobs, then those jobs will be poorly handled.

In fact, our greatest ignorance, it seems to me, is that we

have little knowledge of the kinds of persons we are seeking. In some areas selection appears more sophisticated than in others. For the offices of business manager, dean of students, public relations, and development, top institutional officers usually know what kinds of persons and what kinds of skills are wanted, possibly because the actual functions of these offices are clearly defined before anyone is selected. Also, those functions may vary somewhat less from institution to institution. The kinds of persons as well as their backgrounds are more clearly in mind in the selection process. Moreover—and here higher education differs somewhat sharply from other organized activities such as industry, government, or the armed services—there is limited upward mobility in these offices. Once you are head of such an office, your next step is usually open only through an offer from a larger institution.

But when it comes to selecting the various kinds of departmental chairmen, deans, provosts, academic vice-presidents, and presidents, we have thought too little about the characteristics of persons who can accomplish objectives not only in general but within a specific institutional framework. These positions are dominantly academic in orientation, but beyond academic qualifications, what do we seek? I suggest that the particular institution or unit within an institution must spell out individual and often unique requirements. Let me add that there appears to be considerably greater upward mobility in these areas than among the nonacademic group of college and university administrators. It is therefore all the more important to know the kinds of persons to be placed in these posts, for it is not totally unheard of for a mistake to be "corrected" simply by passing it up the line.

There is greater concern manifest today over these problems as there is more attention paid to actual preparation. Perhaps the area of greatest disagreement lies in that of formal academic degree programs purportedly for administration of various sorts. Graduate courses have sprung up at many if not most large universities, and these often are packaged into master's and doctoral degree programs. Again, for the nonacademic administrative posts, these are less challenged than the dominantly academic positions. Not many deans of students are hired without specific graduate work in guidance and personnel affairs, but who ever heard of a department chairman being selected for a mammoth and unwieldy department because he had special graduate training for the job?

Outside of graduate departments of higher education, there are some persons in graduate faculties of business and public administration who believe that their schools can and should prepare college and university administrators. Many years ago, it was debated whether the Harvard Graduate School of Business should be limited to business or encompass public and educational administration as well. At Cornell, some faculty in the School of Business and Public Administration have interests in preparation for academic administration. At the University of California at Irvine, the graduate work in administration covers business, government, and education—including higher education. Princeton hopes to enlarge the interests of its Woodrow Wilson School of Public and International Affairs to include educational administration, possibly including higher education. In other words, there is growing recognition that academic administration is not totally different from the management of other forms of complex organizations and that therefore the different kinds of preparation have something to teach one another and may be conducted partly in common.

Pre- and post-employment assistance in the form of internships, institutes, and workshops of many sorts for many different posts have continued. One great difficulty has become visible and that is the high cost of year-long internships. The programs of the Ellis L. Phillips Foundation and the Ford Foundation through the American Council on Education have come to an end, and institutions have been asked to carry their own financial costs for interns, a plan that may or may not work in the long run. In one specific area, the business management of our predominantly Negro colleges, it is worth pointing out that the Esso Education Foundation is currently providing consulting and intern assistance through the National Association of College and University Business Officers and the Woodrow Wilson National Fellowship Foundation to beef up the work of the financial management of these institutions.

So the debate continues whether there can be graduate preparation for administration, and if so, in what school of a university it should be conducted. And there is the perennial problem of what kinds of workshops, institutes, and internship programs are valuable and how to finance them.

Four critical problems face our campuses today for which many different officers should be prepared if they are to bring real leadership and statesmanship to their work.

The first is the emerging ethos of student involvement in the educational direction of our institutions. Precisely what this new ethos will be, we do not know as yet. But there are signs that may help. For example, there are the new campus-based experimental colleges organized and directed by students, such as those at San Francisco State College, Dartmouth, and elsewhere. In April 1968, a conference of student and faculty representatives of some twenty of these new colleges-within-colleges met at Hanover, New Hampshire, with the support of the Esso Education Foundation, and discussed experimental curricular and organizational matters. Or consider the joint faculty-student Study Commission on University Governance on the Berkeley campus of the University of California, in which the authors seek "educational regeneration" in part based on giving students greater voice in running the institution, which they want to have broken down into many smaller, more personal units.[1]

But what about drugs and protest on campus? Administrators have a hard time today with the old *in loco parentis* problem and the new problem of student demand for a dominant voice in the direction of their lives. Few administrators have been able to stabilize their own emotions for the guidance of students. Administrators today suffer from the confusion of parents: the desire for permissiveness for creative reasons, and the bent to help adolescents develop autonomous order for their own lives. I think college and university administrators must understand themselves, their culture, their society, and the realities of ongoing life far better than they have. Law and order must be maintained, the campus is no longer an island, and deficiencies of home life must be taken into account. But the problem of administrators today is to be ahead of what is happening, to help guide parents and other adults

---

[1] Caleb Foote, Henry Mayer, and Associates, *The Culture of the University: Governance and Education* (San Francisco: Jossey-Bass, 1968).

as well as students, and to make competent and firm decisions leading to action. This is not an easy task to accomplish. One gifted administrator in working on the curriculum and other aspects of a brand new college used students from other institutions to help him—only to have his thinking classed as antediluvian by those students. But I do see that greater knowledge of and preparation for working with students must be a part of creative administration today. At all levels of education, the generation gap must be closed.

Second, the administrator today faces some new relationships to the faculty for which he must be more adequately prepared. Faculty seek a greater voice in the governance of our institutions, as witness the Statement on Government of Colleges and Universities first developed by the American Association of University Professors and subsequently reformulated with the American Council on Education and the Association of Governing Boards of Universities and Colleges. It is not unheard of for a faculty to vote no confidence in a dean or president, and that is the sorry end-state of an administrator's lack of preparation to work on equitable terms with the faculty rather than attempting to be the sole decision maker.

Another aspect of this same point is emerging in the growing unionization of faculty visible in New York, Michigan, California, and elsewhere. The junior colleges are already affected, and it may not be long before state colleges and universities, and eventually private institutions, will fall heir to collective bargaining not only over wages but many conditions of work. There is a lively debate under way whether collective bargaining will make or break our campuses. What is doubtless, however, is that today's administrators must know what such bargaining really is and how to handle themselves and their institutions productively. Ignorance and unpreparedness here can lead to disaster in short order.

A third area for which today's administrator needs preparation concerns the matter of state, regional, and national planning. At the annual meeting of the Association of American Colleges, Alan Pifer charged that nationally we have not really exerted ourselves for planning our higher educational affairs, and I agree with him. The same may be said of regional and statewide planning, although we have developed three regional groups and many state boards that are forging ahead in a host of ways.

The great debate in this area of planning has to do with public versus private control and finance. In reality, this means that right-minded administrators must devote themselves to the careful integration of efforts on the part of so-called private and public institutions within states, regions, and the nation. This is a new dimension of our administrative task. We have grown up with all the motives of individual institutional pride, competitiveness, and inherent provincialism. Those older motives must not only be eroded away, but insight and skills for coordination of effort among a wide variety of institutions must be within reach of college and university administrators. All strategically located personnel and facilities—liberal arts and other single-purpose units, community colleges, universities, research centers—must be coordinated to meet society's real needs. Indeed we require a national coordinating group outside of government to plan and stimulate toward solution of this problem.

Fourth and finally, accountability in financial matters now has become more critical than heretofore and yet another set of insights and abilities must be possessed by administrators. These are the days when funds are needed for redevelopment of our inner cities, job training for the hard-core unemployed, health, welfare, and a host of cultural developments as well as higher education. Currently about 2.1 per cent of our gross national product is spent on higher education. In relation to other needs of our society we do not know whether that is enough, just right, or too much. We have a national problem of balancing the proportion of our investments in our various benefits to make the mix produce the kind of life and society we really want.

The college and university administrator must know not only how to assess his institution in financial terms with unit cost and program budget analyses. He must now learn something that has grown up in industry and government called *cost-benefit accounting and analysis*. This is an educator's task, not just a bookkeeper's. In Pentagon language, how are we to get the biggest bang for our buck, and therefore what hard evidences have we to present to the federal government, state legislatures, corporations, foundations, and individuals that we are really effective and efficient? Such cost-effectiveness analyses are indispensable for the systems analysis of decision making, which is just beginning at some institutions.

Today's problems facing administrators are many, but I have singled out the new student ethos, the new demands of faculty, the requirements of interinstitutional planning, and cost-benefit controls as precondition for systems analyses of management. However we prepare or assist administrators on the job, they must be able to work effectively and creatively in these areas.

I now turn to what may be happening in the year 2000. Those who think ahead should base their predictions on what is incipient today and appears decisive for tomorrow.

The pressing issue being discussed concerning the future is where the money will come from to pay for higher education and how it will be spent. This I feel is only one issue out of several, but let us divine if we can what administrators may then face. Some believe that virtually all funds must come from the federal government and, if this is so, then federal investment must be directed so as not just to underwrite the way we "do" education today but to finance with great discrimination so that we accomplish nationally our optimum. Others suggest that federal funds will increase from the current 23 to 50 per cent of total costs of higher education, assuming states will continue at present or somewhat higher percentage of costs, and that the way we now operate our institutions is the way we should operate them in the year 2000. This difference of approach will continue, and either one of these or yet a third position may be approved in Washington and in the states.

In any event, the future administrator must be able to cope with national financing, the practical obliteration of the current distinction of private and public finance, and degrees of interinstitutional cooperation and cost-benefit accounting not presently on the scene.

I would suggest that secondly the administrator of the future must approach the whole learning function far more flexibly than in the past in part to make financing possible. Theoretical and applied learning about learning is in its infancy in higher education. We have a few—but very few—research and development centers, and faculty are slow to alter ancient ways for more effective and efficient paths to help young minds develop creatively. Lectures, seminars, tutorials, laboratories, libraries, classrooms—one or all may give way to entirely new modes of learning. Faculty may in the future devote little time to teaching, much to being the architects of learning as well as to research. The many different administrative posts may change radically, and administrators must be prepared for large doses of change.

Finally, I suggest that the locus of learning may be somewhat different in the future and this will alter the very nature of educational administration. Harold Orlans of the Brookings Institution foresees what almost looks like an amalgam of industry, government, and universities. The blending of knowledge and action, and of personnel, may make it hard to know where one begins and the other ends. Stephen Graubard of the Academy of Arts and Sciences looks forward to university cities—a parallel to cathedral and company towns of yesteryear—in which the knowledge industry finally comes to serve mankind in a new and more effective way and with an obliteration of distinctions which now separate educational and other activities. Herman Kahn and Anthony Wiener describe the postindustrial era as that of a learning society primarily because of the rapidity of change. John Kenneth Galbraith has suggested that industry and state and education are steadily being woven into something like a seamless garment.

Perhaps the administrator of the future must be as much at home in industry and government as in education. But how do we prepare future administrators for that diversified life unless, as some suggest, life is really far more coherent in that year 2000 than anything we know today?

Section VII

The Faculty Role in Governance

16

FACULTY AND ADMINISTRATIVE ROLES IN DECISION MAKING

John C. Livingston

Shortly before Thorstein Veblen discovered that higher learning in America was managed by the "captains of erudition," Lord Bryce gave us an account of one institution in which shared authority appears to have been fully developed and working effectively. It was, he tells us, a smaller public institution in one of the "ruder western states":

> I remember to have met in the Far West a college president—I will call him Mr. Johnson—who gave me a long account of his young university, established by

187

public authority, and receiving some small grant from the legislature. He was an active sanguine man, and on dilating on his plans frequently referred to "the faculty" as doing this or contemplating that. At last I asked of how many professors the faculty at present consisted. "Well," he answered, "just at present the faculty is below its full strength, but it will soon be more numerous." "And at present?" I inquired. "At present it consists of Mrs. Johnson and myself."

Unless Mrs. Johnson had not yet acquired tenure, we are entitled to wonder whether even this is an example of completely harmonious faculty-administration relationships; and it would be interesting to know whether President Johnson was setting policy for Professor Johnson or vice-versa. Still, it may be useful to examine some possible roles of the participants as ideal types. I propose to examine these roles by considering them in the context of three alternative patterns of decision making in academic institutions, which may be described as monarchical, democratic, or market oriented. The distinction I mean to emphasize among these three models is briefly suggested by the difference it makes whether an administrative position is regarded as a throne, a platform (or pulpit), or a mediation office.

Academic monarchy need not detain us long. There are still some pretenders to academic thrones and indeed some reigning monarchs. But most of them have made their concessions to the faculty nobility, if they have not agreed to reign without ruling. However much their faculties and their institutions may suffer, they are hopelessly outmoded, even as enlightened despots, and their days are numbered. If they will not share their power willingly, they are likely to share it unwillingly—across a bargaining table, and with a professorial union.

But if an administrative position no longer makes a comfortable throne, even Teddy Roosevelt could not have asked for a bullier pulpit. The traditional professorial view of academic democracy, where the faculty decides policy in town-meeting style and administrators are their emasculated servants, left no room for administrative leadership. But, whatever its validity in an earlier age, this view grossly underestimates the extent to which faculties, lured by the siren song of prominence in their disciplines and

affluence in their consultancies, are no longer moved to imagine
the opportunities and to respond to the challenges of campus
government. The idea of democracy has always been claimed to be
not only a device for giving men equal access to decision making,
but also an arrangement for bringing men's rational and moral
faculties to bear on the identification and solution of problems.
For reasons I hope to develop subsequently, faculty government,
left to its own devices, is now often incapable of fulfilling these
promises. In the circumstances it may properly fall to administrators to provide the leadership that develops analyses of common
problems and proposes solutions involving radical alterations of
habitual ways of doing things. But leadership that is entitled to be
called democratic will regard an administrative position as a platform from which to reason, to argue, to persuade; it will seek only
the influence its creative and persuasive power can bring; it will
be contemptuous of the lure of power and resistant to the temptation to manipulate.

    If academic monarchy is an anachronism, academic de-
mocracy is likely to be nearly as unattainable as it is desirable. It
is a striking and sobering fact that among faculties there are few
who combine a readiness to assume administrative position with
a willingness to rely on the persuasive power of their ideas rather
than the coercive or manipulative power of their positions. Nor
do administrative positions always seek these out. Moreover, administrative leadership of the type described runs counter to some
of the basic tendencies that have been changing the character of
American higher education in recent years. For example, colleges
and universities have become instruments of the existing structure
of society in a way that is radically different in degree if not in
kind from earlier relationships. The university and its members
have become part of the nation's human and intellectual resources, justified as instruments of economic affluence and of a
national purpose shaped elsewhere. Higher education, moreover,
operates in the social climate of fear and mistrust created by the
Vietnam War, poverty, and the civil rights struggle. In this context, the general breakdown of public authority, and public
responses to it, tend to focus on the campuses. Public colleges and
universities especially have become major concerns of partisan
politics, and the public images of private institutions are increas-

ingly difficult to protect and cultivate. The result is that the administrator's other constituencies—students, trustees, legislators, local elites, alumni, donors, and others—make increasingly sharp and insistent demands on his attention and his favor. Insofar as these pressures enter into his view of the institution's welfare, he will play the role of mediator or broker in what I describe as the market-oriented model.

The administrator in this situation is not completely without power. But the power he wields is subtle and hidden from view. He decides which demands are legitimate and he assigns weights to those admitted to the game. He may weigh the balance, within fairly narrow limits, in the direction that corresponds to his own ideas for the institution. But the success of his consensus will depend on how accurately the distribution of benefits reflects the actual and potential power of the various pressures, and not at all upon conscious goals or purposes, his own or anyone else's.

Traditional forms of faculty representation are often themselves absorbed into these institutional arrangements for bargaining and negotiation and for the development of an engineered and watered-down consensus. It is not unusual for faculty members who have thought they were fighting for faculty participation in the definition, deliberation, and resolution of institutional problems to see their victories turn to ashes; their colleagues with whom they have shared the battles were fighting a different war, a war for departmental autonomy and stronger bases of power for departmental bargaining. The result is often a structure of faculty government that insures the representation of vested faculty interests and forces on administrators the role of brokers among these interests, whatever their preferences for a different role might be.

The results are not likely to be happy ones. A large portion of the faculty will be only too willing to play George Meany to the administrator's Lyndon Johnson. The processes of government in the institution will provide no way of responding adequately or even of recognizing clearly the new range of challenges and problems in higher education; as a result, the initiative will be assumed by pressures from outside the establishment (by students or politicians, for example). Able faculty will "vote with their feet" if they find the resulting deals intolerable. Those who decline to take this escape and who cling tenaciously to the vision of an intellectual community whose members share in a rational and moral enterprise will become increasingly frustrated and alienated. They will be driven to greater and greater intransigence, seeming in the eyes of most administrators and many of their colleagues to be irresponsible anarchists and enemies of moderation and reasonableness. But, in truth, their revolt is not against reason; it is, in Ortega's phrase, "reason exasperated"— exasperated in this case by those processes that swallow up arguments in the treacle of negotiated consensus and which substitute bargaining for critical analysis of problems and purpose. These faculty dissidents will be tolerated, with a vengeance; they will be subjected to what Herbert Marcuse has called "repressive tolerance," a toleration that "serves to strengthen the administration by testifying to the existence of democratic liberties, which, in reality, have changed their content and lost their effectiveness. In such a case, freedom becomes an instrument for absolving servitude."

For those who still believe it is the legitimate province of talk to rule the world, the right to speak without the right to be listened to and replied to is futility compounded by fraud. Where the purpose and the outcome of the right to speak is simply the validation of tolerance, where arguments go unanswered and proposals are treated as pressures, speech has lost its meaning. The channels of communication are still intact; they have ceased, however, to serve as means to the rational analysis of common problems and the creative exploration of new possibilities. The college community has been replaced by a pluralism of interests, which, in the final analysis, serves—to use R. M. McIver's phrase—as a "mere bracket to enclose diversity." In these circumstances speech ceases to be communication in any rational or moral sense.

The administrator who is conscientiously convinced that, given existing pressures, he has gone as far as possible to maintain faculty harmony and to meet faculty demands is likely to feel hurt and misunderstood and perhaps even betrayed when the faculty are unhappy with the accommodation he has worked out. He is likely to be driven to the view that faculty are inherently irresponsible, and to fall back on those vicious half-truths of American political folklore: half a loaf is better than none and politics is the art of the possible.

Administrators often live in fear of faculty usurpation of the authority of their positions, without recognizing that their power is already effectively dissipated by the necessity of pleasing their many constituencies. They invoke the politics of the possible in apparent neglect of the fact that the art of the possible in modern organizational politics is the art of manipulation, and the price of successful manipulation is a readiness to be manipulated. Faculty also tend to accept the myth of administrative power, blaming their own powerlessness on the malfeasance of administrators when the real problem is that there has been no feasance at all.

We are forced to conclude, I believe, that the situation in which we are likely to live will inevitably create role conflicts of serious proportion. Why serious? Only a minority of the faculty are likely to be seriously disturbed by the situation and, through the technique of repressive toleration, they can be turned into a somewhat bothersome asset to the system—like the debts one must accumulate to establish his credit rating. The role conflict is serious not because there is conflict but because the conflict is unproductive, because the roles thus played are incapable of shedding light on the nature of our real predicaments, of developing and trying solutions to our common problems, of bringing reason and imagination to bear on the effort consciously to control our destinies. The situation is serious because the alienated minority is the saving remnant whose alienation we cannot afford to manipulate through toleration.

What, then, is to be done? Perhaps, first of all, the roles described above are not mutually exclusive. In some areas faculty and administrators may play mutually reinforcing roles in protecting the fundamental principles on which the academic enterprise depends—such matters as academic freedom and faculty responsibility for the conduct of courses are obvious examples. But, important as these matters are, they do not touch our basic problems. In other areas—the development of new programs and curriculums might be an example—administrators might act as leaders of faculty government. The range of these relationships needs to be extended as far as possible. Administrative leadership holds the greatest promise for encouraging and keeping alive within the institution the flow and encounter of critical and creative ideas addressed to the institution's purposes and its relation to the larger social crisis. Here we can learn something from American politics: Insofar as politicians pay greater attention to interest groups than to conscience or party principles, it is at least partly because interest groups exert so much greater control over their political futures. Administrators need, therefore, to be protected against the reprisals of disappointed or disaffected interests. This might be accomplished by providing that every administrator is to have tenure in some capacity in the institution, and by making him responsible in his administrative role to the faculty. I mean by responsible here not only the existence of procedures to insure that his appointment has the confidence of the faculty but also procedures that require faculty consent to his dismissal from his position.

Still, there are likely some areas in which the judgment of the faculty will be balanced by administrators against other pressures. Here salvation (if it can be called that) lies in the tension between divergent and conflicting roles. The first need is for faculty to be organized to develop, clearly and forcefully, a faculty view of the institution's problems and needs. There is no place in the faculty's deliberations for counsels of moderation, or for conciliatory gestures toward opposing groups. For the faculty, potentially at least, speaks for a perspective that is not likely to be advanced by any other group—the claims of teaching and learning, of what the late Robert Redfield described as "the dangerous duty of the university" to transmit the cultural heritage together with the skills for criticizing and modifying it, the claim of institutional independence from those forces in society which would use the campus as a mere instrument for other purposes. Where administrators, however much they may personally share this perspective, are required to mediate between it and the conflicting demands of other forces, they should nonetheless seek to encourage its organization and its freest and fullest expression. They should, moreover, seek to insure the widest possible audience among trustees, politicians, local elites, the public generally, for the faculty's judgments and arguments. They should actively seek to

create situations in which faculty opinion is heard and considered. This is no small expectation. It asks the administrator to
reveal publicly the discrepancies between the faculty position and
the ground on which he has decided to strike his own compromise.
It exposes him to the ridicule or contempt of the bureaucratic
minds of the elites whose confidence he seeks and who are likely
to see in this conflict of roles only evidence that the chief administrator countenances insubordination among his underlings and
evidence of administrative failure to create a harmonious smoothly
functioning team. Any faculty member who has tried to explain
to friends who work in other bureaucracies why he does not regard
the dean or the president as his boss will understand the difficulty;
a little sympathetic imagination should reveal to him the increased
problems encountered by the dean and the president, who are
called on to confess that their titles and salaries are not indices of
their domination. This difference between academic institutions
and others, however, needs desperately to be understood in the
outside world.

A more immediate reason why the administrator as broker
should encourage the organization of a coherent and forceful
faculty view of the institution's mission and its relation to the
larger society is inherent in the process of compromise. If the administrator is to balance rival claims it is important that the
faculty have some weight to throw on the scales. The institution
and its president himself are seriously handicapped if the president as mediator seeks also to represent the claims of the institution and its faculty, for in that event the faculty's position and its
reasons are obscured and deprived of the weight they might
otherwise have in the resulting accommodation. The lot of the
mediator may be made more difficult but the game will be fairer
and in the long run more productive if there is something from
the academic side to be mediated. One thing seems to me certain:
to expect the faculty to identify themselves with administrators in
their role as brokers, in a vain effort to promote harmony or to
maintain the fiction that the structure of a college is a bureaucratic hierarchy like a corporation or a government agency, can
lead only to disaster. It will disarm the institution in its continuing struggle with outside forces, and it will increase the sense and

the reality of powerlessness felt by faculty and administrators alike.

A. Whitney Griswold has observed that the problem is essentially how we can "make all this organization serve us instead of our serving it." This appears to me the only fruitful point of departure. It directs our attention where it needs to be directed— to those forces and attitudes that have generated the frustration and the futility that underlie the increasing sense of faculty, administrative, and student malaise as well as the increasingly common outbreaks of violence on the campus. More than that, it gets us around an essentially outmoded and irrelevant but persistent way of looking at the world in the traditional terms of power. The fact is that both administrators and faculty tend still to feel that the problem is that the other is in the saddle and exercising arbitrary and unlimited power, when the real problem is that no one is in the saddle; "things" seem to take their own course.

17

THE ALTERNATIVES: PARANOIA OR DECENTRALIZATION

Burton R. Clark

We are not in a time of happiness in the marshaling of campus affairs. Campus government is problematic; faculty unease is part of a general confusion over the proper organization and control of academic work. In one place after another, governance is up in the air and that condition causes many to think it is up for grabs. Eager hands press forward toward the levers of influence and control, to make sure that particular visions are served and particular rewards obtained. The result is often formal educational combat that shocks the sensibilities of scholars, as it takes a regular place in the nightly television review of sensational news. Academic governance has become a new form of popular drama and entertainment.

If we look for the general causes of the current problems of campus governance, with special regard to faculty involvement, we must first turn to the rapid rate at which campuses have been growing in size and increasing in complexity. The rapidity of the change greatly increases the strain. Faculty members who have long had a town hall sense of participation in policy formation, on an old campus now undergoing modernization, feel that the very moorings of faculty government are being swept away. There is so little time on one campus after another to get things under control, to catch up with the problems, to let informal intercourse ease compromise and integration. Governance is problematic, at the present time, first of all because the rapidity of growth keeps problems ahead of the coping mechanisms, formal and informal, that a campus traditionally possesses or can create and make effective in a few months or years.

As cause of the trouble in governance, we must secondly turn to the limitations on individual involvement in policy formation that obtain in large society systems. We have long understood that we cannot run cities and nations by town hall assembly but must engage in representative government. In a representative system, most are slightly involved. The many send one to be active; some among the many then pay attention, but large numbers ignore the whole business. We get a definite stratification of influence. And so it is on the large campus. Within the faculty, there is a small group of oligarchs and activists, maybe 5 per cent of the staff, who are much more equal than others. There is an attentive public, men sufficiently committed or interested to turn out for the dull meetings, perhaps numbering another 10–20 per cent of the faculty. Then there is the inattentive mass, the average citizen in the faculty politic who pays attention to his research and his teaching, his department colleagues and his students, and leaves government to others. The inattentive ones may join the political arena once a year, as spectator citizens, when a hot issue promises some bloodletting on the floor of the academic coliseum.

Many in the faculty, particularly the younger men, will feel they are a long way from central power and policy formation. When issues come along that excite them, the campus then rings with charges of oligarchy, hidden deals, machinations of vice-chancellors and deans. The setting is almost perfect for political

paranoia. Behind the normal passivity of those minimally involved, and their occasional eruptions into action, resides an
age-old doctrine that whispers all are equal and all should participate equally since this is a community of scholars. The wide gap
between this ideal and reality disappoints and frustrates. As involvement in policy becomes thinly sliced for the majority of
faculty on a large campus, major camps of "we" and "they" will
form, leading toward bargaining among major blocs that are
organized or semiorganized as associations, unions, councils, alli-
ances, committees, and cabinets.

The third cause of current troubles in governance lies in
the part-whole relationships among campus organizational structures. The bread-and-butter interests primarily reside in the part
rather than in the whole, strengthening the parts of the faculty
but weakening its central bodies. The department and the professional school are the basic operating units of the campus. They
are also the natural points of identification for faculty members.
Faculty interests in the running of campus affairs are expressed
primarily in these units. Will new positions be added, in my field?
Who is to be hired, fired, and promoted, in my field? What about
salary, office space, secretarial help, a leave of absence? One influences such decisions, and other wider issues, primarily through
the department. At the same time, the fragmentation of faculty
interests in departmental organization causes central faculty bodies, such as the academic senate, to become ever more sterile. The
senate with a membership of 1,500 faculty, whose basic commitments reside in seventy-five departments and fifteen professional
schools, tends to become tangled in its own formalisms, with its
own clerks, its own complicated rule books, its own slow committees. We are all familiar with feelings of helplessness engendered within a large faculty directly by the committee system of
the faculty itself, causing further withdrawal of participation and
loss of interest.

The modern, large campus, then, is not a promising setting
for meaningful and effective faculty involvement in issues pertain-
ing to the character of the whole. If we think about reform that
assists faculty involvement, it is clear that we shall not get very
far if we take the general setting as given and then attempt simply
to improve the old faculty bodies or create new formal ones. In

the short run, of course, it is always helpful to make better use of what we are stuck with. For example, faculties need not be devoted to inefficiency and ineffectiveness in their senates. It is not absolutely necessary for the integrity of the faculty that the executive secretary of the senate be a retired professor of English who answers mail in exquisite longhand. An archaic set of committees can be disbanded and a new set tried. But such reforms by and large mean much hard work simply to hold even or to slow the slide in faculty involvement.

To change faculty involvement fundamentally, we must change the basic organizational structure of the campus, designing changes with an eye for greater involvement of the average faculty member and for the expression of different educational interests, especially those that have been attenuated or overlooked in the massive structural changes of the last twenty years. Greater involvement is possible only if we bring governance down to where the faculty and students are, that is, if we decentralize governance to small units of the campus. A college of letters and science (within a university) that has 16,000 students and 1,000 faculty is not likely to have meaningful involvement; subunits of that college of 500 students and fifty faculty members can. If the subunits have some autonomy, free to develop certain features of their character, then the involvement of the average faculty member, and student, is likely to be much higher. Government is where he is.

The subunits around which authority is devolved in such general reform will include the departments and professional schools. But the substructure need not be limited to these traditional units, and should not be so limited, since the departments and schools serve certain educational interests very poorly. We certainly know well by now that if we wish to serve undergraduate liberal education, we had better get ourselves some units devoted wholeheartedly to its cause. The residential college has been the best unit for this purpose, as a separate college or as part of a university. But in many of the public and private institutions faced with the most severe problems of governance, students do not reside on campus, and subunits set up to support their undergraduate education cannot possess them night and day. Lower-division colleges of about 500 students, for example, with their own names, and with their own staffs and physical locations at least in part, can be organized on a nonresidential basis. It is also becoming apparent that if we wish to connect the full-time researchers of the research centers, and such other important permanent personnel as the librarians, to the government of the campus, we again ought not to rely on departments and professional schools. We need to give much thought about how to cluster the personnel in these fields in structures that have some authority, some self-government.

Finally, then, I do not think it is basically useful to worry about whether faculty involvement in policy formation is advisory, adversary, or legislative. On campuses where the faculty is involved at all in campus government, it is either, in the large places, some confusing mixture of the three, or, on small campuses, essentially a matter of close informal relations with the administration that are not well described by any of the three terms. The crucial phenomenon is that in the rapidly growing places the whole campus is changing as a system of governance. Within the organizational structures to which modern campuses naturally tend, authority flows into bureaucratic molds on the one hand and into a fragmented professionalism on the other. The involvement of the faculty in campus policy will remain inherently unsatisfying to a good share of the faculty if it is contained within these channels.

If we still mean by faculty involvement something that reasonably approaches a full, equitable, and rich involvement in the processes of campus government, then we mean collegial authority; and if we want collegial authority then we must establish the structural conditions that promote it. Collegial authority is finally based on quasi-autonomous, relatively small units of administrators, faculty, and students. Within the massive complexes that we have lately assembled for carrying out the work of higher education in America, the key to meaningful faculty involvement is decentralization.

PART FOUR

Curricular Relevance

The essays of Part Four explore the ways in which the college curriculum can reflect student concerns with large moral issues, with community problems, and with intercultural understandings. The authors of Section Eight—which deals with the first two of these subjects—are Andrew M. Greeley, senior study director of the National Opinion Research Center at the University of Chicago; Donald L. Garrity, academic vice-president at San Francisco State College; William E. Engbretson, professor of higher education at the University of Denver; and William Moore, Jr., associate dean of instruction at Forest Park Community College in St. Louis. Section Nine consists of two essays on the place of intercultural studies in a modern college curriculum. The authors are Joseph Axelrod, project director at the Center for

Research and Development in Higher Education at the University of California in Berkeley (on leave from the Department of World Literature at San Francisco State College), and Glenn A. Olds, university dean for international studies and world affairs at the State University of New York at Oyster Bay.

Part Four opens with the Reverend Andrew M. Greeley's essay, "The Teaching of Moral Wisdom." Greeley's first theme is stated immediately: The moral values of the younger generation are not declining; rather, they are improving. The problem, Greeley asserts, is not that young people are immoral but that "they are almost too moral for the ethical systems that are available to them." The systems available to them are all inadequate, he claims, and he is speaking here of both the traditional Christian morality (whose language, Greeley says, makes no sense to a young person today) and the simplistic "love" philosophies that are so current among youth. This is where the college/university has a role and a responsibility, Greeley tells us. We must teach moral wisdom. But he does not believe that the job can be done by the typical philosophers, theologians, and other academicians on our campuses. His essay reaches a high point of irony as it explains why each one of these campus figures does not have "time" for this sort of problem.

The essays that follow tell of experiences on a number of campuses where the concerns expressed by Greeley are taken seriously—so seriously, in fact, as to affect the curriculum. In the first of these essays, entitled "Response to Student Demands for Relevance," Donald L. Garrity describes three programs that came into being as a response to student demands for relevance. The first of these was the Community Involvement Program, under which fifteen projects were initiated by students, including tenant unions, job cooperatives, and youth counseling services. The second program was the Experimental College, organized and conducted by students, which currently enrolls over two thousand students in more than seventy courses. The third program has just developed in the past year, a program in Black Studies.

Garrity concludes his essay with some comments about the trying year of 1967–1968 at San Francisco State College, the year when there were severe disturbances on that campus in December and again in May. What is needed, Garrity points out, is the sharing of responsibility among all the elements of the college community rather than "the mere application of administrative fiat, the clamp-down that is so often asked for these days." Garrity's essay illustrates how some basic changes in the curriculum at San Francisco State College were achieved by following the principle he recommends.

William E. Engbretson traces the new trends in teacher education programs in his "Curricular Relevance in Teacher Education." One of the important new trends in the preparation of teachers, Engbretson tells us, is the inclusion of work relating to disadvantaged children. He describes four programs that exemplify this trend; they are located in San Francisco, New York, Kalamazoo, and Kansas City. A second trend is the inclusion of direct laboratory experience of a clinical nature, and three programs (at the universities of Georgia, Maryland, and New Mexico) that exemplify that emphasis are outlined. Engbretson then goes on to discuss other attempts to bring the preparation of teachers into a closer relationship with the real world, and he tells of new programs evolving out of the United States Office of Education during this past year.

When William Moore, Jr., author of "Opportunity for the Disadvantaged," spoke on that subject at the Twenty-Third National Conference on Higher Education, he began his talk by presenting his "credentials": he is black; he was reared in a ghetto; he came from a broken home; he dropped out of high school twice; and he ranked in the lowest tenth when he entered college. And he is now a college dean. Moore declares that the American college/university has refused to share in a major educational responsibility—the formal education of the academically disadvantaged student beyond high school. More than six hundred institutions of higher learning, Moore points out, offer "remedial" courses in various fields, but very few have designed a coherent educational program to meet the needs of such students. Forest Park Community College in St. Louis does have such a program, supported by the Danforth Foundation, called The General Curriculum. Moore describes this program in some detail.

Section Nine, dealing with intercultural studies in the modern college curriculum, opens with Joseph Axelrod's essay, the title of which is self-explanatory: "Intercultural Study Versus the Foreign Language Requirement." Axelrod recommends the abolition of the blanket degree requirement in foreign language and the substitution of a degree requirement in intercultural studies. He outlines what an excellent student should know and what attitudes he might hold upon completion of such a course. The essay is a first-person narrative, consisting in large part of an explanation the author makes to a college dean who seems interested in instituting intercultural studies courses on his campus. In the end, however, the dean rejects the idea—in spite of the fact that he agrees such courses are crucially needed if students are to break out of their ethnocentrism. The dean explains the rejection: The faculty on his campus, he says, do not possess the empathy, tolerance, and breadth of perspective that students would be expected to acquire through their experiences in the course. Hence, his faculty would, in fact, not be able to teach such a course. "Not in a million years," he insists. The first-person narrator remonstrates with the dean, assuring him he is mistaken—and suggesting ways of using his rich faculty resources for intercultural goals—but to no avail.

"Foreign Study as Crosscultural Learning," by Glenn A. Olds, is, as the title implies, an attempt to define the purpose of overseas undergraduate programs in such a way as to direct them toward intercultural study. In the first part of the essay, Olds shows why foreign study, as conventionally conceived, often fails. The second section presents a series of basic assumptions that, in the author's view, must underlie programs in foreign study if they are to be successful. The center of the author's thought is reached in the middle section of the essay, which outlines what foreign study can provide to the undergraduate when it is conceived as crosscultural learning. The author hopes that the undergraduate student "will discover that foreign study is as close as the penetration of any difference that stands outside his real understanding, that it can deepen the opportunity and the will to humanize all learning, and that it can provide the ability to scale all walls—linguistic, ethnic, economic, and religious—that shut us out seriously from one another." The last two sections of the essay list emerging patterns in overseas studies for American students and outline some of the persistent problems attending such programs.

The subjects treated in the six essays of Part Four are all intimately related to the curriculum—that element in a college/university "system" that yields the degree. Of all elements in the system, it is the one most jealously guarded by faculty and administration. As a result, basic curricular changes have been all but impossible to effect. Yet the curriculum, like all elements in the system, has been subjected to stress and pressures. In some ways, it has been undergoing slow change. In particular, the walls between the curriculum and the outside world are slowly being broken down. The essays of Part Four give examples of this phenomenon—and analyze some of the problems surrounding it that make curricular change such a painful process.

Joseph Axelrod

Section VIII

Relevance or Revolution

⤳ 18 ⤵

THE TEACHING OF MORAL WISDOM

Andrew M. Greeley

A common theme in current discussions about contemporary youth is the decline of moral values among them. My own belief is that just the opposite is the truth. The moral values of the younger generation are not declining; they are, rather, improving. And the major cause of stress among youth is the inability of systems of morality to keep pace with the increase in man's ethical consciousness.

It is fashionable for journalistic, educational, and ecclesiastical viewers-with-alarm to decry the decline in morality or to assert that we have now entered into a permissive society, complete with pictures of a near-nude Jane Fonda on the cover of the news weeklies. Such affirmations about moral decline usually find their source in the American puritan inclination to equate morality with sex and to argue that sexual behavior is much more immoral now than it was at this or that period in the past. Such heraldings of a new sexual permissiveness are generally unencumbered by any sort of empirical data. But I refuse to take seriously the contention that our society is somehow or other a permissive society. Chastity has never been a terribly popular virtue and if greater lip service was paid to it by college students in years gone by than it is by the college population today—for the evidence shows that student sexual behavior is not so very different now than it was a generation ago[1]—the reason very likely is that the student body is not as middle class now as it was then.

But the question of sexual morality aside, I think the evidence for higher moral standards in other areas of behavior is so overwhelming as to be almost beyond question. Concern about racial justice, peace, service to one's fellowmen, honesty, integrity, sincerity, are, I think, far more explicit in today's highly "personalist" generation of college students than they were in the past. The typical heroes, be they Holden Caulfield in the fifties or Ben Braddock in the sixties, are profoundly concerned about the questions of meaning, of moral evaluation, of purpose, and of responsible relationships. The problem for Ben Braddock and Holden Caulfield is not at all that they are immoral; it is rather that they cannot resolve their moral dilemmas.

It is beyond the scope of this paper to account for the increase in moral consciousness among college students, though I think one could make a case that the long-range trend in human ethics is upward and that the "personalist" revolution is an important factor in explaining the increased ethical consciousness of the college student.

The difficulty, then, is not that young people are immoral, but rather that they are almost too moral for the ethical systems available to them. The repertory of moralities that American society offers to its young people has kept pace neither with the increased moral consciousness of youth nor with the increasing complexities of the moral challenges that youth must face. The traditional moralities have not yet been able to articulate sys-

---

[1] See Mervin Freedman, *The College Experience* (San Francisco: Jossey-Bass, 1967), Chapter Seven, and Joseph Katz and Associates, *No Time for Youth: Growth and Constraint in College Students* (San Francisco: Jossey-Bass, 1968), Chapter One.

tematically the proper responses of the moral man in modern America and indeed have almost despaired of even trying to do so.

It is fashionable to argue that there is no need of a *system* of morality, that all one must do is to love. But in the words that Bruno Bettelheim has made immortal, love is not enough. To say that the moral imperative is really to love is simply to *restate* the problem. First of all, it is quite clear that some forms of "love" are not love at all. He who claims to be loving may merely be exploiting. Furthermore, a *simplistic* morality of love may lead to privatism[2]—withdrawal from the messy, complex problems of a larger society. He who says to youth, "You must love," must go on to explain more precisely what is to be done, how it is to be done, and why it is to be done. A simplistic philosophy of love really does not solve Ben Braddock's problem. Ben is well aware that he must love, but he is not sure whom to love or how to love, or how to direct his life on the basis of love.

The young person, therefore, finds himself faced with the need for constant decision making, decision making fraught with moral implications. Unlike young people of years gone by, today's youth are faced with a vast, almost infinite variety of choices about what to do, who to be, and how to behave. They have been showered with an abundance of riches; they have more alternatives than their grandparents would have dreamed possible; indeed, they have just about everything—except an explanation of reality that would provide them with norms according to which they could make their choices.

The absence of norms, *viable* norms, is defended by some: this is the liberal, democratic, enlightened, progressive way. Yes, so it seems—until one stops to think how truly absurd it is to expect that a seventeen-year-old long on enthusiasm and generosity but terribly short on experience, sensitivity, nuance, and wisdom, will be able to evolve an ethical viewpoint that will be salutary for him and satisfactory for his fellows. Our pretense that the young ought to be able to evolve their own morality is merely an admission of how morally bankrupt we adults are.

To make matters worse, we frequently disfigure the tradi-

---

[2] The term appears to be used here exactly in the sense defined in Terry F. Lunsford's essay, to which the reader is referred. (*Ed.*)

tional moral systems with such an overlay of pompous bourgeois piety that the young person can only conclude that traditional ethics are invalid and indeed grotesque. I am inclined to feel that the ethical vision of the Gospels is at least a challenging one. But there are not many parish churches to which a young person can go where he will hear that ethic preached in a language that makes sense to him. If it is necessary for man to have systems of morality, it is also probably inevitable that these systems will become rigid, juridic, and lifeless unless they are periodically renewed by prophets who reinterpret them in terms of the life challenges of the day. Alas, the prophets—at least for the Christian vision—are in short supply in contemporary America.

I contend that the moral stress that young people are experiencing today can be traced to the fact that none of the meaning-giving institutions—family, church, or school—has been able to provide to the overwhelming majority of young people a vision and meaning of life, a system of general principles of human behavior that is adequate either to the complex decisions that young people must make or the increased explicit moral consciousness that they experience.

If any prophet is to arise who will produce a new morality or unify the traditional moralities, his prophecy will have to redignify the human person. Here is a value that young people do understand. A new ethic that does not recognize this dignity is not worth very much; neither is an ethic of love that does not contend that one ought to *love* one's enemy, for he is a human person too—even if he is also a dean, a president, a Babbitt, or L. B. Johnson. I believe that the traditional moral systems *do* have the raw material for developing such a prophetic moral system, but for whatever reason, it has not yet been done.

Does the academy have any place for the struggle to create new ethical systems? Our philosophers surely must be excused because they are too busy agonizing over whether words mean anything and whether one can talk validly about ethics or about anything else. Our theologians must be excused because they are too busy burying the old God, or being remote scholars, or marching in picket lines. The other members of the humanistic disciplines are busy trying to convert their fields from arts to sciences. The social scientists are counting noses, and the physical scientists are building bombs. All of us, of course, are terribly busy trying to achieve tenure, and any prophet who does not have a good record of publication need not even bother applying. And administrators are busy paying the bills passed by the alumni and preserving law and order. All of us decry war, hatred, and other evils; but if a young person innocently asks us why, we reply that we are too busy to answer such questions. I once asked one of the most sensitive adult observers of contemporary youth, who joined me in lamenting the absence of clear meaning and morality in the youthful generation, what ideologies and moralities *he* would suggest. He shrugged his shoulders and replied, "Look, I'm a third generation agnostic. It's not *my* problem."

I would suggest that it is his problem. It is a problem for all of us. We surely are not going to try to teach morality in the classroom, nor to enforce morality by rules, nor even to make moral development the explicit and direct goal of higher education. Still, I trust we will avoid the simplism of certain college presidents and faculty who divide the goals of education into intellectual and moral and affirm that the university is only concerned about the first. But we are all of us more than teachers, more than administrators, more than instructors, more than rule makers. We are human beings engaged in a cooperative human effort called higher education, an effort that is under great strain and stress at the present time precisely because of the decline not of morality, but of *moral wisdom*. It will do no good to point the finger of guilt at the churches or the family and say, "It's your job," because the family will not hear us and the church is very likely to point its finger right back and say, "It's your job, too." The teaching of moral wisdom to young people *is* the responsibility of the colleges and universities. It is not a question of "whether" but "how"; and responsible curriculum makers ought to set their minds to that question immediately.

19

RESPONSE TO STUDENT DEMANDS FOR RELEVANCE

Donald L. Garrity

In the fall of 1965, a number of administrative officers, interested faculty members, and several "combination" faculty-administrators at San Francisco State College gathered in a series of meetings on late Wednesday afternoons. An unofficial group with no authority whatsoever on the campus, we simply called ourselves *The Group*. The founder had been a chairman of the academic senate and he was at that time the dean of the one of the two largest schools within the college. He and several other members of The Group were fresh returnees from the Danforth Workshop in Liberal Arts, in which our College had participated that summer. His intent in founding The Group was to bring together a number of people sufficiently interested in the harder curricular and curricular-administrative problems to give up two hours they did not have at the end of a hard academic day to discuss them.

One Wednesday afternoon, we were ranging through a number of interesting topics, including one on models for curriculum development and change, when we learned that another largely spontaneous group was developing within the student body itself. Five or six of these young people, some of them graduate students, some of them undergraduates, were invited to join The Group the following week. They explained to us in what was then a somewhat nebulous fashion—but it was nevertheless impressive —that they felt much of the curriculum and other aspects of the teaching and learning process at the college were irrelevant to the student of today.

These students were, I think I should explain for reasons that may become more apparent later, all white students. Their comments on irrelevance were not, by and large, comments born of an ethnic or linguistic difference or from any particular cultural subconsciousness or self-consciousness. They presented themselves and their point of view as largely intellectual and pedagogical in intent; they played down their political, ideological, and sociological views, as such, to The Group. The Group responded sympathetically, but we did have a lot of questions about how comments on relevance, no matter how articulately presented, could be translated into a program in a well-established institution with its own traditions of discipline and orderly curriculum process.

These young people, as an outgrowth of their intellectual, social, and restless energies, developed two new tracks of enterprise within and without the walls of San Francisco State College. They had, prior to their meeting with The Group, already become involved in the community, in tutorial programs, community action programs, and similar efforts, which got them directly attached to the social-economic-educational problems of the disadvantaged young people in San Francisco. In fact, it was this involvement with others, usually on a one-to-one basis, that made them wonder if they had been adequately educated in college to do what they thought was necessary to do as members of a larger community. This is the kind of relevance they were speaking of in the meetings of The Group. This track was developed into what on our campus is called the Community Involvement Program. Student organized and controlled, the C.I.P. has provided an opportunity for students to engage themselves in ways they had thought were closed within the context of a college. With the counsel and assistance of a number of faculty, the C.I.P. invited students to join who were interested in learning about the problems and techniques of community organizing, committed to the concept that an urban college has an action responsibility within the community, and willing to give their time and energy to community action programs. To date the program has initiated fifteen community projects in such areas as tenant unions, job cooperatives, and youth counseling services. It has had an impact upon the curriculum in some departments where new work-study courses connected with the activities of the Program have been instituted.

The second track that was developed by the students who met with us was the now widely known Experimental College, which turned out to have both formal and informal curricular aspects. Exclusive of the normal curricular development, the Experimental College, which was largely a group of young people without a distinguishable academic home, opened itself for business, asking almost anyone with an "idea" to develop a course of almost any content with almost any audience in mind and almost any goal or set of goals—or even changing goals.

During the first three semesters over 5,000 students enrolled in courses proposed, organized, directed, and most frequently taught by a fellow student. Currently, in excess of 2,000 students are enrolled in over seventy different courses. The curriculum offers courses such as these to the student who wishes to compensate for his perceived need for curricular and instructional relevance: God in a Mid-Century Milieu, Utopian Metaphysics of the Three-Fold Forces, Astro-Psychology in Search of Identity, North American White Witchcraft, Sexual Growth, Exploring New Forms of Sexual Relationships, Avant-Garde Music Since 1945, Ways of Life and Means of Livelihood, Effecting Social Change, Innovative Teaching: The Internal and External Environment, Anti-Environments: A Search for Methods of Survival in the 20th Century—to name but a few. I do not think I need to point out that this outburst of curriculum, cocurriculum, quasi-curriculum, pseudocurriculum, and new curriculum—born of a demand for relevance—was revolutionary.

During the past year a third major track has been developed. Led by the membership of the Black Students Union and supported by the black student population and much of the black community, the relevance of the college curriculum admission program, student financial aid program—really the relevance of the college as a whole for the black student on our campus and those who should be there—was brought into focus. Questions were raised about our admissions standards. As these have gone up (in accordance with the California Master Plan) our black student population has dropped from approximately 12 per cent to 4 per cent during the past decade. It is clear that the threat of tuition promises to decrease these proportions even more. Worst of all, curriculum growth has not kept pace. Our curriculum is inadequate in its treatment of material, understandings, and perspectives that are important and necessary to the black person in American society.

With a strong sense of necessity, urgency, and immediacy about their cause, these students have enlisted the support of some faculty and administrators to inaugurate some thirty courses or special sections of existing courses that are responsive and relevant to the contemporary black student. They have helped to recruit, admit, and then support both financially and educationally students who otherwise would not be attending a college. Uncertain as to eventual form, structure, context, or style, the college has been moved to develop a program in Black Studies. Also, it sees the necessity for similar future movements relevant to the Mexican-American, American Indian, and others.

San Francisco State College went through a very trying year in 1967–68. I shall not review here the events of early winter and late spring of that year, as most readers of these pages have no doubt become acquainted with the major incidents through the news media. I do wish, however, to make two or three personal comments.

Those of us who had been trained over a number of years to develop rational methods and processes for dealing with all manner of intellectual and social problems, tried to deal with these issues in the most objective possible way, using carefully established precedent for determining relevant process, calm and representative judgment, and humane and not irretrievable punishment. But we soon found, in this age of relevance, that traditional practice itself can be considered the most irrelevant of all irrelevancies and that a revolution of *all* process, from curricular development to student discipline, was demanded. And we further found that the methods of demand themselves were revolutionary.

How did we respond at San Francisco State College to these demands for relevance? Let me list some of our more obvious responses: extended and searching curricular reviews; the development of a strong academic senate; the encouragement of experiment in the curriculum; the fostering of student strength, through student memberships on all sensitive committees across the campus, even to the acceptance of a student majority on councils that deal with large sums of money and the institution's future; a wide interpretation of admissions policy so that disadvantaged students of promise might have an opportunity at our kind of college; the development of special advising techniques for students in need of them; the welcoming of visiting professors chosen by and completely paid for by the students themselves; and—the list is far from exhausted.

I believe I could say that we have responded in most instances well. Nevertheless I must report that many of my colleagues feel we may be opening ourselves to chaos, true chaotic anarchism, through our kinds of response to demands for relevance. Such demands challenge every aspect of the system—administrative processes, instructional practice, and curricular structure. Such demands are delivered with an immediacy and urgency about them that offends our sense of history and our commitment to thoughtful and disciplined change. Moreover, when the demands are presented through revolutionary tactics and strategies, they produce reverberations throughout the entire college and frequently beyond. The tactics and rhetoric of confrontation, mass pressure, intimidation, and occasionally violence are not only relatively new to the American collegiate scene but offensive to much of our tradition and beliefs. They present contingencies that most of us are ill equipped to handle. It is not an easy experience to live through. We are prepared for dialogue—for reasoning through issues until mutually acceptable solutions are reached—

but we are not prepared for the silent, stubborn, and accusing eyes of confrontation. It is a paralyzing experience. Yet, clearly, the mere application of administrative fiat, the clamp-down that is so often asked for these days, is not appropriate or particularly effective. What is needed (it is easy to say but needs to be constantly repeated) is the sharing of responsibility in judgment making among *all* the elements of the college community.

20

CURRICULAR RELEVANCE IN TEACHER EDUCATION

William E. Engbretson

In the past few years teacher education has been thrust into stage center, especially by the war on poverty and the obvious and well-documented failure of teachers and schools to break the spiral of futility that typifies economically poor and educationally disadvantaged Americans. Minority groups are deprived of their educational birthright, denied teachers who understand their needs and have the skills to really overcome cumulative environmental and learning deficits, denied teachers who can intelligently and meaningfully capitalize upon the strengths of individuals and the richness that does exist in all subcultures, handed all too often decaying firetraps as school buildings, and miseducated or non-educated with a paucity of learning materials that are both too scarce and—when they are available—are unrelated to the young-sters. They just do not make contact, they have no *direct* implica-tions, they represent an unreal world, they are just a meaningless, useless series of exercises apparently designed to defeat children—and they succeed. Despite our accomplishments, and there are many, our educational casualty lists lengthen. The silent scream-ing of children is becoming a raucous roar of urban mobs. The frustration/aggression hypothesis is verified daily. Willingly or unwillingly the education of teachers and supportive personnel becomes a matter of national survival.

In April 1967, the *Southern Education Report* published its survey of teacher education institutions in the southern and border states, assessing how future teachers are being prepared to work with culturally and educationally disadvantaged children. These findings are noteworthy: (1) Of the 281 institutions re-sponding, 269 believed there existed a special responsibility to help improve the education of the disadvantaged, but only 108 think these institutions are, in fact, helping. (2) In actuality, only forty-five—or less than one out of every six—have made any sub-stantive change in their own programs for this purpose in the past five years. (3) For the future, 117 of these institutions—a bit better than two out of five—have any direct intention or apparent desire to change their own program for this purpose. Two additional points bear mention: The survey showed that most changes that do occur get their ideas and initiative from *outside* the institution. Most respondents feel their graduates are either well prepared or fairly well prepared to teach disadvantaged children. And all this from institutions that prepare approximately one-fourth of the nation's teachers and three-fourths of the teachers in the southern and border states.

Barring the urban universities with a major avowed social purpose and commitment, the picture nationally is probably not too different. This is a rather scathing indictment and it is meant to be so.

The first major trend of note, therefore, is concern for the education of prospective and current teachers of economically dis-advantaged or deprived children and youth. Many new programs around the country reflect this deep concern. Prime examples of programs that have evolved are the San Francisco State College-

Sausalito Public School System model, the Western Michigan University Master's Degree Program, Hunter College's Project 120, and the Kansas City Schools-Regional Educational Research Laboratory-Liberal Arts Colleges program at Kansas City.

1. *San Francisco State College-Sausalito Teacher Education Project (STEP).* This three-year old program was originally designed to prepare teachers to be more effective in a dynamic and ever-changing society. It encompasses grades kindergarten through eight in the Sausalito public school system and a deliberately articulated program with the ninth through twelfth grades. The teacher candidates and faculty from San Francisco State College plan, study, and teach in a STEP Education Center.

Included in the program are (a) direct experience in the classroom from September through summer school as teacher assistants, student teachers, and teacher interns; (b) instruction in curriculum concurrent with and related to direct experiences in the classroom through seminars, small group conferences, and individualized attention; (c) weekly counseling sessions of six to eight students to explore and develop the self-image along with the professional image; (d) in-service education activities to parallel or complement the pre-service program; and (e) an evaluation and research program to assess the progress of STEP.

Of major import to the STEP program is a program of communications and community relations and a new careers program designed to seek out deprived students who could be potential teachers. Educational technology for this teacher preparation program is used in an innovative manner and a unique professional and curriculum materials center—used by both students and teachers in the school system as well as by the college faculty—has developed.

2. *Western Michigan University: Masters Degree Program for the Teaching of Culturally and Educationally Deprived Youth.* The basic purpose of the Western Michigan program is to develop teachers' empathy with the lives, values, customs, and difficulties of disadvantaged children they intend to teach. A second purpose is to improve college professors' qualifications for preparing teachers of the disadvantaged through direct involvement.

Features of the program include: (a) pre-service teachers' direct involvement with the disadvantaged; (b) informal seminars with consultant specialists; (c) eight weeks of supervised teaching and camp counseling experience with migrant or inner-city children; (d) faculty fellowships to acquaint them with and prepare them to deal with the problems of the poor; (e) sensitivity training to help both teachers and students to accept and deal with the new educational challenges; and (f) evaluation, which so far indicates encouraging attitudinal changes and preparedness for working with deprived children.

Program results seem to indicate real goal achievement. Both students and faculty are demonstrating a strong emotional and attitudinal commitment to the education of disadvantaged children and youth, a greater understanding of the social forces that create poverty, personalized understanding of the psychological problems of the poor, and a broad understanding of the role that schools can play in helping the poor to a better place in society.

3. *Hunter College: Project 120.* Begun in 1960 at J.H.S. 120 of the New York City Schools, this volunteer student teaching program will have had, by June 1968, 190 graduates in the four junior high schools now participating. Intended to prepare teachers specially for working with students of low socioeconomic backgrounds by use of extra help, conferences, use of teams, visits to social agencies, and so on, the program has succeeded markedly. The Board of Education guaranteed placement in the schools where student teachers were being trained, providing the graduates requested such placement.

At the end of the first three years, 80 per cent of the student teachers were teaching in the schools for which they were trained and none of those had left the school or the profession. By the end of 1964, J.H.S. 120 had over 50 per cent of its full-time staff as Project 120 graduates. The Project has had an effect upon the development of in-service workshops in community study, human relations, and individualized curriculum study. It has also demonstrated the need for continuing assistance to new teachers after graduation.

Another followup was done in J.H.S. 120 in 1966. Of the thirty graduates who elected to teach there since 1960, twenty were still on the job in 1966. Of eighty-eight non-Project teachers who had started at J.H.S. 120 in the same time period, 22 were still on the job in 1966. Which retention rate would you want? Two-thirds or one-fourth? Project 120 graduates are now serving as supervising teachers and "buddies" to the new volunteers. These graduates recommended last fall that all-day student teaching is a must, that methods courses should be more realistic, and more laboratory experiences prior to student teaching are needed.

4. *Kansas City-Regional Educational Research Laboratory-Liberal Arts Colleges' Program.* Profiting from the earlier example of the Inner-City Teacher Education Program of Central Missouri State College in the Kansas City area, last year the Regional Research Laboratory, in conjunction with thirteen liberal arts colleges in Kansas and Missouri, developed an inner-city program with the Kansas City schools. Stimulated financially by the AACTE's NDEA National Institute for Advanced Study in Teaching Disadvantaged Youth, The Danforth Foundation, the Regional Laboratory, and tuition rebates by the participating colleges, students were engaged in a full semester's experience studying, observing, and practice teaching in the inner city. The students were housed in the inner city and faculty were provided from their respective institutions and the Regional Laboratory. Kansas City public school teaching and supervisory personnel have contributed creatively and extensively to the development and conduct of this program.

The above programs also indicate a second major trend that is evolving. This is, in a sense, a return to an earlier normal school kind of concept of direct, sequential, laboratory experiences of a clinical nature with children and youth. It seems to me that a cycle is in the process of being completed. Normal schools at the turn of the century and for several decades thereafter had their prospective teachers working directly with children much of the time that they were in college. Gradually, teacher education became increasingly academically respectable, moved into the university frame of reference, and showed an increasingly great dependence on abstract verbalized learning patterns rather than direct experiences with children. The AACTE Flowers-Lindsay Report on laboratory experiences had the effect of aiding teacher education institutions to develop some sequence in a renewed interest in laboratory experiences.

This sequence has customarily taken the form of a few

hours of observation of teachers and children at work during the sophomore year of college, a few hours of some participatory teacher aid experience during the junior year, and culminated in a term or semester of full-time student teaching in the senior year. In recent years, the internship concept has evolved and it certainly has been stimulated by the grants of the Ford Foundation. Interning demands a higher level of responsibility and accountability than is customary in student teaching, since the intern has direct control over a classroom of children, while a student teacher functions in a subsidiary capacity in a classroom while being directly supervised daily by a teacher who has legal accountability for the classroom.

I see many new developments in the laboratory experiences part of the prospective teacher and in-service teacher education program. Programs are now evolving where tutorials of a prospective teacher with a disadvantaged child take place early in the collegiate years, followed by a much more rapid and intensive induction in direct clinically-oriented laboratory experiences with small groups and with whole classes of children in the sophomore and junior years. These kinds of experiences have different names, such as teacher aid, assistant teacher, and the like, but their effect is to compress more direct experience with children and youth earlier into the pre-service program. Student teaching follows then with a better background of learning through experience, and new programs frequently involve internship before or after receipt of the baccalaureate degree. The crucial questions raised here deal with the quality of the laboratory experience and how well it really sensitizes the teacher and develops the skills that enable him to teach better. Laboratory experiences must be coupled with the knowledge and theory that give them meaning. Because of the internship the five-year program is definitely on the horizon.

Our college students' cries for relevance and the need for prospective teachers' broadened social understandings contribute to a corollary trend, the use of summer VISTA, assignments with Neighborhood Youth Corps, closer working ties with a variety of social agencies, full or part-time work for pay and credit—or purely volunteer—some or all of which begin to characterize many teacher education students. The range of experiences from Head

Start, through Peace Corps, and literacy teaching in Adult Basic Education Programs should be carefully considered by administrators and faculty for their educative values for prospective, as well as in-service teachers.

Let us turn now to three additional institutions whose programs illustrate some of the continuing and changing patterns.

5. *The University of New Mexico: New Elementary Teacher Education Program.* This newly developed program combines the teaching of methods courses and actual laboratory experiences for elementary teachers into a modular approach that features the intensive study of the content and methodology of a single subject in the university, followed by an intensive laboratory experience in that subject in an elementary school classroom. In this approach, the typical one-semester course is compressed into two or three weeks of full-morning instruction, followed by a two- or three-week full morning laboratory experience. Thus, by scheduling courses consecutively rather than concurrently, time is made available for immediate follow-up laboratory experiences.

The program has three major characteristics: (a) an approach to instructional theory and classroom practice, which combines both in a single module of time, (b) the utilization of satellite public schools for laboratory experiences and the staffing of these schools by resident clinical supervisors who coordinate the university program and teach in school in-service seminars, and (c) the utilization of teaching-supervising teams consisting of university faculty, graduate students in education, and the public school educators who are participants in a teacher education exchange program between the university and the cooperating public school system. In addition, the program has an honors aspect to it and is jointly financed by the public schools and the university.

6. *University of Georgia-State Department-Public Schools: Elementary In-Service Mathematics Program.* This program provides in-service instruction to 900 elementary teachers in sixty-four county school systems at thirty-five different centers. The statewide TV network is used for basic thirty-minute presentations twice a week, with follow-up discussions and explanation by instructors at each center. The year-long program utilizes after-school time and carries five hours of undergraduate or graduate

credit for those who are eligible. The course updates the basic ideas of modern arithmetic, utilizes new text materials, draws on outstanding high school and junior college mathematics teachers as instructors, and has functionally reached 1,400 teachers in its first two years. Funded originally by the National Science Foundation, a significant part of the cost is now paid by the county boards of education.

Attention should be drawn to a similar TV utilization in the New England area in the creative NDEA in-service institute conducted last year by Bill Kvaraceus of Tufts University on teaching disadvantaged youth. While the Georgia program used late afternoon hours, the Tufts program concentrated on Saturdays.

7. *The University of Maryland: The Teacher Education Center.* The University of Maryland developed and implemented the teacher education center concept as a unified approach to the study of teaching and supervision. It gained its initial impetus from a mutual desire on the part of the university and the public schools to provide a more effective program of teacher preparation. The program integrates theory and practice and brings together both the pre-service and in-service components of teacher education in a manner calculated to provide unified and continuous instructional service. Each of the fourteen teacher educational centers has a full-time coordinator jointly selected and employed by the public school system and the University of Maryland. The coordinator plans an effective laboratory experience program for university students and coordinates an in-service laboratory program for supervising teachers who work directly with these student teachers.

Each center has a staff that plans, directs, and assesses the development of the undergraduate student teacher's supervised program. Thus, many persons are available to assist the prospective teacher.

The regular university supervisors serve in the capacity of curriculum and teacher education consultants to the center staff. They work more directly with the cooperating teachers than with the individual student teachers. This means the public school personnel assume increased responsibility for the pre-service program and, in return, the university assumes increased responsibility for in-service education.

The honorarium customarily paid to cooperating teachers has been diverted in this program to staff development. So far, the evaluation of data gathered by the University of Maryland and the cooperating public school systems indicate that the program is highly effective. It serves as a model for close cooperation in both pre- and in-service education between public schools and the university, and, in this connection, is closely attendant to the proposed new evaluative criteria for NCATE.

The AACTE media project has had a direct impact on this program, which is utilizing the materials developed on microteaching, interaction analysis, nonverbal communication and simulation in the in-service program with teachers.

Another major trend is the continuing interest of the college and university in the in-service education of teachers. For too long, able people have been lost to the profession through the initial shock of working in classrooms with children, a shock resulting at least in part from lack of adequate preparation for this demanding task. Now colleges and universities are beginning to aid by direct supervision, conferencing, and supportive work of many kinds, following up new teachers in their first crucial years on the job.

Parallel to this trend is a corollary that we might call *professors in the classroom*. For too many years now, professors of arts and sciences and education have been absent from the public classroom scene. In recent years, a fresh interest has evolved on the part of curriculum experts from the academic disciplines in developing content materials for children and youth. This has brought many leading scholars into direct contact with teachers and children in the schools. The NDEA National Institute for Advanced Study of Teaching Disadvantaged Youth funded a program in New England last spring that is noteworthy. The program took approximately fifteen professors in the academic fields and enabled them to work directly in classrooms with disadvantaged children and youth for periods of time ranging from two weeks to an entire semester. Uniformly, these professors felt that this was a highly exciting and desirable experience. Conversely, and rather sadly, I must also report that most of these professors lost academic credibility in the eyes of their colleagues. This is an indictment of the Ivy League faculty ranking, promotion, and publish-orperish sort of syndrome we find in our higher education institutions.

Another significant trend in teacher education at the present time is an increasing utilization of knowledge engendered from the basic disciplines of anthropology, psychology, social psychology, sociology, and the like. I think there is evidence that teachers are better trained in these basic disciplines and the disciplines themselves have become increasingly respondent to concerns evidenced in the public schools. Collateral with this trend is a growing concern with the definition and analysis of the variety of teacher tasks that must take place in order to have effective education for children. For years we have labored mightily on limited research studies that have attempted to define aspects of teacher behavior, teacher characteristics, teacher tasks, and the like. It seems now that there is hope that some real progress will be made along these lines in the fairly near future and that as we more adequately analyze and describe teaching tasks, we will more intelligently be able to prepare teachers for these tasks.

Another discernible trend approaches as the profession takes a closer look at teacher and staff role differentiation. The training of para-professionals on the basis of a variety of models is beginning. The Minneapolis public schools are adapting the "new careers" concepts to the training of indigent poor as professional teacher aides, being certified through the State Department of Labor the first several years, and, for those who can progress to a fully professional level, becoming certified through the State Department of Public Instruction subsequently. A number of junior colleges are now beginning to work with four-year senior colleges in partnerships along the lines of the "new careers" approach. We may quite legitimately expect a new partner in the teacher education enterprise as junior and community colleges enter heavily into the training of para-professionals for education, health, and social services. Federal funding through the Office of Economic Opportunity, the Office of Education, and the Department of Labor is felt in this connection.

The American Association of Colleges for Teacher Education is currently engaging in several developments of note. A proposal jointly sponsored by the Association for Student Teaching and the National Commission on Teacher Education and Professional Standards has been initiated at the request of the Office of Education for an Educational Research Information Center in Teacher Education. Coupling the potential of this ERIC Center with a proposal for a National Center for the study of teaching emanating from the Association's Committee on Studies would pose a two-part organization that might hold tremendous potential for research and communications bearing directly upon teacher education programs. Another effort of the Association is the tentative draft of the proposed evaluative criteria for revised standards of the National Council for Accreditation of Teacher Education. Anyone giving detailed examination to current trends in teacher education must consider the implications of the new criteria.

Finally, two new programs have evolved in the Office of Education over the past year. The Triple-T Project (the training of teachers of teachers) that has emanated from the Bureau of Elementary and Secondary Education's Division of Educational Personnel Training, which will now be administered by the new Bureau of Educational Professions Development, and the Elementary Teacher Education Models Program initiated by the Bureau of Research are illustrative of the major thrust of the Office of Education toward improving teacher education.

The Triple-T Project is developing on the basis of wide involvement of "places" of interested public school, college, and university academic and teacher education personnel. The program is marked by its effort to unify the contributions of these three components of teacher education resulting, hopefully, in new and creative approaches to the graduate education of teacher education leaders. We are told that roughly 10 to 15 per cent of the funds to be appropriated under the new Education Professions Development Act will be allocated to future development of the Triple-T.

The Bureau of Research, taking a broad approach to future programmatic development in elementary teacher education, initiated a widespread request for proposals for plans-to-plan on the part of colleges, universities, and related agencies. This request for proposals resulted in seventy-nine submissions, which have now been screened; announcements will be shortly forthcoming identifying the nine institutions that are being awarded the eight-month contracts to develop models for improved elementary teacher education training programs. These models will then be marketed in a broad request for proposals so that institutions that are productive of elementary teachers can propose project activities over a period of time to implement all, some, or part, of the models that will have been developed by the end of October 1968.

We see, thus, that teacher education today is characterized by increased attention to the problems of educating the disadvantaged, wider use of educational technology, more intensive development of a wide variety of laboratory experiences clinically oriented, more flexible entry, progression and follow-up programs, a new blending of pre- and in-service programs, renewed interests of faculty in the realities of the elementary and secondary schools, a host of innovative programs and packaged materials stimulated largely by federal funding, and growing concern with the definition and conduct of teaching behaviors.

21

OPPORTUNITY FOR THE DISADVANTAGED

William Moore, Jr.

There is an academic and social revolution going on today in higher education. This revolution is dramatized by new techniques for educating marginal students, the unprecedented growth of community colleges, the increased emphasis upon higher education for the masses, the great demand for trained persons in supportive services who are not professional but who need post-high school training, and the emerging demands of racial and minority groups who deserve equal access to more education and an equitable share of its rewards. These and other changes emphasize the growing numbers of disadvantaged students who may be regarded as either a monumental problem or an immense opportunity for two-year and four-year institutions.

From either point of view, higher education is in a raging storm. But, by and large, it is responding as though it cannot feel the rain. In fact, the colleges continue to survive under the phi-

losophy and practices of the nineteenth century and seem unwilling to move forward in time. Students who finish our colleges
know more about Greek antiquity than about the Negro in contemporary America; they can understand the causes of the fall
of the Roman Empire in 476 A.D., but cannot conceptualize the
causes of the devastation of a part of Detroit in 1967. American
students are taught to speak a foreign language by professors who
cannot teach a Mexican-American child or a child from the Negro
ghetto to speak standard English. These things seem incongruous
for the mood and the needs of today.

Although the academically unsuccessful come from all social classes and minority groups, there is a disproportionately
larger number of Negro students among them. The majority of
these students live in the ugly cities. They come from broken
homes, dilapidated buildings, and crippling schools. Only a few
of them are motivated; most of them have been rejected; almost
all of them have experienced some failure; a considerable number have been poor; and none of them have had a second chance
at an education. These are the people who are supposed to inherit
the earth.

Typically, higher education has shown little concern for
youth with educational obstacles spawned by poverty and discrimination, and has refused to come to terms in dealing with
these students. Fewer than 10 per cent of the institutions of higher
learning in the United States provide specific programs for the
academically and socially handicapped. Although more than six
hundred offer developmental and remedial courses, these are isolated and unrelated courses, and cannot be construed as programs.
The colleges say: "It is the job of the preparatory institutions
(high schools and preparatory schools) to develop the readiness of
the student for college." "The academically slow and impover-
ished student will distract from the character and reputation of
our institution." "The financial and academic preparation of our
students are such that a special program for the educationally disadvantaged is unwarranted. We see the need for such programs
and give moral support to them. Beyond this, we can see no reason
for our involvement."

College people insist that they are doing what they are
supposed to do. They reject the awesome burden of trying to

salvage students who are not "qualified" for higher education. Most of them repudiate the idea that they can educate everybody and suggest that post-high school education has to be selective. They contend that they are doing a pretty decent job in preparing qualified professionals. They recommend that some other, more appropriate, educational agency should try to reach that student who is academically unsuccessful. These professors boast that teachers, engineers, lawyers, doctors, and other professionals who now serve the society are trained by them. And they reject the new function of providing an opportunity for the student who cannot successfully handle academic work.

In spite of these claims, many people are asking whether higher education is producing enough of the right people. Our universities produce doctors who can be effective only if they are complemented by a sufficient number of nurses, nurses' aides, pharmacists, medical records librarians, and eight or ten other supportive individuals. It is appropriate for the colleges to produce the professionals. At the same time, however, they have to be aware of the number of people that are involved in these supportive services. Doctors need assistants and their helpers need helpers.

It is as important to make sure that the person who mixes the insecticides in the bakery and the sanitation department knows ratio and proportion as it is for the nurse who measures dosage and the pharmacist who compounds the drugs measured in grams and centimeters. All along the line there is need for sound preparation. It is expected; it is assumed to be there. Many times it is not there. There are many levels of supporting services in all the professions. Here lie many of the opportunities for the academically unsuccessful, inept, and uninterested student. If we provide him the opportunity to improve his skills, we may improve his scholarship; if we give him a chance to develop his self-confidence, we may be able to eliminate his ineptitude; and, if we provide him with incentives, we may motivate him. If we fail to do this, we will be remiss in doing our duty. We already know that the number of unskilled jobs is decreasing while the number of unskilled people, high school dropouts, pushouts, and graduates, is increasing. When these people get sufficiently frustrated they can strike out at any moment and in any direction. A hurled brick has no conscience and a fire bomb does not discriminate.

In this decade, what constitutes a bona fide educational opportunity for the socially and economically disadvantaged that would be beneficial both to the student and to society? It certainly cannot be the traditional attitude of higher education, which says: "This is what we have to offer—take it or leave it." Too few of the inept can take what is offered; and too many of the unmotivated choose to leave it.

Forest Park Community College in St. Louis, Missouri, was able to secure financial support from the Danforth Foundation to develop what is called "The General Curriculum, A Program for the Educationally Disadvantaged." Everything about the general curriculum was developed with the student in mind.

Forest Park Community College is located almost on the boundary where the city meets the suburbs, although technically it is in the inner city. We might describe the college's location as having its east entrance in poverty and its west entrance in affluence and it was planned that way. From both directions and from both economic and social classes, the General Curriculum Division (one of the College's six divisions) attracts students whom we have euphemistically labeled "academically unsuccessful, inept, and uninterested." Students are assigned to this program on the basis of two criteria: high school rank at graduation and percentile rank on the School and College Ability Test (SCAT). These ranks must be lower third and tenth percentile or below, respectively. Both criteria must be met for the student to be assigned to the General Curriculum. The student, however, is not locked into the program. If he makes satisfactory progress (C+) within one year, he may move into the transfer, technical, and career programs.

The General Curriculum Program has been developed on the premise that the educationally disadvantaged students who enter Forest Park Community College will need simultaneous assistance in the developmental areas of basic academic skills (reading, mathematics, and grammar), personal enrichment, and adjustment to self and society. The program provides this assistance through programmed learning, general education, and guidance techniques.

The primary objective of the program is directed toward the student and may be summarized by a single term, placement, which might take any of the following forms: (1) placement in a specific curriculum offered by the college, (2) placement in a training program offered within the community, but not under the auspices of the college, and (3) placement directly on a job consistent with the student's interests and aptitudes.

The secondary objective concerns goals that might be met by the program and that would broaden on a national scale the scope of applicability and usefulness of the general curriculum. One of these goals is the development of a model program for educationally disadvantaged students with a consistent theoretical rationale that could serve as a guide to other institutions, state and federal organizations, and agencies confronted by similar conditions.

The improvement of basic skills has to play a major role in any program for the educationally disadvantaged, for without these skills no gates will open and the student will leave the college after a period of time, as he left the high school, functionally illiterate. The solution to the problem of basic skills is offered through a multimedia approach to programmed instruction. The Forest Park Community College has established a Programmed Materials Learning Laboratory. The programmed approach is especially appropriate for the disadvantaged college student as instruction is individualized. If a student cannot read, then he may be instructed to listen to tapes; if he cannot read well and does not listen well, the two skills may be combined by using the video-sonic (see and hear) approach. Specially trained coordinators who have teaching backgrounds are available to assist him.

Each student works and is tested on material that he can master, he proceeds at his own rate, he works only on those skills in which he is deficient, and his periodic examinations are spaced for maximum reinforcement. He always knows the level where he is working and where he must go to reach his objective. The burden of responsibility for assimilating the material is placed on him. He must take an active part in the learning process. The present laboratory has auxiliary laboratories in writing, mathematics, and reading.

The educationally disadvantaged student knows little about events beyond his day, beyond his age group, beyond his neighborhood and school. Thus, he lacks an understanding of contemporary culture and does not have a basic historical frame of reference. Therefore, the basic vehicle for the cultural development of the student is a one-year program of general education designed to provide him with a stimulating and successful classroom experience under the guidance of an instructor who has both interest and experience in working with the low achiever and who is willing to devote a majority of his time to this area of instruction.

The general education courses in the general curriculum are designed primarily as enrichment courses that will give the students some insight into the world in which they are living and the society of which they are a part. These courses differ from regular courses more in their lack of abstraction and their method of presentation than in the sophistication of subject matter. In addition, they are not designed as prerequisites for any other course, so the instructor has a wider choice of subject material than in regular courses. The courses can help students prepare to do further work in a college transfer or technical curriculum, although this is not their primary purpose. Personal enrichment in the general curriculum program is defined as that minimal body of knowledge necessary for successful participation in American cultural life.

Ideally, integrated patterns or approaches occur at three different levels in the general education part of the program: (1) Instructors of general education courses work together with the academic skills staff and counselors in a team approach to the needs of the individual student. (2) Within the area of general education, instructors aim at a broad-fields pattern of curricular organization, with special consideration given to employing modified core concepts. (3) General education instructors draw on the St. Louis community for resource material for enrichment purposes.

The counseling program, too, is community centered rather than institutionally centered. Counselors are trained to know intimately all facets of the community so that its total resources are at the disposal of the educationally disadvantaged student. The counseling staff works closely with personnel in the public schools to ensure adequate understanding of the program along with the modification of traditional attitudes concerning what is or is not acceptable higher education.

A social worker is employed as a part of the counseling staff to provide a continuing bridge of understanding between the environment from which the student comes and the programs that are developed for him. A low student-counselor ratio ensures that students can be seen weekly if necessary. The counselor and the social worker have the responsibility for conveying the student personnel point of view and for teaching human relations skills to other staff members serving in the program. In addition they assist in coordinating the efforts of other team members through case conferences and in collecting and presenting data concerning student characteristics.

The counseling-human relations team is also responsible for developing, testing, and reporting new methods of counseling the disadvantaged student. While a number of books have been written about disadvantaged students, little has been advanced in the way of special counseling approaches specifically designed to overcome their problems.

Unique features include: the employment of a full-time social worker, provisions for articulation between the high school community and the college, subsidizing of students to attend cultural events, remission of fees for students in the program who cannot meet the financial obligation of attending college, continuing workshops for in-service personnel and on a national basis for those interested in learning techniques of the program, the funds and access to expertise to develop materials and experiment with varying approaches in teaching the educationally disadvantaged students, a deliberate plan to work with the deprived community, and an internship (with stipend) for prospective teachers of the disadvantaged at the college level.

Institutions that are willing to be innovative, those with commitment, and those that want to make a positive contribution to the social order can develop programs like the one at Forest Park Community College to meet the needs of disadvantaged students.

Section IX

The International Dimension

INTERCULTURAL STUDY VERSUS THE FOREIGN LANGUAGE REQUIREMENT

Joseph Axelrod

The scene is the lobby of the Conrad Hilton Hotel in Chicago.[1]
A meeting of the American Association for Higher Education is

---

[1] My thanks to John Warner, editor at the Center for Research and Development in Higher Education, University of California, Berkeley, for his invaluable aid in the search for the right form for this essay and its final realization. I hope the narrative form will not be taken either as a desire to be unconventional or as an easy means to make dull material more "interesting." It is, in fact, intimately related to my message.

in progress, and one of the general sessions has just ended. The lobby is filled with Association members and visitors who stand in pairs or in groups of three or four, talking animatedly.

Earlier in the day I presented a paper, titled *Foreign Language Study*, in which I recommended the abolition of the blanket foreign language requirement for the bachelor's degree and the substitution of a requirement in intercultural studies for all students. Now, in the lobby, I find myself confronted by a certain college dean whom I know vaguely. He is an administrator of the conventional type—at least this has been my impression of him—and cautious about new ideas. He wears a sour expression.

"You and your ideas!" the dean greets me, and I prepare myself for an argument. But to my surprise he adds quickly: "I like them. I like them a lot." And then, as I begin to relax, he says, "There is only one thing I want you to tell me: where do you expect me to find staff to teach such courses?"

And the argument begins.

The argument, however, has already been going on for some time for me. Several years ago, while I was serving as a member of an accrediting team in California, I encountered at a certain campus an unusual lower division foreign language program, one specifically designed for students who were not language majors but who were studying languages to satisfy the blanket requirement for the bachelor's degree. The remarkable thing about this program was that it placed its emphasis on intercultural studies rather than on language skills as such. As a consequence, while the students actually did learn something of the languages they were studying, they really did not acquire a very high level of language skill.

However, this in itself did not worry me. There was ample evidence, I knew, to show that the majority of college students do not in any case develop really usable skills in a foreign language—for example, the ability to read with *real* ease—unless they go considerably beyond the courses needed to meet the graduation requirement.[2] Besides, the program I was observing produced

---

[2] The most recent data relevant to this question are reported by John B. Carroll in his study for the U.S. Office of Education; a summary appears in the December, 1967, issue of *Foreign Language*

something that was lacking in conventional first- and second-year language courses. That something was intercultural understanding—I do not mean merely a smattering of cultural facts, but real understanding at what I discovered to be a surprisingly deep level.

My report to the accrediting association, after our team's evaluation had been made, was to commend the program highly. But I added the recommendation that the names of the courses might be changed. Since they were not concerned primarily with teaching language skills, it seemed to me that their name ought to indicate more precisely what was being taught. I suggested that each course title might start with the words *Intercultural Studies* followed (after a colon or similar device) by the name of a specific language-and-culture.

I discovered later that my recommendation was not put into practice. The reason given by the college was simple and conclusive: neither the Curriculum Committee nor the faculty as a whole would ever agree to the abolition of a blanket foreign language requirement, even if intercultural study were to be put in its place. Moreover, there would arise the question as to whether the new courses in intercultural study—in which language was not to be the main point of emphasis—actually *belonged* in the Foreign Language Department. If they did not, then a financial question would arise. On this particular campus, departmental budget allotments are determined almost entirely on the basis of student enrollments.

At the last Modern Language Association meeting, I bumped into the chairman of the Foreign Language Department from this campus. He told me they decided to leave things pretty

---

Annals. Carroll's data show surprisingly low language skills for foreign language majors at graduation. (He used a representative sampling of 2,700.) His data invite the question: If majors at graduation possess such low skills, what must the level be for non-majors—those thousands upon thousands of students who each year are enrolled in college foreign language courses in order to satisfy the blanket degree requirement? *Newsweek,* in its issue for January 8, 1968, expresses shock over the results of the Carroll study. There are some bright spots, however. It appears, for example, that study or travel abroad, even if only for a brief period, has a potent effect on the language skills of students.

much as they were. I told him I thought they had made the wrong decision. I would bet, I told him, that the total faculty on any campus—including theirs—*would* vote for abolishing the blanket foreign language requirement if the proposal also included the establishment of a requirement in intercultural study. He replied by saying that even if the total faculty could be persuaded, he would still be faced with a major problem in his department. If the courses should indeed be taken away from the Foreign Language Department—as conceivably could happen once the foreign language label was removed—he would be faced with an "excess" of foreign language staff.

I said the solution to that problem was obvious. Since the foreign language staff had been doing such a superb job teaching the courses in intercultural studies (I myself had observed the program and knew this firsthand), obviously they should be assigned to teach them even if the courses were now to come under the jurisdiction of another department. Dual departmental membership for faculty—especially at an undergraduate college—is, after all, not uncommon nor necessarily undesirable, I said. I could not, however, persuade him.

It is this conversation at the Modern Language Association meeting that flashes through my mind now, as the dean and I are speaking in the Hilton lobby. I am therefore able to answer his question quickly.

"Who will teach the intercultural studies courses?" I say to him. "Let the foreign language staff handle it. They would no longer be needed in such large numbers for the first- and second-year language courses because enrollments would drop." I pause, and then add: "And surely they would be excellent for this new assignment."

"And surely you are joking," the dean says.

"Not at all," I say. But I can feel my cheek stinging, so I try really to make a joke: "Look. I am a member of the Modern Language Association and the author of two MLA reports. We could sue you for that remark."

"Sue," he says. "But a member of the Modern Language Association ought to be aware that only about *half* of a foreign language department would be capable of teaching such a course. What about the rest of them?"

"When the International Education Act of 1966 is funded," I say dryly, "we won't have anything to worry about."

He looks at me for a few seconds, then shakes his head.

I wait for the dean to move on. Certainly, I tell myself, he has already dismissed me as an idiot, one of those people who appear at every convention to urge crackpot ideas on the crowd. And I am sorry to have lost touch with a serious mind, to have alienated him. I prepare to move on, too—but he surprises me.

He points toward a couch in the lobby and invites me to join him there. "I am serious," he says. "How would you organize such a course? What sorts of things would be covered?"

I hesitate. "It would take too long to explain. We would miss the next meeting."

"So we shall miss the next meeting," he says. "Tell me."

Since I have been trying for several years to persuade faculties that such a change must come, my response is immediate. To emphasize language only, I tell him, is to miss the largest part of the subject. If we are talking about a requirement that every student working for the degree must meet, then it is intercultural understanding that must be stressed. And I explain that we should not be concerned only with cultures of foreign lands. We should require our middle-class students to become intimately acquainted with several American subcultures, too, other than their own.

"I'm with you on that," he says. "But I wanted to ask you about those language courses where students learn numbers in French by memorizing the dates of events in French history. Someone told me that's the new 'cultural' approach."

"That's *nonsense*. Let me give you the title of an MLA report—"

He interrupts me. "Tell me about the intercultural course, as you conceive it," he says.

"The course I have in mind," I reply, "would include both a patterns-of-culture approach and an introduction to some of the major artistic and philosophic works. You see, it is just as important for Americans to understand how members of the foreign culture regard, say, their leader's mistresses—or Communist Party activities in their country, or the records of Louis Armstrong—as it is for us to know, firsthand, some of the books the culture thinks of as its 'classics.' "

"But surely this course should be an *academic* experience!" the dean says. "It sounds like you're talking about a cultural travelogue, a lot of trivial detail—with a couple of nineteenth-century novels thrown in to make it look good!"

"It *will* be an academic experience," I assure him. "And the detail will not be trivial if it teaches students something about the broad patterns of the foreign culture, the whole network of beliefs and values. Students ought to come out of a course in intercultural studies with a knowledge of such things. Or rather, they should have *both* kinds of knowledge, because both kinds are important if they are really going to comprehend a people and a culture."

I break off at this point to explain to the dean that instead of going on with details of course content, we should be talking about broader aims—things like empathy, tolerance, breadth of perspective. We should be talking about the importance of growth along those dimensions during the college years. I tell him that, in my view, courses in intercultural study could contribute in a significant way to that growth.

"I agree," the dean says, "but I still need to know more about the content of such a proposed course. Maybe not so specifically—but in general. What kinds of things would the student —say, the *excellent* student—know when he finished such a course that he hadn't known before, or couldn't learn from just socializing and watching TV?"

I see he wants me to pick up where I left off, so I repeat that our excellent student will, first of all, finish the course knowing and appreciating some of the cultural monuments that members of the foreign culture take pride in. I assume that is what the dean is afraid would be missing; and so I explain further: "The course, obviously, must include a selection of masterpieces of art and music and literature, as well as some of the outstanding works of the philosophers, religious leaders, historians, scientists."

But I try, then, to show the dean that a matter of overwhelming importance in planning a course in a foreign culture is the recognition that knowledge of the foreign culture cannot be limited to cultural monuments alone. There is another dimension that must be given equal attention—and that is the complex cultural and societal pattern that governs the daily behavior of the members of the foreign culture. The course, I explain, is interdisciplinary. It is not a course in the humanities alone.

I frankly admit to the dean that this is precisely where he may encounter difficulty if he uses language-literature personnel to teach such a course. When faculty trained in language and literature offer a course in the humanities, it is generally heavily weighted toward works that use language as their form of expression. And even among such works, these faculty devote most of their attention to imaginative literature—drama, fiction, and poetry.

It is completely understandable (even as I say this, I perceive I am being defensive) that language-literature faculty should be so excited about works of imaginative literature. In them, language—normally the instrument for daily communication—is converted into an *art* medium. "You see," I say, and I move closer to him as I speak, "literature is a kind of *miracle*. Only in literature does speech become art."

"I know that. But you yourself,"—the dean jabs me on the chest—"you yourself said that literature is only a single segment of the foreign culture."

"That's right. Such a course must not be limited to literary works, or indeed to cultural monuments alone. Not that such courses aren't valuable. They just aren't the course I'm describing here."

"Okay. Fine. Now, what else does an excellent student know when he's finished your course?"

I tell the dean that our excellent student will understand some of the major cultural assumptions which are held in common by members of the foreign culture. He will have some knowledge of the values that guide daily living among the people who share this culture. These values determine what is socially acceptable, and what is ethically and politically acceptable, too; what "losing face" means; and what the differences are between public and private posture, both for the group as a whole and for the individuals in it. I try to make clear that this knowledge cannot be gained by memorizing someone else's generalizations. The students will have to undergo a variety of direct experiences, I explain, that will enable them to understand all of these matters not merely as abstract principles, but as concrete fact. I mention foreign students on campus as a resource for such a course; I mention the "international" communities in our big cities, and professors on campus who are visiting from abroad. And their families, too—for there we have a rich educational resource that we hardly ever use.

"You see," I say, "in this part of the course, students will be learning *intimate* details. These are things that you can learn, really, only from people; like what mannerisms of face and hands and voice carry prestige; what foods and what types of dress carry high or low status; what attitudes and behaviors are typical toward infants, toward children and adolescents, toward the aged; what sort of face and body is considered beautiful, sexually attractive. Our excellent student might learn how names for children are determined, how nicknames are derived (if they exist in the first place in the culture), what family names *mean*. He might learn how affection is shown—"

I stop. I cannot tell whether the dean is frowning or smiling. "You know, of course," I go on, "you know that in many cultures affection is shown differently from the way Americans ordinarily show it."

"Yes, yes. Of course," he replies.

"Or take humor. Our excellent student will have some idea of the kinds of things that are thought funny in the foreign culture. He will know how members of the culture habitually behave when they find something amusing." Again, I notice, the dean appears to be smiling or frowning. "I'm serious about this," I say. "You know how many educated Americans there are who understand a foreign culture so little they would laugh publicly at things no native member would laugh at, even a boorish or stupid person! You know that's true."

"Yes, yes. Of course," he says again.

I go on to say that our excellent student will also come to know something about the myths of the foreign culture. He will understand to what extent they are accepted by members of the culture—people of average education, for instance—as unchallengeable truths. He will understand, too, what risks he will run if he tries to question these "truths" in conversation with members of the culture.

Beyond his knowledge of the traditions and habits of

thought characteristic of members of the culture, I explain further, our excellent student will know something about the nature of contemporary social institutions in the culture. He will know something about family structure, about the courts and prisons, about the educational system, about banks and credit, about transportation and housing and marketing. He will know the approved patterns of courtship and marriage, and he will have some knowledge of the rituals that attend birth and puberty and death. The communications media, advertising, entertainment—these will be somewhat familiar to him. And he will know something about social problems in the foreign culture—juvenile delinquency, poverty, and so on.

When I finish my recital, I see the dean scratching his head. I realize suddenly that I have left out the most important point of all. It was *his* fault, insisting that I give him so many details of content! Before he can say a word, I cry out:

"About method! I haven't said anything about that, and that's really the most important thing. The course has to be taught *contrastively*."

"Contrastively?" he says. "Contrastively with what?"

"With standard *American* cultural patterns." I say this as if it ought to be obvious.

His reaction is immediate. "Now *that* does it," he says. "How is the foreign language staff going to be able to do *that*?"

"But why not?"

"Because most of them don't *like* American culture. At least *my* foreign language people don't like it. So how are students going to learn tolerance and empathy and breadth of perspective —and all those other things you've been talking about—from *them*?"

"I'll bet they could do it," I insist, "if you place the challenge before them. Maybe they could co-teach with people in American studies; maybe you could arrange teams of faculty working together. I'll bet you don't know what strength you have in your foreign language faculty. I'll bet you don't know what resources you have at hand."

"I do know," he says firmly.

"Maybe you haven't been using them in the right way. Maybe *they* haven't been using themselves in the right way. You see, there's a whole new view, now, of the roles a college teacher plays—more a resource person, a model learner, and so on, than actual teacher. Students are learning to teach *themselves* in ways we—"

He stands up abruptly. "You have very interesting ideas," he says. "The only problem is how to make them operational."

I begin to follow him as he starts down the corridor to the meeting rooms. "What is to prevent it?" I ask. "What is the obstacle?"

"Faculty," he says. "My present faculty. And I don't mean just the foreign language faculty but the whole lot of them. They simply could not do in a million years what you're talking about."

"They could!" I say. "They could!"

"Not in a million years," he repeats. And he disappears into a room where a meeting is in progress.

~23~

FOREIGN STUDY AS CROSSCULTURAL LEARNING

Glenn A. Olds

The concept of foreign study for undergraduate students is badly in need of re-evaluation.[1] Each year thousands of American college and university undergraduate students are being sent overseas to study, and each year a large percentage of these students return to their home campuses without having learned anything very profound about the cultures they have been studying. These stu-

---

[1] The original paper prepared for this collection by Dean Olds was submitted in outline form and has been recast in the present form by John Warner of the Center for Research and Development in Higher Education at the University of California in Berkeley. Mr. Warner is former Administrative Assistant for the International Programs of the California State Colleges.

dents have "had an experience," but whether they have truly absorbed any valuable amount of *experience* remains questionable.

Foreign study, in its proper sense, must be understood as crosscultural learning. It must change the student, and it must in some way affect the culture studied. In short, when the student has finished his year of study, the "foreign" should no longer be foreign to him—nor he to it.

Perhaps one of the first obstacles put in the way of the student is the concept of foreign study as "taking a trip." A student goes to a foreign country, and he looks and he listens, but he knows that he is only "passing through." He thus becomes a kind of special tourist, and he brings with him all too often no knowledge of the country, and he is neither prepared nor willing to become a part of the culture he observes.

A second obstacle put in the way of the student is an attitude on the part of certain faculty and administrators, which has been called "academic baby-sitting." Basic to this attitude is the assumption that students—especially undergraduate students—are children and must be constantly watched and directed. And when a student-child is sent abroad on his "trip," the watching and directing must be intensified, lest the impressionable youngster receive some kind of shock. The shock against which the student must be protected is, of course, cultural shock—the knowledge, often sudden and sometimes painful, that there are things in the world different from what he has always known. Presumably, it is precisely this kind of knowledge that the student goes abroad to obtain, but he is prevented from obtaining it simply because he is so carefully watched and directed. The student is kept from shock, but he is also kept from any real encounter with the culture he observes.

Assuming, however, that a student is allowed some encounter with the culture, what can happen to him aside from "having an experience"? A third obstacle is the student himself. Frequently he is not adequately prepared for his experience and, as a consequence, may be left with shock and nothing else. Or, he may be overprepared. Alfred North Whitehead once said that, unlike Adam, in the Garden of Eden, who saw the animals before he named them, we learn their names before we see them. All too often, the student is prevented from absorbing the culture of the country in which he studies because he has been over-oriented in the abstract, and he has created symbolic barriers to a genuine learning situation. Such a student possesses a romantic and generalized view of the culture, which is premature and sometimes false, and he is given no time for discipline and seasoning. This student, consequently, finds himself faced with the necessity for making a choice between clinging to his romantic infatuation or taking refuge in a feeling that his own culture is superior. Either choice, unfortunately, still leaves him outside the culture he has come to study.

A student sometimes chooses to believe that his own culture is superior to the one he is studying because of a kind of "immunity" that he carries with him—another obstacle in his way. This immunity may come from a variety of sources, but chiefly it has its origin in the campus from which he comes. A college or university community, no matter how large, cannot begin to compare in scope with a vast cultural or national community, and an undergraduate student, who has often known no community larger than his campus, makes his observations and judgments about any new culture in terms of his previous knowledge. He identifies himself with his own campus, regardless of where he is attending classes, and he remains ever the "foreign" student obtaining a "foreign" view in the "foreign" country.

Related to the problem of immunity, however, is the problem of maturity. The attitude that maintains that students are essentially children derives some support from the fact that many undergraduate students do not have sufficiently focused intellectual interests to allow them to make knowledgeable decisions about their foreign study. A student who is accustomed to taking the courses outlined in his home campus catalog is often unable to shape his own plan of study in the absence of a set pattern of requirements. He is simply unable to select and evaluate courses offered at a foreign university, and he lacks the ability to adjust to the new and different situation in which he finds himself in relation to his professors and his materials. Such a student often ends up taking just *any* course, merely because it is there and not because it fits either his personal interests or the requirements of his career goals. One might well ask whether this student would not be better off if he remained at his home campus.

What the student does under these circumstances, however, is to accept the next best thing: he enjoys the prestige of studying abroad, but he studies only what is already most nearly familiar to him. He will thus avoid as much as possible anything that is really new to him, and he will be further tempted to make the obvious comparison with home. And if the foreign study program itself is designed to be merely an extension of home campus courses taught in the "foreign" environment, the result is likely to be that the student merely extends or deepens his already parochial American attitudes. Even when he is offered the opportunity to see how "they" do things, he will observe that "we" can do it faster and better. He has, in the end, failed to see how "they" do it at all, for nothing in him has been challenged.

But the real failure in such foreign study programs is that, even when they do provide a student with some amount of real experience, they still remain one-way streets. The student lives parasitically on the culture, dependent upon the good will of the host country or host group, and he makes little or no effort to initiate a countermovement. He takes all and gives nothing. He is not a partner to an exchange but simply an intruder. He has missed a valuable part of the total experience because he has not learned how to carry his own culture abroad and present it in a meaningful form to his hosts. Such a responsibility may be too much to ask of an undergraduate student, but the fact remains that there is no crosscultural learning unless there is absorption of culture on both sides, unless the traffic flows both ways on the street.

One of the main purposes of higher education, an intention intrinsic in its goals, is to provide the student with a knowledge of the comprehensiveness of cultures and a sense of the universality of culture. The comprehensiveness of cultures is seen largely through the differences in cultures, their unique particularity, at a very specific level. Culture is studied as a particular thing—as a culture—and not as abstraction. It is understood that such knowledge is desirable and must not be feared, resisted, or ignored.

It is further understood that this knowledge must involve something beyond superficial acquaintanceship with a culture. It must be intensive, and it must be crosscultural—that is, it must move across any artificial barriers that exist between cultures.

Crosscultural education is appropriate for any discipline at any level of learning—cognitive, affective, or volitional—and it should not be confused with the merely symbolic or linguistic. In this sense, one's own backyard may be a "foreign country" and an untapped laboratory for such education. Also in this sense, "foreign study" becomes a permanent part of higher education because of the technological creation of one world, with mobility of peoples, and the multiple impact of simultaneous communication.

The crisis of the contemporary campus reflects our inability to reform our institutions swiftly enough to accommodate these basic assumptions and to evaluate fully the real climate of our time. The crisis has three aspects: (1) organizational, wherein students and faculty revolt against passive, external, manipulated, or irrelevant roles in college-university life and governance; (2) intellectual, wherein students protest against the sterilized, abstract, and irrelevant nature of much of contemporary learning and demand authentic, holistic involvement in learning as an integral part of a life style; and (3) moral, wherein students and faculty demand institutional and academic integrity relating information and responsibility, knowledge and accountable action in the arena of life where truth has consequences.

If higher education can be conceived as crosscultural learning, then foreign study can become a more complete extension of that learning. A student with crosscultural orientation can then be adequately prepared for his foreign study and will be enabled to make fullest use of it. He will be intellectually independent and will be capable of relying on his own resources outside the security of his own culture and his own group. He will also be capable of experiencing self-transcendence, which is essential to self-identity, self-criticism, and objectivity.

A mark of maturity in a radically pluralistic world is the ability to comprehend and order a variety of differences and their dissonance. A properly prepared student will be able to forge living links within and between peoples and institutions whose national character and self-interest require penetration and accommodation if there is to be any prospect for peace in the world.

The student will also experience the intrinsic joy of the discovery of the genuinely new, fresh, and different, as well as the comparable delight of discovering human continuities in the midst of differences. He will know the challenge, the art, and the science of reconstructing a symbolic and real world in communities with and beyond difference. He will obtain a new view of the discontinuities that break the order of conventional campuses with their lock-step of courses, classes, credits, and credentials, and understand that they yet provide moments of meaning, depths of motivation, and the reconstruction of rational perspectives as new and deeper ground for liberal and liberated learning.

In the end, the student will be involved in "cultural immersion," with both the innocence and frustration of the child's entry into the world, but now self-consciously, with the possibility of the reconstruction of his own educational and personal biography. He will discover that foreign study is as close as the penetration of any difference that stands outside his real understanding, that it can deepen the opportunity and the will to humanize all learning, and that it can provide the ability to scale all walls—linguistic, ethnic, economic, and religious—that shut us out seriously from one another.

Some attempts have already been made to reconstruct the concept of foreign study as crosscultural learning. Following are some of the emerging patterns:

1. Reconstruction of the undergraduate pattern around a global design, with regional emphasis by semester or year (Western College for Women, Friends World Institute, California Western, University of the Seven Seas [Chapman College]).

2. Reconstruction of the undergraduate pattern around foreign college clusters within a comprehensive university—the "study abroad at home" concept (University of the Pacific, experimental projections at the S.U.N.Y. at Buffalo, Binghamton).

3. Reconstruction of undergraduate colleges treating domestic crosscultural learning as foreign study (Springfield College [Massachusetts], Old Westbury [Long Island]).

4. Simulating crosscultural learning on campus through "foreign cultures in miniature" (variations on language houses at Oberlin and at the Indiana University).

5. Multi-institutional exchange with three-way (or more) exchange (the India-Africa-United States link through institutional consortia and undergraduate exchange around common themes—New Paltz, New Delhi, Nairobi).

6. Reformation of conventional structures and resources of the university through introduction of crosscultural materials, new teaching methods with dramatic involvement, foreign students as educational resources—so that students have "foreign study" in conventional classes.

A few persistent problems remain, however, and some opportunities have gone unexplored. We must develop more adequate and effective qualitative measurements for readiness and success in foreign study. We need to develop mechanisms of genuine exchange that can accommodate and equalize the enormous financial differences that prevent many foreign studies from becoming two-way. We ought to provide preparation for foreign study that does not overinsulate or undereducate for crosscultural experience. There remain few tested models of this proper balance. We must provide adequate and dependable ongoing evaluation in the light of objectives and results. We must develop mechanisms for properly converting the world into a campus, utilizing for learning the world's rich cultural resources in their natural setting. Finally, we need to develop comprehensive inter-university systems that build on mobility and complementation but that avoid breakdown over "credit transfer," "cost differential," and similar problems.

PART FIVE

Looking Toward the Future

The two essays of Part Five bring us back forcibly to the issues of Part One—and thus the circle is complete. The author of the opening essay of Part Five is Lewis B. Mayhew, professor of education at Stanford University, 1967–1968 president of the American Association for Higher Education, and well known writer on higher education. The author of the closing essay is Edith Green, United States Representative from Oregon, author of the Higher Education Act of 1965, member of the Education and Labor Committee of the House and chairman of the Special Subcommittee on Education, and recipient of the honorary doctorate from fourteen universities.

Mayhew's essay, "Faith and Despair," picks up the major strands of the preceding parts of the book and recombines them into a sequence of propositions about the present and the future of higher education, culminating in a daring program for the nation's colleges and universities. Congresswoman Green's essay, "Through a Glass Darkly: Campus Issues in 1980," deals with higher education and our national purposes, and then, in the very last paragraphs, moves even beyond our country's boundaries. Of greatest concern to both authors is the all-pervasive problem of the clarification of long-range purposes for the American college/ university.

Congresswoman Green lays particular emphasis on the distortion of educational purposes that inevitably takes place when a society is at war. All wars have this effect, but the Vietnam war, as her essay makes clear, has had a multiple impact on the American people. It has used up enormous—unimaginable—national resources, and these are the very resources that we so desperately need in order to wage the far more important battles we face here, within our own borders. At one point in her essay, there is a powerful passage in which the seventeen million South Vietnamese are contrasted, in a resounding crescendo, first with the nineteen million Americans over sixty-five years of age, then with the twenty-two million nonwhite Americans, and finally with the fifty-six million young Americans who need to be educated— properly educated—for tomorrow.

Beyond its wasteful expenditure of these great national resources, the war, by its very existence, has had other harmful effects: it has enormously aggravated the frustration and hopelessness of those citizens whom it has robbed, and it has fed the anger and despair of all Americans who care about their plight. These concerned Americans include the majority of students on the nation's campuses as well as very large numbers of faculty.

Aside from the hot war, the essay discusses other national priorities that have distorted college/university goals. The need to reverse what Congresswoman Green calls the "inverted national priorities" that are dominant at the present time must, therefore, be of the greatest concern to everyone involved with higher education.

As Lewis Mayhew's essay begins, the author is standing between faith and despair. Faith arises, Mayhew says, when one contemplates how well we have been able to solve many vexing problems in the past. But faith gives way to despair, he continues, when one perceives how great is the gap between our current responses and the ideals we proclaim. It is difficult at this point in time, consequently, "to determine which sentiment will ultimately prevail." After this dramatic—but not exaggerated—introduction to his topic, Mayhew analyzes the unprecedented successes of higher education in solving many of the overwhelming problems it has had to face since World War II. But there is now taking place, Mayhew says, a "profound combination of revolutions," which changes the entire picture. His essay describes the five sets of pressures and forces that constitute these revolutions. They provide Mayhew with a basis for drawing inferences about the future, and in the next section of his essay, he outlines the general developments that he predicts will take place within the next several decades. But these important developments, Mayhew goes on to say, will all go for naught if three major battles are not won: if the Negro community does not move into the mainstream of American intellectual life; if the research and "service" power of the university does not concentrate on the problems of contemporary society; and if faculty and administration do not gain the confidence of students so that the tremendous student power may be used to help build better colleges and universities and communities. This section of Mayhew's essay strikes so close to the heart of the matter that it ought to be reprinted in thousands of copies and appear daily on the desks of all decision makers in higher education.

These final essays in the book show us what two acute observers believe is the order of priorities in higher education at the present time. As the closing sentence of Congresswoman Green's essay tells us: *If we can find the solution in Vietnam and get the priorities of this nation back in order again, we may then direct all our energies toward a 1980 that we will control, and not an Orwellian 1984 that will control us.*

Joseph Axelrod

Section X

Campus Issues in the Years Ahead

~24~

FAITH AND DESPAIR

Lewis B. Mayhew

The future shape and substance of higher education to at least 1980 can be reasonably predicted in broad outline by examining its recent past and by observing developments that are presently taking place. Such an exercise is occasion for both faith and despair—faith arising when we stress the pragmatic quality that has enabled us to solve so many vexing problems, and despair overwhelming us when we see that on certain critical matters emerging responses are so far from the ideals of its spokesmen. At this point it is difficult to determine which sentiment will ultimately prevail.

No analysis of higher education should ever be made, especially analyses leading to extrapolation into the future, without the perspective of the unprecedented successes of higher education in solving the enormous problems society has presented it since the end of World War II. Indeed it can be argued that higher education has been too successful. This has led people to expect too much from it, At the root of much student protest is frustration that colleges and universities do not serve well as a church, clinic, sanctuary, or arbiter of all social values. But these successes are of significance not only for the achievements they signify but also as indications of what is to come. Social institutions function in many ways like biological organisms. Successful experiences are perpetuated and unsuccessful ones are extinguished.

Consider what has been accomplished during the last two decades:

The veteran enrollments were accepted and accommodated and a new conception of financial aid was added to American culture. Current efforts to find ways to channel even more massive amounts of federal funds into higher education are made in the shadow of P.L. 346 and P.L. 16 (G.I. Bill of Rights).

Those born during the post-World War II baby boom have been and are being provided collegiate experience on a scale and at a cost undreamed of in any other society, including the Russian, indeed undreamed of in the United States until the veteran experience suggested what could be done. College enrollments have jumped from 1.7 million in 1940 to 3.2 million in 1958 to almost 7 million in 1967–68.

Faculty salaries, once it was recognized how seriously underpaid college teachers were, have increased by almost 100 per cent since 1958. Salaries are now competitive with almost all other professions and the end of increases is not yet in sight.

The Sputnik-inspired demand for academic rigor has been met with increasingly stringent admissions standards and an increasingly demanding undergraduate curriculum. The two-century tradition of extension of curricular material downward into lower levels of education has been accelerated through such techniques as the Advanced Placement Programs, the new high school curricula in sciences and mathematics, and the paperback book.

Much to the chagrin of some, the apathetic generation gave way to a quite unsilent one whose concerns for values are so acute that the present student generation could set a new stance for the entire society. Student activism was sparked by the civil rights movement, and its present expression is a search for a value system capable of rejecting war as an instrument of politics. Young protestors were taught in American schools and colleges that may have succeeded too well in inculcating liberal beliefs.

The public policy statement of President Truman's Commission that at least 50 per cent of all high school graduates could handle and should have some collegiate education has been achieved and a goal of almost universal higher education (for all youth save the severely mentally retarded) became a foreseeable possibility.

The temporary dilution of the training of college teachers, occasioned through the effort to meet demand, is being rectified, and during the decade of expansion, the proportion holding the doctorate increased from 41 per cent to 51 per cent.

The strong vein of Know-Nothingism in the American character finally gave way, in part, of course, due to the precepts of Pope John; and ways have been found for the religiously related and secular institutions to cooperate and eventually to receive some kind of support from tax sources. The future, of course, will not be all smooth, but it is by now clear that church-related colleges must and will have tax support.

Higher education, once the luxury of the upper and the intellectual middle classes, has now achieved the status of a major —perhaps the major—instrument of national policy to be used in solving the most critical of domestic issues.

The one-time almost complete lack of information about higher education as a social institution has given way to the flood of research-spawned evidence. Most institutions either have or are planning to have offices for institutional research or institutional planning. And the publication of books about higher education is increasing enormously.

The Manhattan Project and other war-inspired liaisons between the federal government and the intellectual community provided the prototypes for such intense research cooperation that some even fear a new power elite has been created consisting of government-military-industry and the university.

These accomplishments have taken place and must constitute elements of any picture of the future we draw here. But there have also been some failures. An ideal of a democratic society is its diversity of institutions so that pluralism of belief may be accommodated. And while this value is proclaimed, in reality institutions seem to move toward a mean, becoming more like one another. The increase in the proportion of students educated in public institutions increases at rates of about 2 per cent a year, and it is possible to anticipate a time when not over 10 per cent of all students will attend private colleges or universities. Thirty per cent of liberal arts colleges now offer graduate work. The teachers college is almost a thing of the past, and this is the fate, too, for separate men's and women's campuses.

Colleges have attempted to solve the riddle of a general or liberal education for undergraduate students, but contrary forces have been too powerful: parental desire that students be trained for a vocation, the specialism of even liberal arts departments, and the lack of appeal of general education as it is currently taught. The general education movement of the forties and fifties has faltered. The attempts to reform the movement have generally not been widely adopted. The free university sort of course now seems to have been a momentary phenomenon and undergraduate faculties are in search of a new mission. While Barzun's thesis may not yet be validated, that is, that the liberal arts are either dead or dying, the interesting experiments to revive or perhaps recreate a viable undergraduate mission have as yet not been sufficiently accepted to make prognosis hopeful.

Colleges have also listened to the argument that other professions have innovated and been able to extend better service to more people at less cost. But as yet higher education has either not found the proper innovative devices, has been reluctant to use them if available, or has been too insensitive to opportunities for innovation. Cost of education has tripled while enrollments doubled. Typically those institutions—with a few notable exceptions—that have emphasized new patterns of instruction have been regarded by standard institutions as not quite respectable. And for various reasons, some of which are not quite compelling, one of the most visible of the experimenting colleges, Parsons, was exiled. That experiment was contaminated, but there is a real question as to whether it was in poorer condition than other colleges reaccredited that same year.

Higher education is evolving, as do all social institutions, in response to both internal and external forces. The following pressures appear to be most operative, for example, in the expansion of graduate and professional education: Society demands highly trained manpower. In one way or another every institution hopes to produce its share of leaders in fields significant to society. Thus interest is declining in theology but increasing in education and urban planning. Moreover, expansion of scholarly disciplines in a way creates a dynamic for growth. As scholarly fields develop, new subspecialities are created; and institutions wishing to remain in the forefront of intellectual life must develop these new fields regardless of the cost. Faculty recruitment is another force toward increased specialization. In order to attract recent products of graduate schools, new specialties must be offered, especially graduate specialties, whether a balanced curriculum needs them or not. In addition, many institutions feel strong faculty pressure for more doctoral work even when such an effort would jeopardize the undergraduate mission. Presidential aspirations must also be considered. In spite of the growth of faculty power and Clark Kerr's mediator-type president, institutions still project the shadow of the president and his interests do find their way into the curriculum. Beyond the president, statewide master plans or role-and-scope studies have had increasingly stronger impact on institutional missions and the pressure has not always been a healthy one. It may, of course, be that these studies simply codify accomplished fact, but administrators do seem to look to them for guidance. Beyond the impact from the state, there is federal influence. One can agree that there has really been little overt federal control of higher education, but still see considerable federal influence. Just the availability of funds for some purposes but not for others is enough to shape an institution's character. Then, too, political pressures intrude. The present shape of higher education in California results in part at least from the belief that political pressures have been applied. And, of course, idiosyncratic forces operate. A vigorous department head, an institution's traditions, or just proximity to an intellectually vibrant urban area help shape evolving futures.

He who would scan the horizon of the future with any degree of clarity must examine how these forces operate and understand characteristic responses. But he must also search for the more fundamental elements within the society that will ultimately be reflected in the activities of colleges and universities. In one sense the years since the end of World War II can be judged the period of the most profound combination of revolutions of any comparable period in human history. It is probably the combination that makes the impact of these revolutions so powerful. They are well known and may be quickly summarized:

The information explosion has created more knowledge than any person or institution can assimilate. As a consequence, the curriculum has been so dislocated that unity becomes almost impossible. How can administrative law, computer science, Negro history, non-Western art, African studies, and consumer economics be added to an already overcrowded list of curricular imperatives?

The fact of affluence poses several different sorts of problems. First, how to develop people who can accept affluence when their ethics, psychology, sociology, and economics are predicated on the universality of poverty and scarcity? Secondly, how to reconcile the fact of affluence with the fact of extreme poverty and then to correct the imbalance that emerges? One could argue that the crises of Hunters Point, Detroit, and Newark were at least in part caused by color television, two-car living, and a hedonism that a majority of a society could afford.

The revolt of colonial peoples is, of course, related. For American education this most clearly means a search for ways of educating segments of the society previously judged ineducable. Much of the research interest of the U.S. Office of Education seems designed to do just that.

The technological revolution provides frequently unwanted leisure. It has been argued that if the defense-related economy were to falter, the productive power of the technology is so great that the needs of the society for goods could be satiated and still not need a major portion of the work force. An extension of this notion holds that unless people are taught to handle leisure, half of the population will have to be kept under sedation by the mid-1970's.

The last of these critical revolutions is, the weapons revolution, which in a sense has made total war as an instrument of national policy intolerable. Theology, demography, law, ethics, and even the arts seem to be struggling to adjust to this one fact. And student protests about Vietnam are not unrelated to that revolution.

These five sets of pressures and forces provide bases for inference about the future. But the future may also be predicted by extrapolation from observable developments and by attending to plans for the future that responsible officials are making. These plans extend from the most casual assumption that an institution will keep on doing what it has been doing to elaborate almost utopian schemes involving automated colleges and narco-education. Indeed, the last half of the decade of the sixties could be categorized as the time of planning. State master plans, institutional self-analysis, and commissioned studies of the future are endemic. Much of what is being discussed will not come about in any appreciable way by 1980 or even 2000. The force of cultural lag nowhere operates more effectively than in higher education. But some things will come about:

It seems clear that by 1980 every state will have a state master plan for higher education and some form of statewide coordination and control. Higher education has simply become too expensive and too significant for state government to allow it to function in the laissez-faire manner of the past. A few states may resist this trend by setting up a formal structure without real power. But the days of institutional autonomy for at least public higher education are numbered. And the same is very likely true for the private sector.

It is also clear that federal involvement in higher education must intensify. Few private universities or major state universities could even survive in their present form if federal support were withdrawn. And states are approaching limits of their own existing taxing powers while the costs of higher education continue to mount. The federal government then is the last recourse, with its nonregressive powerful tax base. The form this support will take is more difficult to predict, for higher education is divided on the matter. At this point it seems most likely that it will involve continuation of categorical aid with some reduction in research contracts, especially for big science.

There will be added some form of scholarship and guaranteed loans to students but with a cost-of-education allowance for the institutions. And federal support for construction of facilities will probably be increased. These seem more likely than any massive direct institutional grants or the creation of an American version of a University Grants Committee. But more centralized federal policy will be needed and by 1980 the cabinet rank for education should have become a reality.

Whether the society needs the products or not there will be major expansion of graduate work so that by 1980 graduate enrollments should be larger than all college enrollments were in 1952. The reasons appear to be these: as the bachelor's degree becomes more common, some other symbol is needed to screen people; retraining professional workers will be the rule rather than the exception; new jobs seem to require more advanced training than just a bachelor's degree; and, finally, the society just cannot use all of the bachelors' degree holders it produces.

Graduate study is socially acceptable and personally not too destructive as a substitute for work. And more and more institutions will be offering graduate study whether or not they have the requisite resources. Teachers colleges, turned state colleges, seriously plan on entering doctoral work. Liberal arts colleges will offer master's work, partly as a bribe for new faculty, and a few in response to local pressures will enter the doctoral field. While a very few institutions will be exclusively graduate, that dream of Harper and Jordan does not seem likely to come true. Undergraduates are too sound a financial investment—almost an endowment—for universities to give them up. It is this fact alone that will negate the claims of junior college theorists that junior colleges will provide the lower division work for a majority of those who will receive a bachelor's degree. In only one state has there been a substantial drop in the proportion of university enrollment in the lower division.

Unless some form of sanitized state or federal aid is provided private institutions, the days of many of them are numbered and the viability of others is threatened. The major private universities have begun to encounter serious financial problems and are responding by deficit spending, using gain from investments, curtailment of programs, and intensifying the search for more funds. Private universities that previously served a local clientele have now priced themselves out of that market and are attempting to find a new one. While in public their leaders sound sanguine, in private many feel that within five to ten years their institutions must join a state system. The examples of Kansas City, Buffalo, Temple, and Pittsburgh are clear.

Private liberal arts colleges are in an even more serious situation. Between 1957 and 1967 many of these have enjoyed their most prosperous years. Salaries have increased, new buildings have been started, and new programs have been launched. But the cost has been high and was met by doubling enrollment and tuition at a time when demand was so great as to allow this to happen. But to maintain progress the same strategy must be used in the next decade. Conditions, however, have changed. Now states have begun to assume responsibility for higher education and have or will have enough spaces so as seriously to restrict demand. Already in the fall of 1967 private colleges were reporting difficulty in filling residence halls.

The first step that will be taken will be a reduction of standards for admission. And this will not be all bad. In a number of institutions, the accidents of demand produced a student body brighter than the faculty. But after that, the future is bleak. Some will merge in a search for economies to scale, some will diversify (although this is dangerous), some will affiliate, and others will continue but by offering a less than adequate program.

Because of its uniqueness and because it is so politically desirable—and powerful—some 'mention must be made of the junior or community college. This, when first conceived, was to be the locus of lower-division undergraduate education. Such a development did not transpire, and for years the junior college served as an extension of secondary education. Since World War II, however, it has become more comprehensive in nature and claims to offer lower-division bachelor's work, general education, technical-vocational education, adult education, and to serve as a center for community cultural interests.

When we examine what in fact happens in junior colleges, their future form comes clear. While two-thirds to three-fourths of all freshmen who matriculate in a junior college say they intend to transfer, not over 15 per cent actually do. Those who do transfer seem to succeed reasonably well in a four-year institution. When we examine enrollment, we find that, typically, evening, adult enrollment is larger (frequently twice as large) than the day enrollment. When we examine attrition rates, we find as much as a two-thirds dropout rate between the freshman and sophomore years.

All of this leads to the conclusion that the junior college will likely make its biggest contribution to the society by extending some limited higher education to those segments of the population that never before expected any, by providing vocational training for one or two years leading immediately to employment, and by providing adult education as one way of helping people cope with leisure. This is what is happening. It is a commendable set of purposes. Some theorists or apologists have just not yet made it *legitimate*.

Higher education in 1980 will, for the most part, be conducted in large institutions located in large metropolitan areas. While some isolated junior colleges will remain small, even they will likely be parts of a large district, as liberal arts colleges will be part of a university created from existing consortia. The typical undergraduate, however, will attend a university of 20,000 students or more located in a city of 100,000 people or more. In some of these there will be attempts to subdivide into cluster colleges or other units designed to provide small-group experience. But one cannot predict too many cluster-college campuses, partly because the problem of departmentalism has not been solved. How can an institution command faculty loyalties from a cluster college and at the same time allow faculty members to develop as research scholars in their departments? Experience thus far suggests that departmental loyalties win and that the cluster college either receives part-time allegiance or a different sort of faculty from the university proper.

As to the shape of the curriculum, the future is unclear. Both undergraduate and graduate institutions are planning major interdisciplinary efforts but actual achievement is so limited as to make hazardous a prediction that such work will enter the mainstream by 1980. There is currently considerable interest in new problems-centered courses, programs, and even degrees. But the powers of departmentalism may prevent these from expanding because of the threat they pose to disciplines. The argument is widely heard that one cannot study urban problems, one can only be an urban historian, economist, or sociologist. The new hardware—television, computer, multimedia classrooms, and automated information retrieval systems—are all available and touted by their exponents. But the walls of academe are thick and 1980 will probably come and go with such devices still classified as experimental.

Students and student life also present an enigma. Clearly students will be made more and more responsible for their private lives. Institutions will gradually relinquish supervision over such matters as the relationship between the sexes, the use of alcohol, and student living arrangements. Indeed some institutions will not only condone coeducational or cohabitational living, as they now do, but actually provide university facilities, in the form of apartment-style residence halls to facilitate it.

Students will have the potential political power to concern themselves directly in the governance of higher education. Whether they will use it is not so clear, or if they use it, whether it will be done wisely and creatively. There is some evidence that the large majority of students are not really concerned, and the minority that is concerned is either worried about the moral dilemmas of the society or views the university as an impossible institution that must be destroyed along with the rest of society before utopia can be achieved.

There will be other developments, too, of course. Faculty salaries will continue to rise into the early 1970's. Faculty research will become more and more attractive. Strong graduate schools will become more and more selective in the limited dimensions of academic aptitude. The college teaching profession may well be unionized in all save a few elite institutions. Large-scale testing will be even larger and more significant in the lives of students.

Higher education will do these things and will succeed reasonably well. However, that success will be hollow and in the end lethal if it does not transcend its own part, its own evolutionary process, and its own mission by attempting to solve several imperatives. Thus far it has not, and to the extent that higher education does not modify its stance, it opens the way for destructive forces to grind colleges and universities—indeed the entire society—to a halt. This is no idle alarm. There is already evidence of the results of ignoring these cultural imperatives. When a handful of students can disrupt a major university, when frustrated humans turn cities into battlefields, and when youth can reject the fundamental values of a culture, a crisis is at hand.

Higher education will have to meet that crisis on three

fronts. First, the Negro community must be helped into the mainstream of the national intellectual life. Further, national leadership from the Negro community at least proportionate to Negroes in the total population must be identified and cultivated. Similar claims could be made for other minority groups, but the Negro community is so qualitatively significant as to deserve special attention.

At this point one cannot be sanguine that higher education will respond. While a few places, such as the University of California at Berkeley, have honestly called for an effort to increase the proportion of Negro students, regardless of the cost, most have done nothing. Graduate schools will accept all qualified Negro students but will not modify admissions policies to enable Negro students to become qualified. Junior colleges will not reject Negro students but will move to locations which, by the sheer fact of distance, deny students from the ghetto. Selective four-year colleges wish for more Negro students but use their scholarship resources for students with the best chance of survival, that is, white Anglo-Saxon children from middle-class intellectual homes.

What is called for is a major revision of what is proper for higher education. The major universities must be willing to support Negro graduate students for a year or two years of pregraduate work. The states must be prepared to offer massive scholarships of two to three thousand dollars for Negro youth, regardless of past academic achievement and regardless of whether or not they appreciate it. The entire enterprise must be prepared to expand capacity to handle 700,000 to a million more students, for this is the enrollment that would come if proportional enrollment were to be accomplished. This effort incidentally could be financed for an entire year with the funds used to continue the war in Vietnam for just one month.

Making such efforts will be no nine days' wonder. One obvious reason is that the white, middle-class, political power establishment may still be reluctant, and they will base their arguments on the myth of "educability." This seems especially clear in the present institutional stance showing unwillingness to modify admissions standards. But another, perhaps even more serious obstacle, is beginning to be apparent. For a host of reasons, many members of the Negro community are becoming suspicious of what might be called *white liberals*. For example, the Urban League has reacted negatively to a desire on the part of one junior college president to extend branches of a college campus into lower-class areas, including some predominantly Negro and some predominantly white. The liberal leadership has been in effect told, "We can no longer trust your motivations or your sentiments."

The only way such reluctance and distrust is likely to be overcome is for the predominantly white community to begin to take drastic steps, all without coercion. To name a few: If every predominantly white institution set as an immediate institutional policy the recruitment of 10 per cent of its total student body from the Negro community without respect to formal admissions requirements, this might signify an interest in reform. If every college administrator would cause his service and social groups to extend immediate invitations to leaders of the Negro community without respect to whether leadership was professional or not, the message might be communicated.

We come now to the second front on which the current crisis is to be met. The research and service power of higher education must be brought to bear, in a sustained way, on the problems of contemporary society—in magnitude similar to the nineteenth-century effort in agriculture. Thus far efforts regarding urban problems, resources, air and water pollution have been episodic, shifting emphases as the availability of project research funds dictated. As a result no cumulative effort has been possible. In some way continuous tenured support must be provided so that men can devote their entire careers to problem-centered research and teaching. Increasingly, Americans live in urban areas and these urban areas are becoming increasingly uninhabitable for human beings. It is in the urban areas that the most critical domestic problems are most visibly manifest. It is just possible that higher education does have the talent, the potential insight, and the skills of inquiry that could help solve the riddle of urbanism.

The solution will come only with the same sort of long-term sustained and supported efforts that made the land-grant colleges viable. This clearly requires a different conception of funding and it implies a different way in which colleges organize their efforts. Presently, professors are given their organizational security from the department. To do what is suggested here will require loosening departmental bonds and creating new structures capable of maintaining tenured professors. Other cities should follow the recent lead of New York City and create new, attractive, and well-staffed colleges and junior colleges in deteriorating parts of the city. Such a decision has the potential of changing the character of a neighborhood if the institution will extend itself into the community.

The third front relates to students. In some way higher education must realize the fact of the upward extension of childhood into the late twenties or early thirties and make adjustments in the curriculum, in custodial relationships, and in the entire private sector of student life. Some of the more militant student protests have come from students in their mid-twenties who are physically and emotionally adult but who find themselves without the full identity that comes from being economically self-sufficient. They demonstrate attributes of adolescence. It now seems clear that students will be expected to mature earlier, as part of the emphasis on academic rigor, but to continue dependency longer. This phenomenon requires colleges and universities to regard students with new eyes. Unless they do, these older children, adolescents or alienated, whichever term suits, can destroy; and they have already demonstrated the power to do so.

There must be a sense of urgency about this matter. This alienation of students who have been denied complete role fulfillment can move quickly into a philosophy of nihilism and despair. On a number of college campuses the leadership of some of the more militant student groups seems at present convinced that society in its present form cannot be repaired. Some of these young people are quite ready to bring the university, as well as the entire society, to a halt. (We might also keep in mind that the age group currently demonstrating such feelings will, within the decade, come close to holding the balance of political power. This will come when the majority of the nation will be below twenty-five years of age.) The responsibility of higher education is clear but the techniques for assuming this responsibility far from certain. Just the first step, however, seems critical and that is for each responsible educator to test every single assumption he makes about the nature of student demands and the relevance of programs for the needs of youth.

The evolving form and substance of American higher education seems remarkably clear but this evolution will justify faith only if these imperatives are considered the most serious of educational and social problems. And we in the academy must be sufficiently flexible to modify in major ways existing and evolving practices.

~25~

THROUGH A GLASS DARKLY: CAMPUS ISSUES IN 1980

Edith Green

We are more determined, today, to control the immediate and distant future than any previous age of men has been. This desire is reflected in books describing the year 2000, in TV programs about the twenty-first century, in governmental decisions that are made with an eye to their impact on generations unborn. Yet this determination is at the same time shadowed by a nagging doubt: Can we muster the intellectual and moral energy to govern ourselves in justice and in dignity? Do we not have the wisdom to avoid self-extermination?

We see through a glass darkly. In 1980 we will be face to face with the effect of the decisions we make now.

I would like to react to Mr. Mayhew's preceding paper

280

by considering three problems he has brought up for consideration: the impact of federal spending on higher education; the
effect our decisions have in limiting and directing the lives of
future generations; and how higher education in America affects
the world beyond our borders.

Experts have speculated about the educational system in
the eighties—its components, its curricula, its scope, and even its
schedule. The explosion of knowledge has made it imperative
that institutional capabilities be used to the fullest. Colleges are
experimenting today with trimester and year-round schedules.
Computers have already made great impact on both the what and
the how of a college curriculum. Community involvement has
replaced the universities' ivory tower.

It is probable that these trends will continue at a sufficient
pace that the university of 1980 will be a distinctly different
entity from the university of today. In order to cope with the
vastly increased number of students seeking higher education, the
college will have to make substantial adjustments. One thing is
certain—higher education will cost more in 1980 than it does
today.

Annual current expenditures of institutions of higher education increased from $4.5 billion in 1956–57 to $13.2 billion in
1966–67, almost a threefold increase. They are expected to reach
$25.3 billion by 1976–77, or nearly double during the projected
ten-year period. While enrollment is not expected to increase at
as rapid a rate as during the past ten years, this factor will be more
than offset by increasing expenditures per student.

Current expenditures are divided into four functional
components: student education, organized research, auxiliary enterprises, and student aid. Student education encompasses general
administration, instruction, departmental research, extension and
public services, libraries, and operation and maintenance. This
figure reflects what it actually costs an institution of higher education to educate a student—a far higher cost than is reflected in
the tuition actually charged. This school year, costs of student
education average $1,400 per student in public institutions and
$1,864 per student in nonpublic colleges. By 1980, the cost of
student education to institutions will have risen to $1,611 for
public colleges and $2,672 for nonpublic institutions. When one

realizes that this figure only embraces the actual cost of educating a full-time student—but does not include other necessary institutional expenses, such as research, student aid, or capital outlay for facilities—the actual cost to the institution of keeping that student in school becomes staggering.

Part of this cost is passed on to the students in the form of tuition. Today, students in public institutions of higher education pay an average of $268 in tuition charges. This cost is higher in four-year institutions ($299) than it is in two-year colleges ($110). Students in nonpublic institutions of higher education pay substantially higher tuitions, with an overall average of $1,782 per student per year. By 1980, these charges will have risen drastically. The average public colleges will charge an estimated $347 in tuition, two-year schools will have an average fee of $140, while four-year colleges will charge $424. Private colleges will show a concomitant increase, to an average of $1,910. Again, I must caution that this figure represents only tuition charges. The additional costs of room and board, plus the necessary student extras of books, travel, entertainment, and clothing, are not included in these figures. The cost to the parent will in many cases be doubled or tripled.

We cannot discuss the cost of higher education without considering the role of federal aid to colleges and universities. How will federal aid affect the purposes of these institutions? Now and in years past, the University of Chicago could pursue its ends as that university community conceived those ends. The University of Oregon could pursue its ends within broad limits established by the Oregon Legislature. In between, hundreds of private and smaller state schools fulfilled the needs of students and society in accord with more immediate individual goals and the goals of relatively restricted social-political units. But what has been happening—and what will continue to be true—is that national goals, as conceived primarily by the various agencies of the federal government, have permeated our society. Are we in any danger that national purposes will dominate the purposes of higher education?

Let us recall that the National Education Act of 1958 had to be called the National *Defense* Education Act to secure enough votes. Federal spending in higher education increased most sharply after Sputnik, which presented a national challenge—not a challenge for individual Americans to engage in the pursuit of individual excellence.

As many know, I have supported federal aid to education at all levels for many years. But it does seem to me there is a need to assess constantly the results of our action as we continue toward 1980. We are determined, I think, that 1980 will not just *happen* to us. We are determined that we will control what happens in 1980. And we are obligated to our children to understand the effect of our actions so that they will have the power to shape the world in which they live. If our deeds bind them within the limits of our priorities and decisions, then we have not transmitted freedom of choice. Thus, as we move toward 1980 I propose that educators begin to press for a policy of general federal aid to higher education with as few strings attached as is politically possible. Obviously, this demand will necessitate a favorable federal response before it can become a reality in terms of long-range practice. But the time to begin the campaign is now. We must convince ourselves and the federal agencies that colleges and universities know what they need and know how best to spend their incomes.

It seems to me, also, that to request this kind of a policy in federal spending will require forbearance on the part of all higher educational institutions. They must hold out for aid to meet *their* priorities as *they* conceive them. Federal money simply must *not* become a force to mold American education into uniformity.

I do not say that national purposes are of themselves inimical to the internal direction and goals of our colleges and universities. Students of the University of Iowa surely grow as individual researchers during the years they work on space satellites. Students and faculty at Stanford benefit enormously from the government-sponsored Electron Accelerator. Yet I believe that public and private universities should maintain their own direction and let government come to them for the brains and programs that government needs. If the procedure works the other way round—government funding for specific governmental needs—then the universities and colleges lose the precious power to determine what is best for them—given their students, their faculties, their facilities, their long- and short-range purposes.

A rather unique case comes to mind that illustrates my point. An instructor at Portland State College—the largest public college in my congressional district—applied last year for a grant from the Defense Department to work on toxic chemicals. The Defense Department makes these grants under the name "Project Themis." A dean, who happened to be a chemist, made the judgment that the research had little value as part of the college's educational mission, and most likely was directed toward biological warfare. The dean did not approve the instructor's application. During the debate that this decision aroused, the Defense Department said candidly: "The Defense Department does not have an educational mission to serve in Project Themis. We are seeking a specific purpose." This statement hardly needs further comment. It illustrates clearly the point: If higher education bends its purposes to fit only the needs of the nation—as interpreted by one or more federal agencies with a great deal of money to spend—then the educational goals of diversity, excellence, and nonconformity may be in danger. The words of Senator William Fulbright are particularly appropriate:

> The corrupting process is a subtle one: No one needs to censor, threaten, or give orders to contract scholars; without a word of warning or advice being uttered, it is simply understood that lucrative contracts are awarded not to those who question their government's policies but to those who provide the government with the tools and techniques it desires. The effect, in the words of a report to the advisory commission on international education is to "suggest the possibility . . . that academic honesty is no less marketable than a box of detergent on the grocery shelf. . . ."
> When the university turns away from its central purpose and makes itself an appendage to the government, concerning itself with techniques rather than ideals, dispensing conventional orthodoxy rather than new ideas, it is not only failing to meet its responsibilities to its students; it is betraying public trust.

As a footnote, I would add that diversity of study in private and public universities is our best guarantee of continued intellectual strength. President Johnson spoke most eloquently of the brainpower we need to build a world of peace. I would say that the foundation of that brainpower is individual excellence in fields of study chosen by the individual.

If education of the people is, in Jefferson's words, one of the prime functions of democratic government, then I would add that this function deserves a voice in cabinet decisions that touch each of us now and certainly will touch us even more in 1980. For at least six decades a proposal for a cabinet-level department of education has been before the congress in one form or another. The House and Senate each had bills proposing this in the Sixtieth Congress, which convened in 1907. Similar bills have been introduced in almost every congress since, including the current Ninetieth Congress. This need has also been a matter of continuing concern to the nation's education community. For example, the National Advisory Commission on Education reported in 1931: "The presence in the government of an officer of cabinet rank . . . would insure that effective contribution of education which is essential to the future political and social welfare of the nation."

The Office of Education now has a larger budget than eight cabinet-level departments of the federal government. Despite this rapid growth and the size of its programs, the Office of Education administers only slightly more than one-third of the eleven billion dollar federal expenditure for education. It shares its educational mission with ten cabinet departments and more than fifteen other federal agencies, fourteen of which spent more than 100 million dollars for educational activities in the 1967 fiscal year.

Although we accord cabinet status to commerce, to housing and urban development, to law enforcement, to labor, to foreign relations, to the treasury, to those functions grouped under the Department of the Interior, to transportation—we relegate education the status of an "office" within a sprawling department that encompasses health, social security, and welfare activities as well.

We deny a full voice to education in the highest councils of our government, and fragment the federal educational mission. No single voice speaks for education in Washington. Instead, department and agency rivalry occurs. No department or agency is responsible for a majority of the federal educational expenditures, and interagency rivalry often leads to empire building as each agency must defend positions it has previously taken.

I think it is time to endow the federal educational effort with the direction, the prestige, the visibility of cabinet status. The parts, the pieces, the fragments of the federal effort are tucked in nooks throughout the federal structure. No unity of purpose nor common goal binds them into an effective force to help meet the educational needs of the nation. There is a time for thought and a time for action. Sixty years of reflection should now achieve fruition. I sincerely hope that long before 1980 this objective will be achieved.

This brings me to my second major point: how our priorities and decisions today limit the range of action our children will have in 1980.

It is often said that President Kennedy possessed a sense of history. I think that is true. And I understand that phrase to mean that President Kennedy knew his dreams and actions were limited by the decisions of men before him, just as *his* decisions will limit and direct the lives of future generations. Open debate about the priorities of this nation has the purpose of broadening the range of action in which our sons may decide how to order their lives. In this context, we are morally and intellectually bound to consider war as a course of action that binds our children to our decisions with a vengeance. Our history may limit us. Our debts are to the future.

It is in this context that we should make decisions about the future. There are remarkably few who would any longer dispute the fact that we are simply not going to have a guns-and-butter economy. We are dropping 3,000 pounds of bombs per minute on North and South Vietnam. We have lost more than 17,000 American lives. We have had well over 100,000 casualties in the field, and we are losing 250 to 300 men each week. We have already invested in this struggle over 130 billion dollars. These are the grim statistics and they become grimmer by the hour. The cost of the war is now over thirty billion dollars a year—about ninety to a hundred million dollars every day.

There are seventeen million South Vietnamese, and there are also nineteen million Americans over sixty-five years of age, many of whom desperately require better housing, more available medical assistance, a decent income, and most of all, the attention and concern of their juniors.

There are seventeen million South Vietnamese, and there are also twenty-two million nonwhite Americans, many of whom are trapped in the urban ghetto, left holding the bag—a bag marked: "Rising expectations—temporarily postponed."

There are seventeen million South Vietnamese, and there are fifty-six million young Americans in an educational system that urgently demands a massive infusion of manpower and resources. But every soldier that we send to Vietnam with fife, drum, and fixed bayonet represents one less potential teacher here at home; and every dollar that we spend on destruction in Vietnam means one dollar less for construction of a classroom, or a recreation center in the decaying urban core. Surely this has an impact on our country in 1980 as well as 1968 and 1970.

The increasing complexity of all our problems will require the most highly trained minds—and many of them. Projections of needs for instructional staff in higher education indicate that we must add 100,000 new teachers for expansion plus 280,000 more for replacement between now and 1975—a net increase of 167,000 above our present supply, in addition to the 1,250,000 teachers we must produce during the seven-year period to upgrade the quality and replace those who retire or leave the profession. Where are these trained people to come from? Our graduate schools, aware of the needs, have increased their capacities to take in more students. Our young men and women have been encouraged at home, at school, and by their peers to continue their education beyond high school, beyond the baccalaureate toward the limits of their capability.

And now a new factor has entered into this top-heavy equation of inverted national priorities. The present draft rules, which provide not only that graduate students may not be deferred after this year, but that the draft shall continue to take the oldest first among the nineteen- to twenty-six-year-olds virtually insures that almost all of those drafted will be college graduates. Further, our military forces will not be able to utilize their skills intelligently. The present draft policy will make about 226,000 graduates at the baccalaureate level, and above, draftable; and most of them will be drafted to fill the expected call for at least 240,000 men during the next twelve months.

What will this do to our plans for 1980? If we look ahead

only four or five years, the impact is obvious. Next year, our graduate schools will lose between 50 to 60 per cent of their beginning graduate students, and half of their second year students. Since the ratio of starting students to Ph.D.'s is essentially constant, our male Ph.D. production in 1972 will drop from our previously expected total of 24,000 men to 12,000. In 1973 when this year's first-year class of graduate students should have reached the Ph.D., we can expect only about 14,000 men and 3,500 women Ph.D.'s instead of the expected total of 32,000.

Since there will be no appreciable number of returning college graduate veterans by September of 1969, we will lose a third half-class of graduate students, and another Ph.D. half-class in 1974, when we expected to graduate 35,000 men and women. Instead there will be only 20,000. Our total loss of Ph.D.'s during these three years alone could reach 42,000. We would be unrealistic to think that the universities could maintain their staffs, their impetus, and their ongoing programs through three lean years. How could they cope with a normal entering class of veterans in 1970? Probably it will take two or three years after returning veterans fill the campuses to return to a normal production schedule. This loss can never be made up.

The direct loss to education in terms of staffing of our schools from kindergarten through the university level will aggravate an already projected shortage. How about our loss of trained technological brain-power? We know that most students of science and engineering tend to enter graduate work immediately on completion of the baccalaureate.

Students in other subjects are more likely to wait a year or two before beginning graduate study. Therefore, graduate students in the sciences and engineering are not only predominantly male but more likely to be under twenty-six and draftable than students seeking a degree in education or in the humanities. This would be serious, but not disastrous, if we could be sure that these men would return as veterans two or three years later and continue their study. However, today's rapidly changing technology poses a double problem for the returning veteran in a technological course: he is out of date, and he has forgotten much that must be relearned before he may make more forward progress.

Today's baccalaureate student will be at least twenty-four or twenty-five years old when he comes out of military service ready to begin his graduate training. He may have acquired responsibilities and aspirations during the interim which will dissuade him from returning to graduate work. Many may feel that continuous study to age thirty to obtain a Ph.D. is not worth the effort. At the very best, we know that we will have permanently lost the number of graduates represented by half of three classes of Ph.D.'s and masters.

New graduates are in great demand today, and the tightened policies of selective service will tend to take into the service not only this year's new graduates, but the young scientists, engineers, and teachers of the past two or three years who have been deferred because their skills and the way they were using them were previously judged to be essential to the nation. Since occupational deferments in the foreseeable future will be limited to those required by community need, it appears that the nation will lose the professional services of many of these young men.

Let me emphasize that I do not favor preferential draft consideration for those on the graduate level. But, because of the "oldest first" practice, the draft call for 1969 will be almost completely from the graduate student population. Most of the colleges and university presidents who have communicated with us believe there should be equal liability for all in the nineteen-to-twenty-six age group, and no deferments. For the last two and a half years we have indeed been discriminating against the boy who was not in school; now we are discriminating against the boy who is.

I should like now to make a few comments on the way higher education in America continues to shape the world beyond our borders.

The world of 1980 to which we aspire should, of course, be a world in which the entire planet is moving ahead. By 1980, the brain drain from the rest of the international community to our own ought to be reversed. The ability of the United States to export teachers, technicians, agricultural experts, and Peace Corps volunteers coupled with our tremendous agricultural capacity could be a power more potent and majestic in a hungry world than all the H-bombs ever manufactured. Yet today we find we are importing professionally trained people to keep our country going. Last year 100,000 students came to the United States from around the world; 13,000 of these students are planning to remain.

Here again we view the tragic inversion of our priorities, for we will increasingly be tempted to fill the expanding gaps in our own professional ranks by continuing the import of technically trained persons from other countries. Among those who immigrated to the United States in 1966, 13,500 were scientists, engineers, and doctors; even more ironically, the future drain will fall largely on the underdeveloped countries. In recent years, Western European immigrants with technical skills could enter at will without exceeding their quotas. Beginning next year, technical immigration will be based on a list of qualified applicants in the order of their application; and the lists are already full for three years ahead with applications from immigrants in the underdeveloped countries.

Surely it is a paradox to talk of aid to developing countries and at the same time siphon off their professionally trained people to supply our own manpower needs in medicine, in engineering, and other scientific endeavours. Our own industries may be compelled to find trained talent wherever it can be found. They may even become envious of Russia, which will produce 138,000 engineers this year compared to less than 50,000 in this country. Already more than 20 per cent of our doctors of medicine, added to our supply each year, come to us from foreign countries. What is the price of such replacement, both to their homelands and to our own?

If we find the solution in Vietnam and get the priorities of this nation back in order again, we may then direct all our energies toward a 1980 that we will control, and not an Orwellian 1984 that will control us.

Index

AAHE   A publication of the

AMERICAN ASSOCIATION FOR HIGHER EDUCATION
A Department of the National Education Association
1201 Sixteenth Street, Northwest
Washington, D.C. 20036

LEWIS B. MAYHEW, President
C. ADDISON HICKMAN, Vice President (President-elect)
BRUCE DEARING, Conference Planning Committee
                    Chairman
G. KERRY SMITH, Executive Secretary

The American Association for Higher Education, a self-governing department of the National Education Association, promotes higher education and provides a national voice for individual members.

AAHE, founded in 1870, is the only national higher education organization open to faculty members and administrators alike—without regard to rank, discipline, or type or size of institution. The Association is dedicated to the professional development of college and university educators, to the achievement of their educational objectives, and to the improvement of conditions of service.